Routledge Revivals

Prelude to Modern Europe

First Published in 1972, *Prelude to Modern Europe* provides a political narrative, the social and economic background of events in Europe from 1815-1914. Woodward's own deep sense for social values and the quality of life emerges conspicuously in his long introductory chapter on European civilization. This is followed by chapters on the major powers, France, Germany, Russia, Italy and the Habsburg Empire. Finally, there is an epilogue describing and discussing the breakdown of the 'great power' system. Throughout the book, the author deploys all his unrivalled skills in historical and philosophical commentary.This is a must read for scholars and researchers of European history, modern history, and history in general.

Prelude to Modern Europe
1815-1914

Sir Llewellyn Woodward

First published in 1972
by Methuen & Co Ltd.

This edition first published in 2024 by Routledge
4 Park Square, Milton Park, Abingdon, Oxon, OX14 4RN

and by Routledge
605 Third Avenue, New York, NY 10017

Routledge is an imprint of the Taylor & Francis Group, an informa business

© 1972 Executors of Sir Llewellyn Woodward

All rights reserved. No part of this book may be reprinted or reproduced or utilised in any form or by any electronic, mechanical, or other means, now known or hereafter invented, including photocopying and recording, or in any information storage or retrieval system, without permission in writing from the publishers.

Publisher's Note
The publisher has gone to great lengths to ensure the quality of this reprint but points out that some imperfections in the original copies may be apparent.

Disclaimer
The publisher has made every effort to trace copyright holders and welcomes correspondence from those they have been unable to contact.

A Library of Congress record exists under ISBN: 0416201806

ISBN: 978-1-032-82864-0 (hbk)
ISBN: 978-1-003-50671-3 (ebk)
ISBN: 978-1-032-82867-1 (pbk)

Book DOI 10.4324/9781003506713

Prelude to Modern Europe
1815–1914

SIR LLEWELLYN WOODWARD

METHUEN & CO LTD
11 NEW FETTER LANE LONDON EC4

First published 1972
by Methuen & Co Ltd

© *1972 executors of Sir Llewellyn Woodward*

printed by Cox and Wyman Ltd,
Fakenham, Norfolk

SBN 416 20180 6 Hardback
SBN 416 20190 4 Paperback

This title is available in both hardbound and paperback editions. The paperback edition is sold subject to the condition that it shall not, by way of trade or otherwise, be lent, re-sold, hired out, or otherwise circulated without the publisher's prior consent in any form of binding or cover other than that in which it is published and without a similar condition including this condition being imposed on the subsequent purchaser.

Distributed in the U.S.A.
by HARPER & ROW PUBLISHERS INC.
BARNES & NOBLE IMPORT DIVISION

Contents

PREFACE	*page* vii
INTRODUCTION	1
1 France	59
2 Germany	104
3 Italy	148
4 Russia	180
5 Austria–Hungary	220
EPILOGUE	256
BOOKS FOR FURTHER READING	279
INDEX	287

Publisher's Note

Sir Llewellyn Woodward died on 11th March, 1971. The MS of this book was entirely ready for the printer except for the checking of a few facts and dates. This has been done by his colleague, Mr H. G. Pitt of Worcester College, Oxford. He and Mr John Turner have also compiled the reading lists and seen the book through the press. We are very grateful to them for all the work they have done.

Preface

This short book is based upon lectures (revised and brought up to date) which I gave in the University of Oxford twenty years ago to undergraduates about to begin a study of European history between 1815 and 1914.

Since Europe in the nineteenth century was the most important centre of high civilization, I began my lectures by asking what a high civilization was and why this civilization should have developed in Europe. I explained that civilization brings danger as well as achievement – if there is such a thing as progress, there must also be a possibility of regress – and that one of the most dangerous features of European civilization has been that politically it has taken form in a number of independent, sovereign states without an overriding authority to ensure that their respective aims, fears and rivalries should not lead to war and mutual destruction. I described the efforts made, after every great war, to avoid a repetition of calamity – efforts such as the attempt to secure a balance of power – and the reasons why these efforts failed to bring lasting peace.

After these and other general considerations affecting Europe as a whole, I considered in turn the history of each of the five continental Great Powers, France, Germany, Italy, Russia and Austria-Hungary. This method of separate treatment seemed to me essential if I were to avoid a mere summary of the external relations of the Powers. The difficulty of the method was how to avoid repetition; for example, should the Franco-German War of 1870–1 be described as an event in French history and then be retold as an event in Prussian or German history? I hope I have avoided this dilemma, while making each chapter intelligible in itself, but I would ask the reader, before he comes to a judgement on the matter, to read the book as a whole, since only then can he decide whether my 'dovetailing' has fitted all the separate pieces into a pattern.

In a brief epilogue I ask the question whether the failure of the greater nation-states, when the leadership of the world was in their hands, to avoid internecine war, showed that the political organization of human societies in units of independent, sovereign states had become totally inadequate, whatever their contribution might have been in the past to the high civilization of Europe. I cannot, of course, answer this question in a few pages of a short book, but I have put forward some doubts about the value of 'total historical damnations' based on after-knowledge, especially of failure and disaster, and I have given some reasons why national governments did not give more attention to possible ways of preventing the outbreak of war, and why they did not expect a war, if it should break out, to be the immense disaster we can recognize it to have been. Finally I mention very shortly, as a matter of interest, what kind of forecasts of the future were made by nineteenth-century critics of their own age, and what problems they thought they were leaving to posterity, that is to say, to us.

Anyone who attempts an outline of a vast and complicated subject such as the history of Europe in the nineteenth century, will know that whatever plan he may choose, his main difficulty is not what to put in his book, but what he can safely leave out. Here again I would remind the reader that I have attempted no more than an introduction which may save his or her time in discovering what to look for in longer and more detailed books. A serious student must go to these larger books. History has no more short cuts than any other branch of learning.

Oxford, 1971.   Llewellyn Woodward.

Introduction

I

Europe could have been described in 1914, and in spite of all that has happened since 1914, could still be described, as the centre of the highest civilization which the world has known. What is meant by a 'high civilization'? Why should such a condition have developed in Europe? The word 'civilization' and the spatial metaphors 'higher' and 'lower' imply judgements of value. Civilized society is regarded as 'better' than barbarism, and barbarian society as 'better' than mere savagery. Over three centuries ago the philosopher Thomas Hobbes described what he called life in a state of nature, that is to say, life without the restraints and order of civilized society, as 'solitary, poor, nasty, brutish and short'. One can safely agree with Hobbes, and waste no time in discussing whether there ever was such a state of nature, and, if so, whether it was or could have been more desirable than the civilized societies which have taken its place. It is also unnecessary to bother about the coteries and 'dropouts', ancient and modern, who in fact have not wanted to lose the main advantages of civilized society, but merely to avoid taking part in the labour and submitting to the restraints and conventions required to uphold it, and who would be at a loss if other people did not provide the drains, dentists, transport systems, textile factories, tools, police protection, printing presses and the like to keep civilized society going.

For my purpose I need not narrate stage by stage the transition over an immense period of time from what may be called the earliest human societies to those in which we live. This transition – the control of fire, the invention of the wheel, the domestication of plants and animals and countless other innovations – can be described as one of 'progress'. Progress implies an end – getting somewhere; there is no progress on a treadmill. The idea of progress as a cumulative improvement (interrupted at times by regress) is relatively new. The Greeks inclined to believe, not in progress, but in recurrent cycles of change, a rising to a climax and then a time of falling back; they thought themselves to be living in one of the long phases of decline – the golden age lay in the past. Even so, they accepted qualitative differences in judging contemporary societies, differences so great that they distinguished between themselves and barbarians who might be enslaved without offence to natural justice. The Christian thinkers of the Middle Ages could not regard temporal society as capable of lasting improvement since it was corrupted by original sin and destined to destruction in the fires of judgement. Nevertheless the Incarnation had been something new, and the age of the Church and of our salvation was something qualitatively better than anything which had preceded it.

The idea of an advance which could be traced in history was not put forward until the eighteenth century. Observation of savage tribes and especially of American Indians had led to a theory that such communities represented the original condition of all human societies. At the time of the French Revolution Condorcet[1] made an attempt to show the stages of development from the primitive state. If the title of Condorcet's book – *Esquisse d'un tableau historique des progrès de l'esprit humain* – is taken as a general formulation of the principles of human progress, it is important to notice that the book was written about 1794 before the Industrial Revolution had had any great effect in France, and that Condorcet's judgements did not depend on the evidence of recent material invention;

---

[1] The Marquis de Condorcet (1743–94) was a distinguished mathematician and philosopher. He took the side of the Third Estate at the outbreak of the Revolution, but broke with the leaders after the fall of the Girondins. He was arrested in 1794 and seems to have taken poison in prison. The *Esquisse* was written while he was in hiding in the months before his arrest.

for example, he does not mention the steam engine. The idea of progress is not, as is often assumed, merely a deduction from the existence of labour-saving machinery or improved methods of transport.

On the other hand, Condorcet did not deride material advances. His English successors in the next two or three generations may appear to us to have put too much emphasis on them. Our Victorian ancestors tended to equate the progress of civilization with good plumbing and an adequate water-supply; the better the plumbing, the 'higher' the civilization. There is something in this view. If you read Charles Kingsley's novel *Two Years Ago* or Sir Henry Acland's *Memoir of the Cholera at Oxford in the year 1854*, you will agree that the Victorians had good reason to speak of the moral benefits of sanitary engineering. Political advance could be shown to depend upon material invention. Universal suffrage could not have been introduced with safety into Hogarth's *Gin Lane*. The first stage in the shrinkage of a debased proletariat – dangerous to itself and others – in the great cities was a rise in the general conditions of living, an improvement which is still very far from complete, but which none the less during the last two centuries has been without parallel in human history. It is indeed unnecessary to demonstrate the non-material consequences of the improvement of things. The railways, which Ruskin and Matthew Arnold, two enthusiasts for education, regarded with such disdain, enabled thousands of children to go daily to secondary schools otherwise out of reach of their homes.

One of the marks of a high civilization is thus, age for age, an increasing fund of technical skill and inventiveness. In other words a high civilization means a high material standard of living for those, maybe only a minority of the population, who are civilized. Technical skill and invention are cumulative in their effects. To that extent the high civilization of the nineteenth century possessed advantages of an absolute kind over the high civilizations of the ancient world. The plagues which devastated Athens in the later fifth century B.C., or those which six or seven hundred years later the Roman armies carried with them from the east to the west of the empire, or, again, the pestilences which attacked western Europe in the fourteenth century, seemed at the time totally unpreventable.

Furthermore, as they accumulate, these technical skills require a greater rationalization of life. This rationalization is another mark of a high civilization. The Industrial Revolution had been called the embodiment of mathematical thought in material things. Compare an ancient or medieval ship with a modern liner, a medieval fair with the workings of modern exchange controls, or the methods of accounting in the medieval English Exchequer with those of a great industrial company. Rationalization is primarily a means to secure a greater production of goods and services, but the skills required to keep a high civilization going demand, from a minority, a long and elaborate training, and from everyone a certain level of instruction, intelligence and discipline, a level at least high enough to enable the average man to use the machines, manipulate the gadgets, learn the rules and accept the adjustments of instinct and habit necessary for the artificial conditions of a modern industrial community. These adjustments are difficult. They need a considerable degree of self mastery which every generation must learn for itself. Hence such a community must provide for its members at least a minimum of education. There will also be differences of function within the community, that is to say, a diversity of choices. Even in the lower grades of a highly civilized society a man today has far more choices than in a savage or barbarian tribe. He has greater freedom of movement, a wider range of occupations, more alternatives as a consumer. The combination of these two things, education and freedom of choice, lead to greater differentiation of the individual. There are less desirable features of this differentiation of the individual; I will discuss them later when I mention the dangers inseparable from a high civilization. Let me point out now, however, that much nonsense is talked about this matter. The so-called 'mass man' is not just the product of modern industrialism. The 'mass man' is the savage, obedient to his tribal customs, respectful of every tribal taboo, terrified of the local mumbo-jumbo and the local witch-doctors, responding in all his acts to narrow and pre-determined canons of behaviour. The medieval serf (and serfdom lasted into the nineteenth century over large areas of Europe) was the 'mass man'. The view of our own high civilization as a kind of 'waste land' has some truth in it, but on the whole it is an over-sophisticated, drawing room view; it is certainly not the opinion of those living in environments other than that of a high civilization.[1]

The freedom of choice, the development and extension of personality and the liberation of the individual require a considerable degree of political organization; a regular government, a legal system, a complicated administrative service. Rousseau had these things in mind when (contradicting his earlier statement that 'man is born free') he said that outside civil society man is 'un animal stupide et borné', but that within it he becomes 'un être moral et intelligent'. Aristotle a wiser and more consistent thinker than Rousseau, had put the matter more clearly in his phrase that the state came into existence in order that men might live, and continued in order that they might live well. Thus another mark of a high civilization is the establishment of an organized state. A more elaborate argument would distinguish between 'the state' and 'society', but I need do no more here than point out that the political organization which is an inseparable accompaniment of freedom of choice implies a certain minimum of territory and population. I use this vague term 'a certain minimum' because highly civilized states have varied in size. There is no ideal size; Athens was too small; the U.S.S.R., China and possibly the U.S.A. may be too large.

Once you can postulate a fairly large population, living in a given territorial area and accepting a uniform system of government and administration, you are brought to consider this

[1] In a literal sense our own creation of a waste land by the destruction of the environment is not without parallel in earlier civilizations, as any traveller in North Africa, Greece, Italy or large parts of Asia Minor can see for himself.

organized power of the State. Such organized power is another mark of a highly civilized community. Power, as such, is not limited to civilized societies, but there is a qualitative difference between the organized and continuous power – the expression of a high technique – exercised by a modern state and the rudimentary, haphazard power wielded by savage or barbarian hordes or even by a feudal king in the Middle Ages. I shall have much to say later about the misuse of power. I would like to notice now that, contrary to a good many present day misconceptions, power itself, power as the instrument of right has a noble side. Such has been the view of the greatest masters of the imagination. Consider Virgil's words on Rome or Dante's vision of Eternal law or Michaelangelo's figures in the Sistine Chapel or the hosts of angels in Milton's *Paradise Lost*. The phrase in the Anglican liturgy 'whose service is perfect freedom' is a good expression of the idea of righteous power commanding immediate and willing assent. The sin of Lucifer was an attempt to overthrow a cosmic order. The emergence of a high civilization is thus a qualitative change which, from the point of view of human well-being, can be described in terms of progress, and among the marks of this progress are a high material standard of living, based upon an ingenious and improving technique, an advanced degree of rationalization in the production of things and the supply of economic and other services, an increasing freedom of choice for the individual, both as producer and consumer, the existence of an organized state and the exercise by this state of authority and power.

I would add several cautions. In the first place, the idea of human progress in the sense of a qualitative improvement of life has to be carefully defined. One would not assert that the art of sculpture had been 'improving' since the time of Pheidias or that Shakespeare was an 'improvement' on Dante. Whatever one may think of modern music in its various modes, one would not call it qualitatively 'better' than the music of Gregorian plainsong. Nevertheless it is possible to say that in the course of historical time more opportunities have developed for artistic expression – new forms of art, such as the drama, new forms of construction, such as the arch, new musical instruments – and that these innovations have led to an enrichment and a greater variety of human experience. Similarly the existence of libraries implies that there is something qualitatively valuable about the accumulation of knowledge. The argument from the 'absolute' excellence of artistic masterpieces – cave paintings many thousands of years old – does not undermine the concept of progress as a general qualitative improvement.

In the second place, one must not assume that such progress has been inevitable in the sense that it was bound to follow from the geographical and other physical facts I have mentioned. History is much too complicated and uncertain to allow interpretations of this kind. The natural setting gives opportunities which may or may not be taken. The fact that since 1750 most (not by any means all) colonial settlement has been carried out by English-speaking people can be correlated with other facts such as the exceptionably favourable situation of the island of Great Britain for oceanic trade and expansion. The island is relatively large, and until recent times has been easily defended. It has not suffered from foreign invasion, other than insignificant raids, for over 900 years. It is rich in harbours and in mineral deposits near the harbours. Its climate, whatever Englishmen may say about it, is at least as well suited as any other in the world for health, industry and most types of agriculture.

Nevertheless the future of North America, indeed one might say the future naval control of the world, was disputed between England and France in the eighteenth century and an observer at the beginning of this period might well have thought the odds in favour of France. France had many of the advantages of location possessed by Great Britain. In 1700 she was richer, more populous and industrially more advanced. Remember also that in the sixteenth century England might have become at least for some time, a dependency of Catholic Spain, and, on the other hand, that in the fifteenth century Christopher Columbus, who was not a Spaniard, might well have set out across the Atlantic from some other country than Spain, just as John

Cabot, a Venetian citizen who had settled in England, sailed to the New World from Bristol.[1]

My third caution is even more important. I have said that if you recognize the facts of progress, you must also accept the possibility of regress. We are, and have been for over half a century in many respects passing through a period of regress. Since the war of 1914–18 – an immeasurable calamity for Europe – there has been a European schism, deeper and more disastrous than the religious schism of the sixteenth and seventeenth centuries or the long, confused epoch of the barbarian invasions which we still describe as the 'dark ages'. No one in 1914 foresaw such a schism. Nineteenth-century revolutionaries who wanted to change the structure of European society did not expect to divide it as the Protestant Reformation and the Catholic Counter-Reformation had divided it. Karl Marx never supposed that the social revolution would succeed in Russia and in no other great European state, or that the revolutionaries, having established themselves in power in one country, would set up in place of the bourgeois controlled regime an even more powerful state machine which would fall almost at once into the hands of a man like Stalin. No one imagined as a possibility the horrible parody of a civilized society devised by Hitler and given blind obedience by millions of Germans. When I was twenty it would have seemed to me fantastic to suggest that torture would be introduced into the judicial processes of any country in Western Europe. Every one of the marks of a high civilization has been degraded in Europe into a mark of the beast. Technique has been employed for hideous destruction. Rationalization has been pushed to an extreme in which whole classes have been exterminated in the interest of rapid economic development and millions worked or starved to death in so-called labour camps. Political and administrative organizations have been distorted into

[1] Christopher Columbus had sent his brother to England to solicit the patronage of Henry VII. The king was sufficiently interested to invite Christopher to London, but meanwhile Ferdinand and Isabella of Spain had closed with an offer to him. There was one Englishman among the sailors in Columbus' ships.

instruments enforcing blind obedience. The liberation of the individual has meant the domination of whole societies by types conditioned to cruelty and the uninhibited use of power. Power has become an end in itself, a wild anarchic passion. Finally, human beings have devised weapons whereby their entire civilization could be dislocated beyond recovery in a few days or even hours. The older agricultural societies possessed a resilience which our complicated and interconnected economies have lost. The successive visitations of the plague known as the Black Death in England killed off in the fourteenth century about a third to a half of the population without a catastrophic break in the development of English society; for us such large-scale dislocation would be more likely to bring a total collapse.

The unexpected regression of the last half-century has led some social and political thinkers and more artists and poets to deny, in spite of the evidence, that the concept of progress has lasting validity. There is no need to get into an intellectual panic about our modern *dégringolade*, but we have strong reason to examine more carefully our fundamental assumptions. If we have no warrant for rejecting all our knowledge of the past or for thinking that the nature of the historical process has changed in our time, we can certainly point to one mistake made by the philosophers of the eighteenth century, and repeated, with less excuse, by thinkers like Marx and Comte and Herbert Spencer. These writers assumed something like 'automatic' progress. Many of them took for granted that each stage in social development was safer than the last; all of them expected safety in the end. Marx's philosophy is indeed a striking example of the view that there was only one more crisis to be surmounted or, in the words of a once popular parody, there was only one more river to cross before reaching the promised land. Once the capitalist system had been overthrown, there would be complete safety for all.[1]

The Greeks made an opposite mistake. They observed the

[1] See also below, p. 72.

strange and terrible nature of man,[1] the unforeseeable effects of chance. Since, as I have said, they knew very little history, they ignored the cumulative achievements of mankind (much of what they could see or hear of the past was a mass of ruin and failure). Their mistake was in a sense less dangerous because it did not lead them into accepting the kind of messianic or apocalyptic determinism which gives the Marxist view of history the appearance of a melodrama in a number of acts with the conventional happy ending. Once you take into account all the facts about the nature of man, there is no inconsistency in saying that the idea of progress does not mean increasing safety. It means increasing danger. There is more to lose because there is more to gain. The Latin saying, borrowed, like so many Latin sayings, from the Greeks, *corruptio optimi pessima* gets near to the truth. So also, though not in the way he intended it, does Nietzsche's talk about 'living dangerously'. Civilized men, and for that matter uncivilized men, have always lived dangerously. The higher the civilization, the greater the danger. Let me point out some of these dangers. In the first place the advance of humanity has not been at a uniform rate. This is true not only in the sense that the physical, material opportunities for advance have differed in various regions; even where they have been fairly equal some societies have taken advantage of their opportunities and others have not thought of doing so. The Chinese, for example, are said not to have built ocean-going ships until the latter half of the second century B.C., nearly eight hundred years after the Emperors of the Chou dynasty had consolidated Chinese civilization. They did not build such ships because they felt no need for them. Their empire, though constantly engaged in border warfare, was too vast, too homogeneous and too well-protected by nature (and after about 200 B.C. by the Great Wall) to be really on the defensive for long periods. Along their coastline the Chinese had nothing to fear and seem-

---

[1] 'There are many strange and terrible things, but nothing is more strange and terrible than man.' It is difficult to find an English rendering for these words of Sophocles, but the Greek phrase implies the terror as well as the incomprehensibility of a tornado.

ingly nothing to gain from foreign intercourse, peaceful or warlike.

Even with the more favoured areas of the world the advance has been unequal. It has been argued that a high civilization has always been the precarious work of a small minority – certain élites living for the most part in great cities. This argument might be supported by the fact that until recently there has not been enough accumulated wealth to provide the material conditions of high culture for more than a minority, and that such culture had to be the privilege of the few and to be based on the exploitation of the many by conquest, slavery or agricultural serfdom – the labour, in a Chinese phrase, of the 'innumerable black-haired people who grow rice'. The problems of poverty, more perhaps in maldistribution than in an absolute lack of sufficient productive facilities, still exists within the areas of high civilization. Outside Europe these problems are far more serious, and it is impractical to suggest that they can be solved within a single generation. Attempts to 'jump' what J. S. Mill once called the 'one possible order of progress' have led always to disaster.

The difference among Europeans themselves in the degree of acceptance of the requirements of a high civilization has been one of the main causes of the sudden and terrible regression of the twentieth century. Large sections of the European population are 'backward' in the sense that they are relatively untouched in outlook, habits and emotions by the obligations and restraints of a high culture. Among the more civilized Europeans – the élite, if you wish – the rate of progress has not been uniform. It has been more rapid technologically than in the social and political fields. Compare, for example, the intellectual clarity of an investigation in nuclear physics with the muddled arguments in a parliamentary debate. Furthermore, as I have pointed out, the most subtle and delicate discoveries, and the power conferred by them, can fall into gross hands and offer temptation to primitive and debased instincts.

The conditions of a high civilization do not allow a censorship of the mind. It is equally impossible to separate out and sterilize politically the elements of extreme danger in the inventions of human intelligence. Leonardo da Vinci, if he so wished, could keep to himself some of the practical results of his curiosity because he feared that a wrong use might be made of them.[1] The methods of work in modern science and technology do not admit this private culture. There is no getting away from the enormous risks involved, and indeed one element of safety probably lies in a realization of the risks. Until very recently the masters of the natural sciences tended to regard themselves as the pioneers and even the saviours of society; they did not consider sufficiently the risk that they might be providing society with the instruments for its own destruction. We can no longer be unaware of the danger; nevertheless, the way out of our troubles is not to call a halt to scientific research, but to apply similar skills and a similar discipline to the study of political communities.

The problem is fundamental. We do not know whether human beings can endure the strain which civilized life puts upon organisms which have evolved to meet very different conditions of life. The strain is continuous; it increases with every step taken away from the life of instinct common to the higher animals. Every adjustment to the constraints and rationalized ways of civilized communities implies effort and brings frustrations of which we may not be consciously aware. These adjustments indeed began thousands of years ago, yet there is a sense in which most of them have to be made by every individual as though for the first time in the history of mankind.

These facts are too well known to need elaboration. There is all too little scope for 'joy in work' in a modern factory, too little sense of individual 'participation' in the elaborate organization – the 'facelessness' – of the modern state, little advantage in the greater variety of choices if none of them gives lasting satisfaction. Is it then possible to speak of 'progress',

[1] The Brescian mathematician Tartaglia (1505–27), one of the earliest scientific students of gun-fire, is said to have refused to design for King Henry VIII a gun of especially large calibre, on the ground that the use of such a weapon was immoral.

when the attempt to establish high civilization seems certain to fail because it is too much like stretching a bowstring until it breaks? A historian is going beyond his subject if he claims to be a prophet or to offer cures to humanity. All he can do is to try to interpret what he has learned about the past. The facts of past history, as I have said, show beyond dispute a qualitative movement which can be described as progress. One of these facts is that we are much more able than past generations to analyse the causes of our own regress. Sophocles could describe the strange and terrible nature of man. He could not envisage any means of changing it. We are at least not helpless before the facts of human pathology. 'Strange and terrible' states of mind and body can already be modified, for example, by the use of iodine or thyroid or by the skills of surgery. The age which has produced fascism has also produced the concept of social medicine. Before I discuss in detail the nineteenth-century background to the unquiet and in many respects terrible world in which we now live, I would remind you that Freud and Hitler were fellow-countrymen – Freud was thirty years older than Hitler – and that the creative work of the one and the corruption and nihilism of the other would have been impossible outside the environment of a high civilization.

II

I have defined in outline what is meant by a high civilization. Why has this type of civilization developed in Europe, or perhaps it would be safer to ask in what respects have European conditions favoured such a development?

What is Europe? The simplest answer to this question is to look at a map.[1] Europe is not, like Australia, an island continent. It is the western end of a great land mass extending from the Atlantic to the Pacific Ocean; the boundaries between Europe and Asia are generally taken as the Ural and Caucasian mountains, and the Caspian and Black Seas. The Ural mountains are not very high; the flora, fauna and physical conditions

[1] It is useful, in looking at a familiar map, to turn it upside down, when you will often notice features and shapes not previously obvious.

are similar on their western and eastern slopes, but as you move westwards you come into an area which is geographically a peninsula of peninsulas, including the now detached British Isles.[1] This western area has been the true centre of European civilization during the last five centuries. The area can be delimited rather more precisely by a line drawn from Danzig to Vienna and thence prolonged to Naples. The line would turn west from Naples to Lisbon and then north from Lisbon to Dublin, Glasgow and Aberdeen, and finally pass through Uppsala and Stockholm to Danzig.

The European peninsula of peninsulas is set about midway between the North Pole and the Equator in a temperate zone well suited to human beings, animals and plants. About two-thirds of the world's surface are covered by water; the centre of the so-called 'land hemisphere' is not far from a diagonal between London and Paris. The European coastline is favourable to the movement of men and goods in ships. Europe is not quite a third of the size of Africa, and yet it has a greater length of sea coast. The port of Duisberg-Ruhrort on the Rhine had in 1914 a water-borne trade greater than the ocean trade of Hamburg.

It is not surprising that such a favoured region should have become densely populated. In 1914 about a quarter of the world's inhabitants were collected in this continent which had only 7 per cent of the total land surface. Europeans had accumulated in their hands about two-thirds of the tangible wealth of the world and invested a great part of it outside their own continent to produce half of the commodities consumed by the world. The growth of population in Europe was extremely rapid in the nineteenth century. There are no accurate figures before 1800 but the increase seems to have begun in the seventeenth century. The estimate for 1800 is about 200 million. By 1870 the figure was not far short of 300 million and in 1900 just above 400 million. The change in the distribution of people between town and country is no less

[1] During certain epochs the British Isles have formed a continuous land mass with the European mainland, but these times are so remote that the historian need not take account of them.

remarkable; for example in 1871, the year of the foundation of the German Empire, only 4·8 per cent of the German population lived in great cities and 63·9 per cent were still in the country. In 1910 the percentage in the great cities had risen to 21·28, while the country percentage had fallen to just under 40 per cent.

What were the consequences of this growth and transfer of population and of the activities which made it possible to keep alive so many more Europeans, in addition to the thirty million or more emigrants, mainly to America, who were born and brought up in Europe? It would be absurd to condemn all such activity and enterprise in terms of selfish exploitation as it would be to regard the fluid, haphazard, social and political order under which they took place as something morally satisfying for all time. The astonishing achievement of the nineteenth century rests upon effort and intelligence. Taken as a whole, the so-called Industrial Revolution, which is still continuing, has brought what one might call in cold statistics an economy in human material; less waste of the pains of childbirth and the lives of children; better food and medical knowledge; better conditions of living. Consider the ghastly urban slums of the eighteenth century. Well-to-do citizens once lived in closely packed tenements which we should think uninhabitable amid a stench (the palace of Versailles was noted for it) happily unknown to us and a water supply which we should regard with horror.

Within this geographically favourable area the states of modern Europe have developed. The development has not been tidy; history, outside textbooks and works of ideological propaganda, is rarely tidy. The European states did not take their present shape because they were convenient units for modern administration and the exercise of power. No European frontier runs in a straight line like the boundaries of the American states of Wyoming or Colorado or follows a latitudinal parallel like the Canadian–United States frontier for about 1,500 miles between the Lake of the Woods and the Straits of Georgia.

The ethnological distribution, such as it is, of peoples in Europe has little or nothing to do with present political boundaries. Much nonsense – dangerous nonsense – has been written and believed about 'races' in Europe. 'Race' is a scientific concept in the sense that there are different varieties of the human species and that the individuals who make up each of these large groups, if such a term may be used, differ from the members of other groups, to a greater or lesser extent, in certain physical and perhaps psychical characteristics of a hereditary nature (in contrast with characteristics acquired by tradition, education and the influence of the environment). The physical geography and political history of Europe have produced a racial mixture which makes generalization impossible except in the widest sense that most Europeans belong to sub-groups of the white or Caucasian race. Classification of these subgroups is still open to differences of opinion. The common division into three main sub-groups, Mediterranean, Alpine and Nordic, does not coincide at all uniformly with the existing divisions of Europe into separate political entities. Geographers have often been more rash than historians in laying down laws or habits of behaviour according to real (or imagined) racial types. It may therefore be safe to quote the words of a geographer that 'the types intermingle, one dare not venture to link physical traits to any great extent with physical characteristics'. The geographer adds that 'the various physical types do tend to contribute in various characteristic ways to the life of the different nations of Western Europe. It is one of the unrecognized problems of politics so to order the public life that there may be opportunities of the kind required if all the various types . . . are to be enabled to give their contributions freely.'

The existence of different linguistic areas is more important, since it has produced differences of national outlook and sympathy which are especially significant in a small, crowded continent such as Europe. There is a point beyond which translation from one language to another cannot go. You cannot convey to one nation exactly what it is that constitutes the spiritual life of another nation; differences of language make nations colour-blind to one another. The existence of bilingual or trilingual nationalities offers no solution. These nationalities are in a small minority. In the case of Belgium the co-existence of two languages in one state has worked against national unity. Owing to the peculiar geographical character of Switzerland the Swiss Confederation has been able to survive where it could not have done so under normal European conditions.

As well as keeping nations apart, differences of language have had another consequence. The language areas in Europe do not coincide always with political frontiers. The language boundary between French and German, for example, in the upper Rhone valley crosses the river at a right-angle east of Sion; it does not run along its banks. Similarly the linguistic boundary between German and Italian in the eastern Alps did not coincide before or after 1914 with the political frontier or with the military frontier as conditioned by modern weapons. There are large 'mixed' areas in south-eastern Europe and small linguistic enclaves on the Baltic coast and so on. The political consequences of these blurred outlines have been continual unrest, due to the efforts of the European states, large and small, to bring the border areas of other states under their own political control; in other words, language has been, as in Alsace, the basis of a demand for annexation, or, conversely, of a demand for political independence. The question is raised as one of right. German or Italian-speaking peoples should be politically German or Italian citizens. The matter is even more complicated in the case of cities like Constantinople and Salonika, which have three or even four different names.

The accidents of earlier political history have determined the boundaries of the European states, in the sense that these states are for the most part consolidations of smaller and more ancient communities. Some European states are multi-national; some nationalities are dispersed over more than one state. The term 'nation-state' is less precise than it sounds because it is not easy to define what is meant by 'nation'. As I have said, one need not spend time over the concept of race; it is more profitable to list a number of attributes of which some, but not necessarily all, must be present if a community is to be called a nation and to possess the power-organization of a nation-state. The list would include a common language and culture, a common tradition and religion, a continuous geographical location, common economic interests, a willing submission to a common authority, a sense of 'belonging together' and of difference from other communities. In a French phrase, 'qui se ressemblent, s'assemblent'.

Historically the term 'nation-state' has been applied rather loosely to the groups of independent sovereignties formed in Europe between the fifteenth and nineteenth centuries out of the feudal miscellany of kingdoms, principalities and cities of the Middle Ages. Independent sovereignty was at first a more important feature of the nation-state than common nationality.[1] When Henry VIII wished to assert the juridical independence of his dominions in matters ecclesiastical as well as temporal, he did not describe England (and Wales and Ireland) as a nation-state. He used the word 'empire' and the only empires of which he knew were far from being compact nation-states. Moreover this independent sovereignty was not vested in the 'nation' but in the person of the ruler. Henry VIII did not transfer papal jurisdiction to the English people; he transferred it to himself,[2] and the nation, through parliament, recognized the transfer. Any other form of transfer would have been inconceivable. Sovereignty implied power, and the organized power of the community was vested in and exercised by the prince. Power – the theme of Machiavelli – was the attribute upon which princes insisted and which they were reluctant to share with their subjects until the latter compelled them to do so. This process of compulsion was not evenly timed throughout Europe. It had already gone a long way in England

[1] The term 'nation' was used at medieval universities (and has survived in Sweden and Scotland) without a political connotation to cover groups of students from the same neighbourhood or community. Chaucer writes of the 'English nation', but the word 'nationalism' is not older than the nineteenth century.

[2] For that matter Henry VII also transferred to himself papal jurisdiction over the small area of France – Calais and its neighbourhood – which was in English occupation.

at a date when in France Louis XIV might still have used of himself the much-quoted phrase 'L'Etat, c'est moi'.[1]

At the beginning of the twentieth century the change had not come in Russia and was not complete in Germany, although the German Reich had been provided with a representative assembly elected by universal male suffrage. The turning-point in continental Europe was the French Revolution of 1789 and the significance of this revolution is summed up in the French contrast between 'la nation' and 'le roi'. Henceforward the idea of national sovereignty in a literal sense was widely accepted in Europe and its complete realization seemed only a matter of time. After 1815 absolutism, not popular government, was on the defensive.

National sovereignty, the sovereignty of the citizen, meant even more emphasis upon closed areas, demarcated by obvious features such as the sea, rivers, a mountain range or, in default of such natural objects, by frontier posts.[2] In the first excitement of substituting 'la nation' for 'le roi' the French and their imitators elsewhere, having removed the princes in whose names wars had been waged (Frederick the Great had inscribed on his cannon the words *ultima ratio regum*), believed that wars would cease. Within a short time they demonstrated that a nation could be as Machiavellian as a prince and as ready to grasp at territorial or other extensions of power such as colonial possessions or the inclusion of national minorities within the metropolitan state. None the less the belief, or rather the illusion, persisted that the satisfaction of the claims of 'nations' to independent sovereignty would add to the chances of general peace. Mazzini was perhaps the greatest exponent of this belief in the nineteenth century. President Wilson in the early twentieth century qualified his own optimism about the doctrine of national 'self-determination'

---

[1] There is no record that Louis XIV actually used these words, though he came fairly near to them.

[2] Accurate frontier delimitation was impossible before the improvement of cartography during the eighteenth century. The first trigonometrical survey of the United Kingdom (from a base on Salisbury Plain) was not completed until the middle years of the nineteenth century.

by insisting upon the very considerable limitations put on the exercise of independent sovereignty in the Covenant of the League of Nations.

Mazzini is out of fashion today and so, in the main, is President Wilson. The co-existence of a number of independent sovereign states is so obviously a potential danger[1] to peace that almost every writer on public affairs puts in his passage about the need to clip these autonomous units of their power and to set up some larger ecumenical authority. The organization of the United Nations was intended to improve upon the facilities for international action provided by the League. Like the League, it has been of some practical value, though it can hardly be said to have done much to diminish the importance of the greater nation-states, and it has brought an embarrassing increase in the number of smaller aspirants to independent sovereignty.

In spite of the castigations of the respectable, the nation-state, like play-acting under the Puritans, shows such vitality and maintains such a hold upon its subjects that one wonders whether it is altogether the outmoded entity which it seems to most political Brahmins. Until people in the mass will make, for some other form of political union, the sacrifices they are willing to make in defence of their national independence, it is unwise to speak of the nation-state merely as a dangerous anachronism or as a retrogression from a more universal arrangement. Phrases like the 'break-up of Christendom' suggest that at some point in their history Europeans rejected a world order and lapsed into anarchy. There is little warrant for this notion of a political fall of man or for the belief that a return to an earthly paradise can come only from the establishment of world government. A government covering all civilized states has never existed. The Roman Empire at the height of its power only included part of the civilized world as then known to the peoples of the Mediterranean. It was smaller than the U.S.S.R. today. Its economy was based upon slavery. It was so much disturbed by civil dissension – a long series of wars between powerful commanders – that the so-called *pax romana*

---

[1] See also below, p. 45.

was relatively short-lived. The cumbrous administrative system of the Empire (even when it was divided into two parts) was often too corrupt and always ruinously expensive; the cost of the bureaucracy and army was one of the causes of the collapse of the most enterprising classes under the weight of taxation; an indirect consequence of this collapse was the development of serfdom in western Europe. The western Empire failed to defend itself against barbarians using more primitive tactics and weapons. The failure was due in part to the fact that the citizens gave up thinking that their empire or indeed anything else was worth fighting for.

After the political collapse of the western Roman Empire something more than the memory of it was upheld and transmitted from generation to generation by the Church. It is not easy to guess the significance of the Carolingian Empire to its subjects or even to be sure what his coronation in A.D. 800 by the Pope as Emperor of the West with the old title of Caesar Augustus meant to Charlemagne himself, or to know what importance should be given to the laments of monastic writers who regarded as a calamity the partition of the empire after Charlemagne's death. Between the sixth and the tenth century, or later, few people in western Europe considered questions of law or sovereignty in abstract terms, or knew anything of geography beyond their own immediate neighbourhood or of objects (apart from a few luxury goods) from other civilizations.[1] Nevertheless, the fact that nearly all the border lands and coasts of western Europe were under almost constant attack by fierce invaders gave Europeans a certain consciousness of unity. The momentous victory won in A.D. 732 over the Moslem invaders by Charles Martel (the grand-

[1] Many of the luxuries, or rarities, imported from the East represented a higher degree of technology than that of the West, as words like damask (Damascus) and muslin (Mosul) show. Jewels and the like needed no artistic knowledge for their appreciation, but western owners of eastern objects of art often had no inkling of their significance. When, after much wandering during the Scandinavian invasions, the body of St Cuthbert was finally enshrined in Durham Cathedral, the silk wrapping in which the remains were laid was of Mesopotamian origin with the Islamic text 'There is no god but God' worked on it in Arabic-Kufic lettering.

father of Charlemagne) is described by a contemporary as a victory of the 'Europeans'. Seven centuries later Pope Pius II lamented the conquests of the Ottoman Turks 'in our Europe'.

The unity of western Christendom during the high Middle Ages was at best something more flexible than that of the Roman Empire; it was not the kind of universality we have in mind today when we speak of a world state. Anyhow united Christendom, when it was united, did not include the known civilized world, though very early it extended its own boundaries by civilizing, that is to say Christianizing, contiguous pagan areas. The Byzantine Empire was either remote from it or even hostile to it; western crusaders sacked the city of Byzantium in 1204. Christian Europe was hostile, at least in theory, to the Moslems of North Africa and Asia Minor.

Within its own confines Christendom was never a single sovereignty, but a dyarchy of Pope and Emperor; the disputes between these high potentates, spiritual and temporal, over the limits of their respective authority were the main reason for the collapse of oecumenical rule by either of them. Again, although the Pope had something like universal recognition and a universal administration, the universality of the Church was one of persons – clerks as opposed to laymen – and, as every reader of Chaucer knows, the representatives of the papal administration were disliked in every secular kingdom. The medieval Empire also had an administration of its own, but it never covered the whole of western Europe. In economic matters, medieval group life was more exclusive than that of the later national states, and medieval politics were full of local wars.[1]

The truth is that the nation-states were an advance on the political realities of the medieval world. They developed out

---

[1] The greatest of these wars, the Hundred Years War between England and France, began as an ordinary squabble over feudal claims and ended as a war between two nations. Nevertheless Joan of Arc regarded the King of France as a feudal sovereign, not as the head of a modern state, and the French parties who took the English side in the war were not traitors or 'collaborationists' in a modern sense.

of new and healthy demands. They implied the existence of distinct vernacular culture in which laymen as well as churchmen could share;[1] the fact that Latin ceased to be an international language in general use was an inconvenience, but not a misfortune. The nation-states implied also a rising standard of living, the beginnings of the economic rationalization of which I have spoken, and the growing importance of a social class (one might say classes) impatient of the relative anarchy and administrative incompetence of semi-literate feudal magnates. In an age when travel was difficult and dangerous[2] the exercise of power to secure local peace required a prince set above all rivals, but such action was possible only if the rivals and the centres of disturbance were within the prince's reach. Hence the importance of the invention of cannon which could deal with the fortifications of a baronial castle, or the differentiation of ships of war from merchant ships; the time soon came when no private ship could fight a king's ship of the line, and private armies and their equipment became too expensive for the feudal magnates.

Finally one cannot imagine the emergence of self-government or freedom of thought without this transitional stage of closed national sovereignties. Difficulties of communication alone would have made the frequent assembling of representatives impossible except over fairly limited areas; anything larger than the nation-state would have been too big. For the same reason the sense of common unity which ultimately equated the state with the nation and not merely with the sovereign could not have been given too wide an extension; it required more than a city or a province but less than an empire. As for freedom of thought, a universal church cannot tolerate heresy, but most new ideas begin, from the point of view of the orthodox, as heresies. Toleration is still a problem of political society. One cannot suppose that it would have obtained even nominal

[1] In 1362 the use of the English language was made compulsory in the English law courts. A year later parliament was first opened in English.

[2] The Litany in the Anglican prayer book, after a general petition for persons in danger, combines in one sentence an appeal to Divine Providence on behalf of 'all that travel by land or water, all women labouring in childbirth, all sick persons, and young children'.

acceptance more quickly if the nation-states had not already asserted themselves against political uniformity.

I have said that with the French Revolution the nation-state passed into a new stage in its history and that after 1815 absolutism, not popular government, was in general on the defensive. The first phase of the nineteenth-century nationalist movement among those peoples who had not already attained national unity was liberal, politically and economically. What did contemporaries mean by calling themselves, or their opponents 'liberals'? 'Liberal' is one of those terms with a long and shifting history. Before the age of printing it was commonly used to denote the arts and sciences (if one may distinguish between them) which were worthy of cultivation by a free man. The word acquired a political connotation much later, at the turn of the eighteenth and nineteenth centuries, first in Spain and France. For some time it appeared in English in its Spanish or French form. The 'liberals' were the heirs of the French Revolution, the party of those who questioned tradition, authority and established institutions. As such, liberalism carried a threat of disruption and anarchy. It is interesting to notice the use of the term by Cardinal Newman. When Newman was writing his *Apologia* in 1864 he commented on the change which had come over the associations of the word. 'The liberalism which gives a colour to society is now very different from that character of thought which bore the name thirty or forty years ago. Now it is scarcely a party: it is the educated lay world.' Newman still condemned it as 'nothing else than the deep plausible scepticism ... the development of human reasons as practically exercised by the natural man', but it had lost some of its ferocity. 'When I was young I knew the word first as giving the name to a periodical set up by Lord Byron and others.' 'The most serious thinkers amongst us' (that is to say, Newman's fellow-Anglicans of the Oxford Movement) 'used as far as they dared form an opinion to regard the spirit of Liberalism as the characteristic of the destined Anti-Christ.'[1]

[1] Newman, *Apologia pro vita sua, passim*, (Everyman edition, 1912) and especially pp. 233-4 and 176.

The secular governments which had been restored in Europe in 1814–15 tended to think in similar terms about the liberal attacks on the established political order. They had indeed some reason for fearing that, after twenty-two years of almost continuous war begun ostensibly in the name of popular sovereignty and the rule of reason, Europe could not stand another outburst of Jacobin enthusiasm. Metternich was once upbraided by a friend for refusing to support constitutional reforms of a reasonable kind. He replied that his task was not to reshape society more in conformity with the Divine will, but 'to save it from the destruction with which it is threatened by open and determined enemies'. These fears were absurdly exaggerated. The liberal demands for a free press, freedom of speech, responsible and representative governments, administrative services open to talent, an economy free from the survivals of serfdom and outmoded fiscal restrictions were not unattainable and were much more likely to preserve society from anarchy than the squalid misrule of the Neapolitan Bourbons or the political constraints of Prussia, Austria–Hungary and Russia.

The practical form taken by the liberal demands had the support of the most solid as well as the most intelligent minority of the populations concerned, and were in keeping with the best political and economic thought of the time. They meant the disappearance of internal customs dues, a uniform tariff policy, greater mobility of capital and labour, in fact all the advantages proclaimed by the Manchester School in England. Liberals like Mazzini assumed that this association of liberalism with nationalism would be lasting, and that world peace would thereby be advanced.

The liberals, however, had great weaknesses. They had little mass support. The European peasants had grievances enough, but were too ignorant to be moved by general ideas or to support a general programme of administrative reform. Moreover, liberalism was soon attacked from the left as well as from the right. The early socialists regarded it as altogether a sham and a façade behind which the new forces of industrial capitalism were tricking and robbing the workers. The liberals themselves, hardly less than the high conservatives, were on the side of property and as blind as Metternich to the emotional force and the arguments of the Communist Manifesto drawn up in 1848.[1] With no allies, as it were, below them in the social order, the liberals alone could not defeat the strong vested interests, or break the bonds of habit and custom (and, one must add, loyalty and discipline) which upheld the existing reactionary governments of Europe. Above all, the liberals did not understand the significance of organized power in the hands of those who feared and hated political change.

The year of disillusion came in 1848 when for a short time the liberals seemed to have overthrown their enemies on the right. I shall have to show later how and why this triumph was short-lived. In France, fear of anarchy and revolutionary socialism gave Napoleon III the opportunity to undermine and then to supplant the second French Republic. In Austria, the conservatives in control of the army overthrew revolution in Vienna and used force against it elsewhere in the Habsburg dominions. In Prussia, the king, with the support of the army, withdrew most of the constitutional concessions which he had granted in days of confused panic, and the German liberals who had assembled at Frankfurt to decide upon the form and constitution of a united Germany just had to go home. In Italy, the revolutionary movement collapsed except in Piedmont where a constitution remained (insecurely) as a basis for future advance. The Pope regained his temporal power; the Bourbons came back to reign in Naples; and the Austrians continued to hold Lombardy and Venetia and to dominate the smaller principalities. None the less the demand for political unity in Germany and Italy remained as strong as ever. This unity was secured, not by liberal methods and on liberal lines, but, especially in the case of Germany, on an authoritative basis and by force and ruse. What was won by force and ruse had to be kept by such methods, and this

[1] This manifesto was drawn up by Marx and Engels at the request of a conference of Communist exiles in London. The manifesto did not have much circulation until later years. There was no English edition of it between 1848 and 1888.

success brought a contempt for the idealism which had failed before 'realist' strength. I do not mean that France under the anti-parliamentary rule of Napoleon III, or the new Germany under Bismarck, or Austria-Hungary with its attempts to stifle the national aspirations of the Slavs, were aggressive in the sense of aiming at the domination of Europe. Bismarck had a sense of limits, and, unlike Napoleon III in too many of his larger projects, was never a mere political adventurer. Bismarck always calculated the means at his disposal and never set himself an end which seemed to him beyond them, but his objective was solely German and, in the last resort, Prussian. Liberals like Mazzini had little of Bismarck's grasp of the strength of existing forces, but the European community which Mazzini envisaged went far beyond the increase in power of an Italian state, and might have avoided the calamities in the first half of the twentieth century.

The defeat of the liberal movements in 1848 was, however, ominous for the future of Europe. Politically over most of the Continent the next decade was one of reaction. Economically these years were particularly important because the pace of industrial development accelerated in western Europe. Even in Great Britain, where the changes had begun earlier, few people in 1815 outside a small circle of scientists and engineers had the least notion how immense a transformation was opening on them. The governing minority in the continental states a generation later showed a similar lack of discernment. The liberal view that the sum of the economic interests of the nation-states was the same thing as the general economic interests of the world (or at least of Europe) faded out within a generation. The 'will of all', as Rousseau had pointed out, might well be contrary to the general will. The separate interests of each nation-state seemed to be the development of its own industry and agriculture without regard to and even at the expense of other states. The protection of agriculture was as important as the protection of industry not only, in the continental monarchies, for the financial benefit of the landlords, but because in an age of conscript armies the governments wanted to keep the peasantry – their surest source of recruits – on the land. The nation-states sought for power. They were ready to sacrifice economic and political liberalism to national power, and to some extent at least economically there might seem to be no sacrifice since power brought an economic return. Thus, not at once, but slowly and almost completely, occurred what might be called a bending of economics to conform with the demands of nationalist politics.

This phenomenon is so important for the history of the later nineteenth century (and the early twentieth century) that it is worth while looking a little more closely at the rise or revival of a harsh economic nationalism at the very time when technological changes seemed to be leading Europe in an opposite direction. The technological changes were so manifold and so closely interconnected that it is hardly possible to single out any one of them as predominant.[1] The transformation brought about by railways did most to change the attitude of people in general towards machinery and to suggest almost unlimited possibilities of 'improvement'. The building of the railways was the greatest physical achievement hitherto carried out by the human race within a short period of time.[2] The railways brought immediate advantage to all classes. They were open to 'persons in the lower stations of life' (as the directors of the Great Western Railway put it in 1840) and not only to the rich. Migration to a distant place no longer meant for a poor man practically total exile from home and friends. Moreover, the machines which made this rapid and cheap travel possible were not used by industrialists to the detriment of hand workers. Nevertheless the magnitude of the social and economic consequences of the railways were not understood at once; the first British promoters – the steam-driven locomotive was a British invention – almost ludicrously underestimated the amount of traffic which their lines would attract.

---

[1] See *History of Technology*, C. Singer et al., vols 4 and 5 (Oxford, 1958). Their first volume covered the whole period before 700 B.C., the second volume covered another 1,800 years, the third volume about 150 years, the penultimate volume 100 years and the last volume only 50 years.

[2] The work could not have been done in so short a time without the use of steam power for drainage, haulage works, pile-driving, etc.

They did not carry passengers at all until 1825; one scheme for trunk lines assumed that six lines of rails would be enough for all traffic coming into and going out of London.

The construction of railway 'systems' came much more slowly on the European mainland than in Great Britain. The first railway lines in France – from Paris to St Germain and to Versailles – were not completed until 1837 and 1839, and even in 1860 France had only 6,000 miles of lines open to traffic. Russia had only about 250 miles of railway at the outbreak of the Crimean War. Between 1861 and 1878 the total continental mileage rose from just over 30,000 to nearly 90,000.[1]

The increase in the size and output of European manufacturing enterprises came mainly after 1850. Even in Great Britain progress had been slow. Only 500 of Watt's steam engines had been built before 1800, mainly because there were not enough skilled men to set them up.[2] The first British steam-powered loom came into operation in 1806, and by 1835 there were nearly 100,000 of them while France had fewer than 5,000. Nearly all the most important modern machine tools were invented between 1780 and 1880 but the great expansion of the metallurgical industries followed the discovery of the Bessemer steel process in 1856; even so the transformation of an iron into a steel age did not take place until after 1870.

As with manufacturing industry, so also with agriculture. Mechanization in a small way had begun early, but the use of

[1] The Mont Cenis tunnel was completed in 1870 and the line through the Brenner Pass in 1867. The opening of the Suez Canal in 1869 shortened the time of a voyage from Europe to Bombay by nineteen days. European telegraph lines increased threefold between 1858 and 1870 and again almost doubled in the next decade.

[2] Again the history of the use of words is useful to the historian. The word 'engineer' was known to Dr Johnson only as a description of a type of military man who constructed fortifications and 'engines' of war. (The Corps of Engineers in the British Army dates back to about 1716.) Civil as contrasted with military engineers become important in the latter part of the eighteenth century in road and bridge-building, etc. Only in the nineteenth century did the word 'engineer' as such come to be applied to the men who made or supervised the working of steam engines and heavy machinery. The first 'engines' in the modern sense were fire-engines.

agricultural machinery did not gain momentum until the 1850s; owing to lack of capital and education the change came very much more slowly in southern and eastern Europe. The employment of chemical fertilizers during the 1860s in French agriculture (which was more backward than that of Great Britain, Germany and several smaller continental countries) led to an increase in productivity amounting in terms of money to the equivalent of the indemnity imposed upon France by Germany after the Franco-Prussian War.

One could continue almost endlessly with the facts and figures of the rapid increase in the tempo of change in Europe during the 1850s and 1860s. Consider only two other inventions which had important social as well as economic consequences in ordinary life. Gas-lighting came early in the nineteenth century; it spread rapidly after 1812, but owing to the lack of suitable installations was employed almost solely for the lighting of streets and large buildings. Petroleum, mainly for light, and available, without any special form of installation, for small lamps, began to be used on a large scale (it was known a decade earlier) in the 1860s with far-reaching effects upon domestic life. Gas-lighting indeed may be taken as an example of the good and evil resulting from technical invention. On the one hand the lighting of factories made possible excessive hours of labour in them; at the same time public halls, libraries and similar large buildings – the familiar Mechanics Institutes of mid-Victorian England – were available more easily for recreation or public discussion.[1]

This unanticipated expansion of productive capacity after 1850 (leading also to a rapid growth in the number of clerks and other black-coated workers) would again have been impossible without a comparable development of banking and credit for the financing of industry and the provision of easily

---

[1] It is perhaps significant that one of the earliest pictures of large-scale gas-lighting is John Martin's painting of *Satan in Hell* presiding over a council of fallen angels in a huge chamber lit by gas flares. Browning's mention of 'the quick sharp scratch and blue spurt of a lighted match' in *Meeting at Night* (1845) is an early example of the introduction of a recent and humble invention – the ordinary 'lucifer match' – into English poetry.

accessible means for the investment of profits and savings. The adoption of the principle of limited liability, first in Great Britain in 1855-6, and then in France, Germany and elsewhere, gave an immense impulse to industrial investment, though at first it encouraged dangerous speculation. With the exception of the Bank of France, nearly all leading French banks and the four great German banks – Deutsche, Diskonto, Dresdener and Darmstädter – date from the years 1850-70.

There was also, especially in France, a remarkable development of companies interested mainly in overseas investment. This development was itself a sign of confidence in the international political order. Some investors may be fools, and others may be influenced by their governments for political or military reasons, as French investors were persuaded to support the tsarist regime in Russia,[1] but in general the readiness of the people of one country to entrust their money to the governments or citizens of another country shows a belief in the continuance of world peace. These foreign investments were on a very large scale. There were odd instances of an admixture of business enterprise with a certain idealism about some of the companies. The Crédit Foncier was founded under the Second Empire to put to productive use the savings of catholics; its founders had in mind the wealth of the religious orders. They spoke of 'Christianizing the Rothschild business', and their pious ambitions received papal approbation.

The counterpart to the channelling of savings into the provision of capital to states unable to find it from their own resources[2] was at first a fairly general lowering of tariffs. The so-called Cobden treaty between Great Britain and France – a measure carried through on the French side largely owing to the personal influence of Napoleon III – was the highest point

[1] See below, p. 124.

[2] The bad side of this international lending can be seen in the loans to Levantine potentates who accepted ready money on ruinous terms and wasted most of it on feckless expenditure, resulting, for example, in Egypt and Turkey, in defaults with far-reaching political consequences. It is one of the incidental services of the English to India that their supervision largely prevented a similar exploitation of Indian rulers (and taxpayers) by western financial adventurers.

in the international movement for greater freedom of trade. On the other hand, the drift back within the next twenty years to protection was an outstanding example of what I have called the bending of economics to politics and the resurgence of an economic nationalism which had seemed to be lessening in force.

As far as Europe was concerned, the decisive turn began in Germany. The doctrine, if one may call it such, of the pursuit of national power by 'exclusive' economic measures had once been general in Europe; it appeared to be dying out in the later decades of the eighteenth century (Adam Smith's *The Wealth of Nations* was published in 1776), but it was propounded earlier in the nineteenth century by prominent Germans, notably Fichte in his book *Der geschlossene Handelstaat* (1807)[1] and later in the 1840s by Friedrich List in *Das Nazionale System der Politischen Ökonomie*.[2] For the first few years after the foundation of the German Empire the liberal policy of the old German Zollverein[3] remained unchanged; as late as 1876 protective duties on imported iron goods were abolished. After this time, however, Bismarck turned to protection and in 1879 set up a general tariff. As Napoleon's example in supporting free trade in 1860 had been followed by other states, so Bismarck's policy was followed by a move among the continental states towards protection. Russia indeed had already raised her tariffs in a characteristically indirect way; there was no increase in rates, but payment was demanded in gold, and not in the depreciated Russian paper currency. Spain put into force a high tariff in 1877, Italy in 1878 (Italian duties were raised in 1887); French tariffs were increased in 1881 and more generally in 1892; Germany increased duties on foodstuffs in 1885 and 1887. After increases in duties during the 1880s Russia in 1891 practically excluded coal, steel and mach-

---

[1] 'The closed commercial State'. 'Fichte deliberately denied almost everything that Adam Smith had taught.' See R. D'O Butler, *The Roots of National Socialism* (London, 1941), p. 36.

[2] List, however, believed ultimately in international free trade after a necessary protective period had been passed.

[3] See below, p. 108.

inery. Austria–Hungary raised almost all her protective duties between 1881 and 1887.

As I have said, each nation could produce reasons for this economic nationalism. Europe between 1873 and 1895, in spite of the continual increase in productive activity, trade and wealth, was passing through a long period of economic malaise with recurrent crises. The trouble was not due to a single cause. There were successive years of bad harvests, calamities like the spread of phylloxera which almost completely destroyed French and Italian vines, severe outbreaks of animal diseases. The competition of crops grown on the vast American prairies – made possible by cheaper transport – brought a fall in prices which was catastrophic for western European agriculture. These troubles were overcome slowly, and in Great Britain only by the turn-over of much arable land to pasture and the development of horticulture. The industrial depression was intensified by over-confidence and, especially in Germany, by over-building. There were also serious and unforeseen monetary difficulties owing to the disequilibrium between gold and silver. After the discoveries of gold in California about 1848–9, no further important increase in gold production took place until the finding of gold on the Witwatersrand ridge in South Africa in 1885–6; during the interval, with a shortage of gold, world prices tended to fall.

Whatever the reasons, the effect of these national protective barriers was cumulative. As the American historian Hayes has pointed out, they 'subordinated the concept of individual enterprise to national enterprise' and transferred competition between individuals to competition between nations. This deliberate increase of national power at the expense of a general international exchange of commodities strengthened the sense of exclusiveness in the national states and heightened the importance of their closed sovereignties. The tariff walls gave to the protected states a definite character much as encircling walls and market tolls had given a particularity to the trade and industry of medieval cities. The United States, the British Dominions and the Latin American Republics followed the example of Europe, and throughout the civilized world almost every form of economic organization which might have been used to break down political barriers between nations became the means of increasing them.

It was thus inevitable that the nationalist economies of Europe should be projected, as it were, into the areas of the world which had remained untouched by high civilization. This projection is commonly known as 'imperialism', though the term was not applied to it before the last three decades of the nineteenth century. In 1815 Great Britain was the leading colonial power. She had lost her American colonies, but had kept Canada and had ousted the French from India; her predominance at sea had enabled her to keep most of the naval stations captured from the French, Spanish and Dutch during the revolutionary and Napoleonic wars. The growth of the British Empire before 1815, however, can hardly be called planned either in the sense that it was foreseen or that it followed a definite design or purpose other than the extension and protection of British overseas trade. The piecemeal extension of British authority over India was due largely to a 'power vacuum' in India itself. The British did not set out to 'conquer' India but to trade there. It would not be inaccurate to say that India had been left on their hands. The acquisition of African coastal territory was relatively easy because British traders and explorers happened to be the first in the field over many areas of the continent. In the early part of the nineteenth century British naval interest in the west African coast was mainly due to efforts to suppress the slave traffic across the Atlantic.

For almost two generations after 1815 British opinion tended to regard these haphazard and diverse acquisitions as an encumbrance and an embarrassment. There was no 'theory of empire'.[1] The loss of the American colonies was recent enough

[1] The view of colonies as more of a burden than an advantage was not confined to Great Britain. In the year 1867, when Russia sold her rights over Alaska to the United States for £7,200,000, the Russian Ambassador in Washington wrote to the Foreign Minister, Prince Gortchakov, that Great Britain wanted to be rid of Canada. He added: 'If Spain, France, Portugal and even England must lose or give up their colonies without any advantage, can we expect to be any more fortunate?'

for Englishmen in the first half of the nineteenth century to accept – if they wanted to theorize on the matter – Turgot's well-known saying about colonies, when they were ripe, dropping like fruits from a tree. If this were generally true, and if, as Cobden and his supporters argued, a preferential trade with the colonies was harmful to the mother country, British public opinion regarded the colonial empire merely as involving the taxpayer in expensive colonial wars.[1] The absence of any imperial consciousness can be noticed in the official terms used to describe the empire. Slavery, for example, was abolished not in the 'British Empire' but 'throughout the British Dominions' or 'throughout the colonies'. The term 'United Empire Loyalist' taken by those who left the former American colonies after the secession of the latter meant loyalty to the old empire, not to the territorial acquisitions after 1783. Palmerston rarely used the term 'empire', and indeed in his later years most of his fellow-countrymen understood by the word not the possessions of the British Crown but the French Second Empire. This Napoleonic 'imperialism' was criticized in England as implying the subversion of parliamentary institutions in the interest of personal rule. As late as 1878 Lord Carnarvon (then Colonial Secretary) said in the House of Lords that he had heard of 'imperial policy' and 'imperial interests' but that 'imperialism as such' was 'a newly coined word' to him.

Nevertheless a change had already come and was accelerated after about 1884 by the partitioning of Africa. The area of territory annexed by Great Britain between 1871 and 1914 was $4\frac{1}{4}$ million square miles, with a population of 56 million. France acquired during this time $3\frac{1}{2}$ million square miles and 26 million people. Germany started a colonial empire with a million square miles and 13 million people. Great Britain had annexed New Zealand earlier in the century to put an end to the

[1] The objections of Cobden and the Manchester school to the acquisition of colonies had little in common with later attacks on 'colonial exploitation'. Cobden represented *laissez-faire* capitalism; his attacks were made against the protectionism of 'feudal landlords' as supporters of protectionism and colonial and military power.

anarchy in the country (if left to uncontrolled private traders) and to forestall occupation by the French who might have shut out British trade. As long as Great Britain retained authority over the fiscal policy of her colonies, they were not brought within protective walls. There was no official British support for the 'closed commercial state'. British policy towards China favoured the 'open door'; Hong Kong was an open port.

The change of attitude in Great Britain towards the colonies was thus fundamentally a reaction to the threat to British interests from Russian, French and German acquisitions of territory which would be buttressed by a protective system and by military power which the small British Army could not equal. The British Empire, however, was not merely a collection of tropical or semi-tropical dependencies. As far as the older 'colonies of settlement' were concerned, the Empire was an association of free peoples, with enormous potential resources. The spread of Anglo-Saxon institutions over so large a part of the world (including from this point of view, the United States) was suddenly seen as a matter for pride. This reassurance expressed itself easily in a mood of 'jingoism', as well as an unpleasing tendency to moralize British self-interest in terms of a mission to bring civilization to the backward races of the world.

In the present state of British opinion there is a tendency to exaggerate the swagger and humbug of the imperialist period and to forget that these qualities appeared also in other countries. Cecil Rhodes is regarded as the chief exponent of imperialism in practice and Rudyard Kipling as its chief literary panegyrist. Rhodes, however, did not support what might have been called 'Pan-Britishism' (the word never existed) as many of his German contemporaries were 'Pan-German' or as many Russians were 'Pan-Slav'. Rhodes believed in a 'mission' for his fellow-countrymen to civilize Africa, but it was not an exclusive mission; he was especially concerned with Anglo-American (and Anglo-German) co-operation, and indeed with something which, in a not altogether crude or hypocritical way, he took to be the duty of civilized men towards uncivilized races. Kipling, the only writer of genius in the literature of imperialism, composed the *Recessional* as well as the *Barrack Room Ballads* and was not much interested in Africa, of which he knew little. He was impressed above all with the *Pax Britannica* in India – the peace and order upheld by the work, energy and prestige of a small number of Europeans (Scots and Irish as well as English) in an immense sub-continent. Kipling was not a militarist, for all his praise of the British regular soldier. His picture of the rank and file of the British Army was made at a time when English public opinion still accepted the services of a voluntary army – Housman's 'mercenary army' – while underrating the sacrifice and devotion which these services implied. Kipling discovered the private soldier as a disciplined being, not a drunken nuisance. A similar awakening of opinion was not necessary in countries with conscript armies. In any case the mood of imperialism in Great Britain did not survive the South African war of 1899–1902.[1] This war, in the reaction from an early patriotic fervour at the time of its outbreak, tended to be regarded after its conclusion as an unjustified and unnecessary attack on the liberties and independence of two small republics in the interest of a number of cosmopolitan financiers and mining millionaires.[2] A similar anti-imperialist reaction to the annexation of the Philippines took place in the United States.

Furthermore, throughout the whole period of awareness in Great Britain of the need for a concentration of power to meet the rival imperialisms of the continental states, there was always, as I have mentioned, an important difference between British opinion and that of France, Germany and Russia. Even after the acquisition of huge African territories, the colonies of predominantly Anglo-Saxon settlement were in fact the most significant part of the British Empire. The English and Scots who went to make their homes in the colonies carried with

[1] It may be noticed that, after the outbreak of war in 1914, the best-known (and only remembered) recruiting poster displayed the words: 'Your King and Country' (not your Empire) 'need you.'

[2] These charges, which had anti-semitic undertones, were unfair in the sense that the leading capitalists, the 'mining millionaires', did not think war necessary or inevitable and tried to avoid its outbreak.

them ideas of self-government which were taken for granted in the homeland.[1] The British Government could not, if it had wished, and did not in the long run wish to withhold from the colonists the control of their local affairs; such control would lead ultimately to independence. This development, which had been realized and had been implicit in the earlier attitude towards the settled colonies, was bound to affect public opinion and policy towards the backward countries under British rule.[2]

No such historical or practical considerations applied to the more consciously directed imperial expansion of France and Germany.[3] The British Empire had developed largely as an unsought by-product of commercial and defensive naval power. The emigration which had peopled the settled colonies with English-speaking citizens had been for the most part unplanned by the British Government. German colonial expansion had to be more deliberately undertaken. The German Reich began its existence in 1871 without colonies and practically without ships of war. If the German Government wanted to continue the logic of the protected nation-state, aiming at the increase of national power, they would set out to acquire colonies and to build a fleet, but before they could do so, they had to convince the German people that colonies and a fleet were neces-

[1] This generalization also applies to Irish emigrants to the colonies in spite of their hostility to British rule in Ireland.

[2] India was not theoretically excluded from the development of self-government under Anglo-Saxon hegemony and example, but Indian conditions in the nineteenth century seemed to relegate this possibility to a distant future. The radical J. S. Mill wrote in 1859: 'The sacred duties which civilized nations owe to the independence and nationality of one another are not binding towards those to whom nationality and independence are a certain evil or at best a questionable good.' (*Fraser's Magazine*. 1859: quoted from Mill's *Dissertations and Discussions*, vol. 888, pp. 167–71 in R. Koebner, *Imperialism*, ed. H. D. Schmidt, 1964.)

[3] The French occupation of Algeria after 1830 is an exceptional case. Algeria was close to France across the Mediterranean and, although Moslem resistance, often very fierce, lasted for half a century, Algeria was regarded as an 'overseas prolongation of France' and assimilated consitutionally with it. In 1911 the population of Algeria was $5\frac{1}{2}$ million, of whom less than $\frac{3}{4}$ million were of French origin.

sary to their Reich. The German Government had therefore to play loudly on the themes of German national power and prestige. I shall have to discuss later the international consequences of this attempt to beat up German feeling, especially in regard to a powerful fleet. The demand for colonies came earlier and was indeed pressed upon Bismarck who was mainly concerned with the position of Germany in Europe. It is unwise to put too much emphasis upon dates, but there is a significance in the fact that an organized drive for colonial power was in some respects slightly earlier in Germany than in Great Britain where it was still the belated recognition of an accomplished fact. In 1867 one L. Buchar published in the *Norddeutsche Allgemeine Zeitung* a series of articles advocating List's ideas and mentioning the connection between colonial development and national power. In the same year a 'Central Society for commercial geography and German interests abroad' was founded in Berlin; the Royal Colonial Institute in London (later the Royal Empire Society) was not founded until 1868. In 1881 a German lawyer and explorer, Hubbe-Scheiden, wrote a book, *Deutsche Kolonien,* on the theme of colonies as evidence of a nation's strength. In 1882 – two years before the publication of Seeley's *The Expansion of England* – a Colonial Society with propagandist aims was founded in Germany.[1]

The British reaction against imperialism was greatly influenced by the writings of the economist J. A. Hobson. Hobson, who owed much to Marx, and who in turn much affected the thought of Lenin, put forward in 1889, and more explicitly in later books,[2] a theory of under-consumption to account for recurrent economic crises. Too much capital accumulated in the hands of too few people; this 'over-saving' by the rich minority in capitalist countries reduced the demand

---

[1] P. P. Leroy-Beaulieu's important book *De la colonisation chez les peuples modernes* was based upon a prize essay submitted in 1870. In later editions of his book Leroy-Beaulieu argued that colonies were necessary to France.

[2] The most emphatic exposition of Hobson's view is in his book *Imperialism,* published in 1900.

for consumer goods (or rather the ability of the working class to pay for them) and thus led the capitalists to look for new sources of investment, new markets and cheaper labour abroad. Hence the use of military power by governments under capitalist control to support colonial expansion, whereas the real remedy for domestic under-consumption was a more equal distribution of wealth in the colonizing countries.

This theory was not altogether unsound. There was, in fact, under-consumption. There was also capital investment in colonial territories, the opening of new markets, the exploitation of cheap labour, but the economic results of 'empire-building' were far less important than Hobson (and, for that matter, the empire-builders) assumed. Germany, for example, gained far more from her trade with the 'open' British colonies than from her own closed colonial possessions. As late as 1914 trade with her own African colonies was only a half of one per cent of the total German export trade. At the height of the 'imperialist' activities, export markets were still mainly continental and, as in the obvious cases of Austria-Hungary, Switzerland and the Scandinavian countries and, at the receiving end, the south American republics, capital investment abroad did not imply acquisition of territory.

The investment of private capital abroad was also not directed primarily to colonial territories. Private investors put more of their money into foreign countries than into the territories which their own governments had acquired as colonies. In 1913–14 more than twice as much British money was invested in Europe and almost ten times as much in the United States as in the British colonial empire. The investments of Frenchmen in Spain and Portugal were as much as, and those in Austria-Hungary not far short of, the amounts invested in French African colonies. Germany invested before 1914 nearly twice as much in Canada and almost as much in Russia as in the whole of Africa.

Whatever the motives – and conservatives with a high view of state power contributed as much as bankers and industrialists with a special interest in colonial profits – the projection of national power outside the metropolitan territories of the nation-states had the dangerous effect of making collisions between co-existent closed sovereignties more likely. The change from competition between individuals to competition between nations became, as I have said, more marked, and the tempo – often the acerbity – of this competition greater and more dangerous to international peace. Nevertheless in the end we must return to nationalism in Europe as more significant than imperialism outside it. Imperialist rivalries were a contributory cause, but the two great wars of the twentieth century began out of disputes arising from local conflicts between national groups in Europe. These facts make it necessary to carry the analysis of nationalism and the nation-state a stage further.

III

An inquiry into the nationalist movements in Europe after 1815 brings out an element in them which is not found to the same extent in earlier times; an element of protest, or even fear, fear of the disintegration of the group to which one belonged, fear almost of a loss of identity and of being left an atom in a world of atoms. Such a fear was greater when other groups – family, church, craft, city were losing much of their old significance and the individual, especially in urban areas, though more free to choose, was also feeling himself more alone. The association of like with like had been one of the reasons for the formation of nation-states. Medieval loyalty was not to countries, but to persons or small groups; even for churchmen, attachment to a particular order, at times a particular religious house, was a more dominating fact of life than membership of the Church as such. A sense of common achievement or common danger might produce a feeling of more generalized loyalty and this feeling might be attached to the prince; in a later French phrase, 'le royalisme, c'est le patriotisme simplifié'. The splendid words about England in Shakespeare's historical plays come from one or the other of these sources: a sense of common achievement or common danger, and loyalty to a person. These words were not propagandist; they expressed an emotion already in existence. There is nothing we should call chauvinist in the dialogue between Henry V and the three soldiers on the night before Agincourt. The French are the enemy; they are not as good as the English, but they are not 'lesser breeds without the law'. A few nation-states (including city states such as the republic of Venice) could show within their 'moats defensive', if they had any, something like national patriotism, but there is practically no such thing outside them. As late as the early eighteenth century the transfer of territory from one sovereign to another was not regarded as an affront to political morality. The retention of Gibraltar and Minorca by Great Britain in the Treaty of Utrecht of 1713 was not considered by the losers as a moral offence. Gain of territory was the result of victory; loss of it, the result of defeat. A hundred years later the proceedings at the Congress of Vienna caused scandal to enlightened minority opinion in Europe. Transfer of territory had now become barter of souls, something against which this enlightened opinion protested as it protested against slavery. After another hundred years recognition of the right of national groups to determine their own political allegiance was thought essential to the removal of the causes of war. The Vienna treaty of 1815 put certain different national groups under a single sovereignty; the treaty of Versailles in 1919 divided multinational states as a means to lasting peace.

Why was there so much greater self-consciousness about national feeling in 1919 than in 1815? In the two centuries before the partition of Poland the Czechs were the only important nationality to be deprived of their sovereign rights by military defeat. The Dutch Netherlands and Portugal had rebelled successfully against Spanish supremacy. The republics of Venice, Genoa and San Marino continued to exist. Changes of sovereignty indeed took place over the heads of subjects, but rarely brought rapid changes of habit. There might be a fusion of sovereignty by agreement, as in the case of England and Scotland, where there was already a personal union of the two crowns, and the legislative union of 1707 safeguarded the religious and legal systems of the Scots; or by marriage, as in the case of the Habsburgs; or by conquest, as with Alsace. In the latter case the transfer was not one of complete sovereignty and actually led to later disputes about rights,[1] though, as far as the Alsatians were concerned, this transfer was not at the time thought a violation of German national feeling. So far from there being a separatist movement in Alsace, Strasbourg was a centre of revolutionary fervour at the time of the French Revolution. The Marseillaise was composed there by an engineer captain as a *Chant de Guerre pour l'armée du Rhin*.

The first partition of Poland (1772) was a warning to the lesser European states that a change of sovereignty could well mean more than the substitution of one ruling house for another and might mean the annihilation of a nation's institutions. From this point of view it is significant that in 1789 the centralizing reforms of the Emperor Joseph II[2] brought about a revolt in the Austrian Netherlands (later the independent state of Belgium) for the restitution of local privileges and customs. This Belgian 'throw-back', as one might call it, was soon forgotten in the French revolutionary avalanche which asserted in a literal sense the sovereignty of the nation, not of the prince. The result of the shaking of Europe between 1792 and 1815 was to bring to self-consciousness latent feelings of national identity. This realization of separateness was due both to an imitation of French achievement at home and a resistance to French aggression abroad. French ideas were one thing; French armies and tax collectors were an unnecessary oppression. Castlereagh, an aristocratic conservative, realized this fact when he spoke of using 'national'

---

[1] See Sir George Clark, *The Seventeenth Century* (Oxford, 1st ed., 1929) pp. 144–5. Sir George Clark points out that the earliest instances in a treaty allowing the inhabitants of a transferred area to leave it with their moveable possessions date from the seventeenth century. Apart from the confusion and overlap of feudal rights, medieval frontiers tended to be 'marches' or areas in the absence of obvious physical marks of demarcation (such as the Thames, the Lea, and Watling Street in the treaty of about 886 between King Alfred and the Danes). See also above, p. 19.

[2] See below, p. 223.

forces against Napoleon. The continuous remaking of the old political map of Europe by Napoleon had brought home to Europeans the two facts that national independence could be lost and also that it could be won. In the smaller national groups, which hovered between political extinction and a somewhat illusory independence (the consolidation of independent sovereignties into homogeneous nation-states was another matter), the new nationalism took the form of a protest, a defensive assertion of separateness. The smaller the group, the more shrill the assertion. The national song of the Luxemburgers, for example, asserts that they are neither Prussians nor French. Vernacular languages and peasant dialects in which no literature other than folk-ballads had been composed for generations were studied, spoken and taught to children in schools, often at the price of lowering their cultural and economic opportunities. Political lobbying went to secure legal status for these artificially preserved forms of speech. In the twentieth century a fourth language, Romansch, spoken only by about one per cent of the Swiss population, and most of them peasants in the Grisons, was added to the existing three official languages. Once established, the small new nationalities used tariffs and industrial subsidies, often against their own economic interest, in a fight against geography. It is also worth noticing how many nationalist leaders have come from border or near-border areas, and how easily, by slight political accident, they might have been on the other side of the fence. Garibaldi was born at Nice, Mazzini in the extinct republic of Genoa; Cavour spoke Italian with a slight French accent and belonged to the nobility of the 'mixed' kingdom of Savoy-Piedmont. Masaryk came from Slovakia and, for that matter, Stalin from Georgia.[1]

I have already warned you against regarding the nation-state as altogether a creature of sin. I must repeat this warning in relation to the phenomena of nationalism as a form of protest. It is idle to ignore the strength of feeling behind these protests and unimaginative to describe them as childish and

[1] Joan of Arc was born in a village which was partly in Champagne, partly in Lorraine, and away from the centre of the kingdom of France.

beneath the dignity of contemporary thought. If 'modern' thought cannot comprehend these matters, modern thinkers are merely repeating the superficiality of the so-called enlightenment of the eighteenth century.[1] The defensive element in nationalism is, of course, not limited to small states. Over three centuries ago Thomas Hobbes in his book *Leviathan* used words which apply today: 'Kings and persons of sovereign authority, because of their independency, are in continual jealousies and the state and posture of gladiators, having their weapons pointing, and their eyes fixed on one another, that is, their forts, garrisons, and guns, upon the frontiers of their neighbours which is a posture of war.'

Obviously the nation-states have been aware of the consequences of this posture of war, and have tried to avoid them by some kind of political arrangement. All such arrangements have broken down, because the source of the trouble lies, as I have said, in the nature of man as man has developed over immense periods of time. Hobbes, who reached his conclusions by logical deduction from an atomic materialism long since discarded, exaggerated the element of aggression. Continuous aggression is not usual in 'nature'. Lions do not rush around all the time killing every creature within reach. Purposive aggression, both in animals and human beings, has been directed to getting or keeping something of which there never has been enough to go round – food, a particular 'territory' or mate. In this respect it is not true that aggression has never paid. In the millennia of scarcity it was the instrument of survival. We are heirs of countless generations of successful aggressors, but the conditions of life have changed. Technology and reasonable population control could do away with scarcity,

[1] A comment by the writer Joseph Conrad is relevant to this point: 'It requires a certain greatness of soul to interpret patriotism worthily, or else a sincerity of feeling denied to the vulgar refinement of modern thought which cannot understand the august simplicity of a sentiment proceeding from the very nature of things and man.' One might add that a similar 'vulgar refinement' often fails to understand the patriotism and loyalty evoked by great states. There is a tendency to regard the patriotism of a small country as legitimate and noble, and that of a large country as something of which to be ashamed.

while technology has also made large-scale aggression suicidal. Until we can bring masses of men to realize imaginatively what these two propositions mean, we cannot hope to keep the peace of the world by a form of political jugglery. We shall not get rid of the 'continual jealousies' until we have got rid of the fear of being, as it were, the odd man out. There is little difficulty even now of securing organizations on an intergovernmental, world-wide basis if there is no fear of the consequences of their operations. Consider one such body which has flourished almost for a century. The International Postal Union conducts no propaganda. No politicians testify allegiance to it. Few people know where its headquarters are, yet its business affects every citizen in every state.[1] The International Postal Union is not an object of controversy or prestige because no one is afraid of it. Until all international relations can be treated in this humdrum way, until the allocation of food, raw materials and power is as much a matter of routine and excites as little jealousy as the distribution of letters, civilized societies are unlikely to succeed in adjusting themselves to a world of plenty.

Meanwhile we must consider the secondary safeguards against war between co-existent national sovereignties. There have been, in general terms, two different types of arrangement; a permanent, overriding authority so strong that no one can attack it with a hope of success, or an equilibrium, a balance of power which states will not disturb either because they are satisfied with it or because, again, they cannot hope to upset it. Both types of solution go back in history beyond the nation-state. Perhaps the earliest expression of the balance of power is in the words of the ancient historian Polybius about the middle of the third century B.C. – 'you must not allow anyone so much power that you cannot subsequently dispute your claims with him on an equal footing, however just these claims may be'.[1] On the other hand, with the extension of the Roman Empire,

---

[1] The coupons of the I.P.U. are the only documents available for purchase in every British post office upon which instructions are printed, among other languages, in Russian.

[2] Polybius, i, 83.

the idea of a paramount authority became recognized. Although as I have said, the Roman authority was never properly oecumenical and never established on a sufficiently firm basis, the memory of it continued long after it had disappeared. The noblest of all political tracts, Dante's *De Monarchia*, set out the idea of a dual authority, the Holy Roman Empire in temporal, the Pope in spiritual matters, strong enough to compel all lesser sovereignties to peace.[1]

The break-up of religious unity and the rise of national sovereignties, however, made Dante's remedy impracticable. If a solution of the problem of an international order were to be found, the solution had to be of the other kind, the creation of a balance of power. Here again the facts existed before the theory, and the theory itself has undergone such changes in the last three centuries that in our own time the conception has been largely misunderstood. With the emergence of wholly independent sovereign states – the modern Great Powers – the idea of Christendom did not altogether disappear, though the constituent elements in it had changed. The theory of the balance of power took account of these changes and regarded the nation-states as forming a community, almost a federal league, of which the purpose was the preservation of a certain political order. This order was described by the jurist Vattel (1711–67), a Swiss from the principality of Neuchâtel, as such that in it no one prince or state should predominate and dictate absolutely to the others. Since every state had an interest in maintaining the equilibrium, every state also had a duty to interfere, if necessary by force, when one of their number was likely to upset it.

This doctrine has two important features; the idea of a common bond of interest uniting all the states of Europe, and, resulting from this bond, the duty of intervention. About the time of the English revolution of 1688, Archbishop Fénelon expounded the matter to the duke of Burgundy, son of the heir to the French Crown. 'This care to maintain a sort of equality and equipoise between neighbouring nations is a guarantee of the general tranquillity. In this respect all

---

[1] See, especially, *De Monarchia*, III, 16.

neighbouring nations, trading with one another,[1] form one great body and a sort of community. This Christendom is a kind of universal republic which has its interests, its fears and its necessary precautions.'

Fénelon's views were not merely held by theorists. The settlement after the Thirty Years War was an attempt to put these views into practical effect. For the first time a congress of representatives of all the interested states (which included most of the continental states) met to bring a great war to an end by mutual satisfaction of interests. The Congress of Westphalia[2] was, in theory, a mediating action between catholic and protestant belligerents by France, Venice, Sweden and the Papacy. The agreements embodied in the final treaties secured an equilibrium in Germany by reasserting the principle reached nearly a century earlier in the treaty of Augsburg that subjects were to follow the religion of their prince: *cuius regio eius religio*. Three orthodoxies, Catholic, Lutheran and Calvinist, were thus territorially established.

The Westphalian settlement did not bring lasting peace to Europe. The ambitions of Louis XIV destroyed such balance as had been obtained. Other Powers including England, intervened against Louis XIV until the wars which he had provoked ended in another general settlement, the Treaty of Utrecht, in 1713. This treaty stated definitely that a 'just balance of power' was the 'best and most secure foundation of mutual friendship' in a lasting general agreement which still echoed the idea of Christendom in a reference to the 'peace and tranquillity of the Christian world'. The English Mutiny Act, which legalized the discipline of a standing army, and which continued to be renewed annually until its replacement by the Army Act of 1879, described in its early form the purpose of

---

[1] This reference is interesting. Dante did not mention economic questions in the *De Monarchia*. Fénelon writes of the economic community without reference to religious differences. Trade, not religion, was becoming the common factor.

[2] The Congress met simultaneously in the two towns of Münster and Osnabrück. The French and other Catholic representatives assembled at the former, the Swedes and other Protestants at the latter place. This somewhat odd procedure avoided insuperable difficulties of precedence.

this army as 'the preservation of a balance of power in Europe'. From the point of view of theory also, a balance of power seemed to be supported by an analogy with contemporary physics. The Newtonian view of the universe was not unlike Vattel's idea of a political equilibrium among a harmonized group of states. Every age has its own set of political metaphors; those of our own day, 'dynamic' for example, tend to emphasize movement; those of two hundred years ago tended to emphasize stability, an equipoise of forces in a universe controlled by its Great Architect.

It is commonly pointed out that this notion of a balance was politically valueless because no one was willing to maintain it. Wars were fought throughout the eighteenth century, nominally to uphold the balance of power but actually to disturb it in the interest of a single Power or alliance of Powers. No system of keeping the peace could have been proof against the cynical practice of a man like Frederick the Great, but the difficulty of maintaining a balance of power in the century after the Treaty of Utrecht was that the factors which had to be balanced were changing more rapidly than ever before. In any case the lack of accurate statistical information about the real strength and resources of the states of Europe (though this deficiency was being remedied during the eighteenth century) made it difficult to strike a balance between them, but something altogether new and outside previous reckoning was being introduced. The scales were upset and there was no instrument for measuring the new elements.

In the seventeenth century Austria, France, England, Spain, Sweden, the United Netherlands and the mosaic of greater or lesser German and Italian states (with the Habsburg monarch as titular emperor) formed the significant membership of the European community outside the Ottoman Empire. In the eighteenth century first Russia, through the extraordinary westernizing innovations of Peter the Great, and then Prussia, by the *tours de force* of her sovereigns, entered the circle of the Great Powers. On the other hand, by 1700 the decline of Spain had already gone so far that she could not be regarded as more than a second-class Power, although the Spanish possessions on the mainland of the American continent by mere inertia resisted attack. Above all, English and French expansion in North America and India introduced a new factor; oceanic sea-power now became, in the long run, more important than land-power.

A further change took place with the partitions of Poland and the annexations or extinctions of sovereignty during the French revolutionary and Napoleonic wars. The doctrine of the balance of power and its corollary, the idea of intervention, took on a sinister meaning. Intervention to maintain the balance was pushed as far as to destroy lesser and middle states in the interest of an equilibrium between the Great Powers. The partitions of Poland were crimes against international morality, but the partitioning Powers asserted that they were acting in the interest of European peace. On this view an equilibrium might indeed be maintained, but it was more like that between the Walrus and the Carpenter at the expense of the oysters. If this version of the balance of power had continued, the political map of Europe might have been changed without general war, but with the disappearance of the weaker states.[1]

The violent acts of Napoleon following upon the violent acts of the Jacobins did indeed bring a new situation. When the victorious powers of the last coalition against Napoleon met to discuss terms of peace with France, they had to discuss a new settlement of Europe. They could not just restore the *status quo* of 1792. The republics of Venice and Genoa, the ecclesiastical principalities of the Rhineland, the Empire itself had disappeared and could not be re-established. The plenipotentiaries of the Great Powers – the Great Powers, since they and not the small Powers had overthrown Napoleon – had to agree upon some principle of resettlement. Inevitably they chose a return to the principle of balance, with the precautions of which Polybius had spoken long ago. This return to the earlier conception of a balance of power meant also a

[1] As the French statesman Vergennes pointed out, the partitioning of Poland introduced a change in the 'system' of a balance of power, since the three Powers concerned were merely balancing among themselves their own territorial accretions.

recognition of the rights of small states as well as large, a general equilibrium, not merely a balancing of Great Powers against one another, with their appetites satisfied at the expense of their weaker neighbours. The new, or newly thought out conception was expressed in relation to domestic sovereignty in an old-fashioned way as a recognition of the rights of legitimate sovereigns, not legitimate sovereign peoples. Even so it was not complete, yet it was something that there was a question of principle.

These decisions of principles were taken, as always, for reasons of fact, but a restatement of the doctrine of the balance of power had already been made by the publicist Gentz in a work 'Fragments on the Balance of Power'.[1] Gentz became after 1812 the confidential man, one might say the stooge, of Metternich. He was personally somewhat contemptible – the kind of man who is too fond of chocolates and is willing to write clear and clever memoranda for anyone who will pay him; he was paid by the British Government and by the Hospodars of Wallachia as well as by Metternich. Gentz defined the balance of power as a 'constitution subsisting between neighbouring states more or less connected with one another, by virtue of which no one among them can injure the independence or essential rights of another without meeting resistance on some side, and consequently exposing itself to danger'. Gentz, obviously generalizing from recent events – the figure of Napoleon is close to his thoughts – based this 'constitution' on four propositions: (i) no state should ever become powerful enough to coerce all other states, (ii) any state acting in such a way as to secure for itself this predominance of power may be coerced by other states, (iii) fear of coercion would thus keep all states within the bounds of moderation, and (iv) a state defying the warnings of other states should be treated as a common enemy.

Here we have once again the idea of some bond uniting all the states of Europe, small as well as great – Gentz believed

[1] Friedrich von Gentz (1764–1832) began his career in the Prussian civil service. He went to Vienna in 1802 and published his book on the Balance of Power in 1806. He was secretary to the Congress of Vienna.

that his 'principles' would preserve the smaller states – and the doctrine of intervention, the right to coerce an offending state in the interest of general peace. These ideas were, of course, not a peculiar inspiration on the part of Gentz. Pitt had made a more practical suggestion in a paper of 1805 which influenced Castlereagh. Pitt wanted to give 'solidarity and permanence' to a treaty to which all the principal Powers of Europe should be parties, by which 'their respective rights and possessions as they then have been established shall be fixed and recognized'. They would bind themselves mutually to protect and support each other against any attempt to infringe them.

The Great Powers at the Congress of Vienna acted to a large extent (not completely) on these principles, even to the point of threatening those among them who wanted to act against the general interest. Great Britain joined with Austria and France, their former enemy, in threatening to go to war with Prussia and Russia if they insisted upon demands about Poland and Saxony which would have destroyed the balance of power. The action of the three Powers was 'precautionary'; they had good reason to suppose that Prussia at least would give way, since a war would have been fought on Prussian territory and Prussia would have paid the price of defeat. No one would have been rash enough to repeat Napoleon's mistake of invading Russia.

The Vienna treaty had a bad press, to use a modern term, because it neglected the new assumptions of popular sovereignty. The aim of the Vienna settlement was to provide against the misuse of organized state power; the means employed, the restoration of a balance between groups of states, seemed more important than the recognition of the right of subjects to determine their own political allegiance. As late as 1864 Lord John Russell, in refusing to support a French proposal to decide by plebiscite the status of the duchies of Slesvig and Holstein,[1] wrote that 'the Great Powers had not the habit of consulting populations when questions affecting the Balance of Power had to be settled'.[2] The pleni-

[1] See below, pp. 145–147.
[2] *Origines diplomatiques de la guerre franco-allemande*, vol. ii, p. 368.

potentiaries at Vienna thought that in the past twenty-five years Jacobin ferocity and its consequences had shown what was to be expected from windy doctrines of the sovereignty of the people. Castlereagh indeed realized the importance of the new movements in Europe. He did not believe that they could be stopped, but they could be retarded and the hazards which might come from their acceleration could thereby be reduced.

The idea of an equilibrium was followed without vindictiveness (except towards a few individuals) in the treatment of the defeated French. France was necessary to the European balance, and it would have been impolite to 'punish' her people. The settlement of Germany was also included in the general treaty of Vienna, and all changes in the boundaries of the continental states were registered in it. Every state thus had the right to invoke the authority of the treaty. The idea of a balance was not legally connected with the idea of intervention by the inclusion of a guarantee in the treaty, but Castlereagh hoped to develop a new kind of diplomacy by conferences between the Powers. The treaty of alliance signed by Great Britain, Austria, Prussia and Russia in November 1815 stated that these Powers would meet at regular intervals – the term used was 'fixed periods' – 'for the purpose of consulting upon their common interests, and for the consideration of the measures which at each of these periods should be considered the most salutary for the repose and prosperity of Nations, and for the maintenance of the peace of Europe'.

The conceptions of a Concert of Europe and of a balance to be maintained in the general interest, the consideration in common of measures required by this interest, and the assertion of an overwhelming superiority of force against a disturber of the peace were not very far from those of the League of nations, and the recognition of the special position of the four Great Powers was not wholly unlike the arrangements of the United Nations. From a practical point of view, however, the machinery of execution was deficient. There was no secretariat, no permanent representation of the Powers, no regular times of meeting – the 'fixed periods' were not really fixed, but were only *ad hoc* gatherings to consider questions which had arisen. These defects might have been surmounted; they mattered less in an age when international crises did not often develop with the terrifying rapidity of today. The trouble with the meetings which followed the Vienna settlement came from the misuse of the doctrine of intervention. 'Intervention' was employed not to stamp out the beginnings of international aggression but to further the special purposes of certain Powers. Under the pretext of defending the common interests of Europe, the autocratic Powers, Russia, Austria and Prussia, intervened in the affairs of small and weak states to put down movements in favour of liberal reform. The association of jacobinism with external aggression and of every kind of constitutional movement with jacobinism made it possible for the autocratic states to allege that their interference was necessary to safeguard the balance of power.

The break between Great Britain and the continental autocracies over this issue is well known. The British Government refused to accept the absolutist interpretation of the doctrine of intervention and left the meetings of the Powers. The Vienna treaty was still valid, but the 'European Areopagus' in Canning's phrase, had lost its moral credibility. British opinion now became divided between those who thought that British interest required intervention in this or that crisis in order to maintain the balance of power and those who believed that behind the shield of her naval predominance the country could keep out of continental quarrels. The Crimean War, an attempt to maintain the local balance of power between Russia and Turkey in the Near East, was the last forcible intervention by Great Britain in Europe before 1914. Mr Gladstone later called the Crimean War 'just but unnecessary'; popular opinion soon after it was fought regarded it as unnecessary and was unlikely to accept interference in any other continental war. If the continental Powers themselves would not continue to defend the Vienna settlement, Great Britain could not uphold it alone. The Franco–Italian War of 1859 against Austria brought an important change in the balance of power, but the treaty which registered this change was negotiated without the participation of all the Great Powers. Within the next twelve years the Vienna settlement was entirely upset and the old doctrine of the balance of power had disappeared. Two unsuccessful efforts were made to assert the collective interest of the European community in any important changes. Napoleon III, who had realized too late the risks to France in his own policy, proposed in 1863 a congress for revising and re-establishing the balance of power in Europe under the title of an International Council. On paper the scheme sounded well, but the pursuit of separate aims had gone too far to allow a sudden change of direction. Lord John Russell (Foreign Secretary at the time) made the mistake of rejecting the plan in brusque and sarcastic terms, though his objection that discussions would only make matters worse really begged the question. Palmerston (then Prime Minister) was equally blunt in a letter to Russell. He wrote that 'there being no supreme authority in such an assembly to enforce the opinions and decisions of the majority, the congress would probably separate, leaving many of the members on worse terms with each other than they had been before'. This might have been true, but it would have seemed the deepest pessimism to Castlereagh and also to Metternich in 1814–15, since it was a denial of the idea of the collective authority of Europe. (In Pitt's phrase, 'a Concert is an agreement to do something, not an orchestra'.)

The terms as well as the fact of Russell's refusal offended Napoleon III and gave him very soon afterwards a reason for refusing to support Great Britain in defending the rights of Denmark in the duchies of Slesvig and Holstein as affirmed in the Vienna treaty.[1] Palmerston wanted to oppose the illegal action of Prussia and Austria, though he did not realize the immense significance of the matter.[2] If the rights of the small state of Denmark had been upheld, the political career of Bismarck might well have come to an abrupt end. Bismarck and the Prussian Army were, however, allowed a free hand to

[1] For the Slesvig–Holstein question see note at the end of the chapter on Germany.

[2] Palmerston, who had been born five years before the French Revolution, had at least some excuse for failing to realize the significance of the methods and policy of Bismarck.

destroy what remained of the public law of Europe in regard to the recognition of sovereignty based on treaty right, and to set up in the new German Reich the military predominance of one Power which the advocates of a theory of balance had regarded as the greatest danger to European peace.

After 1871 the old conception of the European balance of power disappeared. An English publicist, Henry Reeve, writing about 1875, put the matter as follows:

> 'The balance of power, as it was understood fifty years ago and down to a more recent time, has been totally destroyed; no alliance can be said to exist between any of the Great Powers, but each of them follows a distinct course of policy, free from any engagements to the rest, except on some isolated points; the minor states can appeal to no certain engagement or fixed general principle for protection, except perhaps as far as the neutrality of Switzerland and Belgium is concerned; and for the last two centuries there has not been a time at which all confidence in public engagements and common principles of international law has been so grievously shaken. Where the reign of law ends, the reign of force begins, and we trace the inevitable consequence of this dissolution of legal international ties in the enormous augmentation of military establishments which is the curse and disgrace of the present age.'

Reeve went on to explain why the old idea of balance had broken down. He pointed out that it was impossible to equalize the strength of nations and to regulate and control the growth and development of their forces, which depended not on territorial possessions alone, but on their industry, their credit, their natural resources and their internal institutions. It was impossible to weigh this relative power and influence in 'nice' scales. On the other hand Reeve thought it essential to civilization that 'certain mutual obligations and principles of public law' should be recognized. He concluded with the words:

> 'We trust that before another great catastrophe arises from this state of disguised hostility, a truer balance of power may be established by a return to sounder principles; for peace

can never be secure unless it is protected by the concurrence of the leading nations of the world, and by their determination to oppose a combined resistance to those who have no object but their own aggrandizement and ambition.'

Such was a thoughtful English view of the situation. Reeve was not writing for a handful of experts. The sentences I have quoted come from an article in the ninth edition of the *Encyclopaedia Britannica*. One may contrast them with a marginal comment written by Bismarck on a communication received from the Russian Government a year of two later during the Near Eastern crisis of 1877–8. The Russian Foreign Minister Gortchakov had referred to the public opinion of Europe. Bismarck's comment was 'Europe. Notion géographique', and a few lines lower down, 'Qui parle Europe a tort'.

There was an equilibrium of sorts in the fifty years before 1914 and it was generally called, or rather miscalled, a balance of power. This new balance was different from the conception of Fénelon and Vattel, and later Pitt and Castlereagh. It was a balance between two groups of states, not a general system of weights and counterweights in an equipoise of satisfied Powers. One might describe it in terms of interlocked wrestlers or of a boxer's clinch. There was no real equipoise because each group tried to tip the scales in its own favour. Bismarck once said that in a world of five Great Powers it was better to be one of three than one of two, and Salisbury summed up Bismarck's policy as an attempt to get his neighbours engaged in pulling one another's teeth out. Bismarck's plans failed. They were concentrated after 1871 on the isolation of France and therefore upon preventing a breach between Russia and Austria–Hungary which would compel Germany to choose between these two latter Powers. Bismarck wanted to avoid such a choice because he was bound to support Austria–Hungary and might thus drive Russia into alliance with France. The Franco-Russian alliance did not come into existence during Bismarck's tenure of power and when it came it was in fact pointed as much against Great Britain as against Germany.[1] Nevertheless, as

---

[1] See below, p. 207.

soon as the alliance was formed and France was no longer isolated in Europe, the new equilibrium began to take shape; the dual alliance of France and Russia on one side and, on the other side, the triple alliance of Germany, Austria-Hungary and Italy, in which Italy was always a doubtful partner. This situation was extremely dangerous to peace. Germany could not afford to let Austria-Hungary grow weaker and Russia could not allow her to become stronger, but Austria-Hungary must either grow weaker by concessions to the nationalist movements within the monarchy or stronger by suppressing these movements and those of the neighbouring Slavs who supported them.

Each of the two European groups of Powers continued to add to their armaments and to try to break up opposing combinations. Each group came to regard as preparation for aggression measures which the other group considered as legitimate precautions against attack. Every Power tended to develop a myth about the intentions of its neighbours; these myths were accepted and even fostered by the other party. The German belief in a deep-laid British plot to encircle the Reich was the most fantastic and dangerous example.[1] In these circumstances it is not difficult to understand why and how a brutal act of assassination in Bosnia on 28 June 1914 led to the outbreak of general war in Europe.

[1] At the moment in July 1914 when British opinion was becoming convinced of the German intention to initiate an aggressive war for the domination of Europe, the Emperor William II could write and obviously believe that the war had been arranged by England, France and Russia for the annihilation of Germany, and that a plot to this effect could be traced back to the machinations of King Edward VII. *German Documents on the Origins of the War*, No. 402.

1. France

Hitherto in this introduction to the study of the nineteenth century I have discussed certain developments which have affected the larger sovereign nation-states. I want now to bring each of these states into sharper focus. I shall not thereby dogmatize about 'national character'. National character exists; otherwise the term 'nation-state' would have little meaning, but talk about 'typical Frenchmen' or 'typical Germans' is as elusive as attempts to draw political conclusions from the fact that there are physical differences between races.

Nevertheless these different national characteristics have left a visible mark on the landscapes of areas otherwise geographically similar. An American historian said to me a good many years ago when aeroplanes flew lower and less fast than they do now, that the journey by air from London to Paris was of greater interest than any other short journey in the world. On either side of the English Channel there were similar geographical and geological features – chalk cliffs, small river estuaries and so on, and yet behind them the look of each country from the air was so very different. For centuries past the landscapes have been man-made and only a knowledge of history can explain the differences of pattern in similar areas divided only by a comparatively narrow sea-channel.

Up to 1914 France was (I should say that it still is) the most interesting of the continental nation-states, with the oldest 'national' history, unless the Dutch make this claim for themselves. France was a unified nation-state when Germany was composed politically of 300 and more units under the shadowy sovereignty of the Holy Roman Empire. In the seventeenth century French civilization came to dominate Europe and was imitated in all continental countries except Spain. This imitation continued until the later years of the eighteenth century; the alarm with which the French Revolutionary Terror affected Europe was largely due to astonishment that such things could happen in so enlightened a centre as Paris.

The French themselves were conscious of their pre-eminence and this feeling of superiority had important political consequences. Frenchmen travelled little outside France and knew little about other countries. They disliked the English, and the English disliked them. They underrated the Germans or thought of them too long in terms of Madame de Stael's sentimental ideas about Germany.[1] Thus down to 1870, and in many respects even later, French opinion tended to ignore, if I may use a jargon phrase, the relative power potential of other European states. European civilization had but one centre, France, and one capital, Paris.

French 'insularity' was, of course, matched by English insularity. Against French unwillingness to borrow from English social and political experience, one may set English complacency about the peaceful development of free institutions in comparison with French revolutionary violence. One must remember also the limited extent to which one nation can ever learn political lessons from another. Nevertheless the extreme confidence of this highly individualized French nation in their civilized primacy contributed to the fact that they were less affected than one might have expected by the frequent and turbulent changes in their own political regime.

The existence of a national state of France before the nineteenth century meant that the French did not have to concern themselves, like Germans and Italians, with the elementary question 'who is a Frenchman?' or with a French irredentist movement or with forming a single state out of a number of different-sized units. The peace settlement of 1815 did not leave France with serious territorial grievances. There was no strong

---

[1] Madame de Stael (1766–1817) was the daughter of the French financier Necker (who had been born in Switzerland). She married a German, Baron de Stael. Madame de Stael left France in 1792, returned after some years, and was exiled again by Napoleon. Her book *De l'Allemagne* (1810) introduced German literature to French readers who had hitherto accepted Voltaire's view that the Germans needed 'fewer consonants and more wit'.

nationalist agitation behind Napoleon III's demand for the cession of Nice and Savoy – they would probably have come to France in any case when Italy became a united nation. On the other hand the French-speaking inhabitants of Belgium and Switzerland did not want to be joined politically to France and the Bretons and Basques had no wish to leave the French state. The annexation of Alsace and Lorraine to France had taken place before the rise of modern political nationalism; the Alsatians and Lorrainers were not discontented with their status. As far as domestic policy was concerned, the French could therefore concentrate on what might be called the problems of a modern nation-state which had accepted the principle of popular sovereignty: what is the best form of government for such a society, what should be the relations between Church and State, how can a regime of liberty be combined with one of equality and also with adequate governmental authority, to what extent is administrative decentralization desirable in a popularly controlled government?

The French indeed were bound to concentrate upon these problems because they had destroyed, in a decade of revolutionary experiment, a large part of their old political system without establishing anything stable in its place. They had posed sharply the question of popular sovereignty without learning how they could prevent it from degenerating into a new kind of tyranny. After getting rid of a centralized monarchy based upon divine right, they tried in turn between 1789 and 1814 a limited constitutional monarchy, an 'emergency' Jacobin dictatorship, an unstable (and corrupt) oligarchy – the Directory – and the military, authoritarian dictatorship of Napoleon. From 1815 to 1870 they repeated these experiments. Between 1815 and 1830 they maintained an uncertain compromise between parliamentary monarchy and monarchy by divine right; from 1830 to 1848 constitutional monarchy under a restricted franchise. In 1848 they went back to a republic about which opinion was divided between those who wanted something like an anti-capitalist dictatorship of the working class and those who supported something more like parliamentary monarchy without a monarch. The conflict between left and right, social revolution and social conservatism, opened the way to another authoritarian regime, the dictatorship of Napoleon III based on plebiscite and claiming to be an unaggressive continuation of the system of his uncle Napoleon I. This second imperial regime had begun to move towards constitutional monarchy when it collapsed in military defeat. After the suppression of another revolutionary movement in Paris a third republic was set up which lasted, at times precariously, until a more complete military defeat in 1940. In the seventy years between 1870 and 1940 there were ninety to a hundred different ministries – it is not easy to count them because some of them disappeared before meeting parliament. There were fifty Prime Ministers (Presidents of the Council) and Foreign Ministers, and in all about 450 to 500 Frenchmen held ministerial office under the Third Republic.

I shall say more about these rapid changes and why they contrast, paradoxically, with a remarkable social stability, one might say conservatism, in French life. Let me first mention a few important facts about France itself, the physical background of all this political activity. France, by western European standards, is a large country, twice the size of Great Britain, and bordering on the North Sea, the Atlantic and the Mediterranean; a great river, Seine, Loire and Rhone, flows into each of these seas. Most of the country is extremely fertile, with varied products. It is less rich in coal than Great Britain, a fact of greater importance in the nineteenth than in the later twentieth century. There were, and are, fewer great cities than in Great Britain; in 1900 a far higher proportion of people in Paris than in London had near relations working on the land and much less food was imported into France than into England.

The population of France in 1911 (thus excluding Alsace-Lorraine) was under 40 million, the population of the German Reich was nearly 65 million, and of Great Britain nearly 41 million. In 1815 the figures were about 30 million for France and about 13 million for Great Britain. Paris was a much smaller city than London in the nineteenth century; Marseilles and Lyons were smaller than Birmingham, Liverpool, Manchester and Glasgow. The French population had been growing more slowly than that of their neighbours; between 1871 and 1914 the French increase was 3½ million, or about 10 per cent, and the German about 23 million, or over 50 per cent. It is meaningless to assume, as some German writers have assumed, that a relatively stable population necessarily implies some kind of inferiority or decline in vigour, though there are cases of such correlation. There were special causes for this relatively small French increase in numbers; the caution of peasants not to multiply overmuch the numbers to be maintained from a single holding – a tradition of this kind, once established, can easily be carried over to other modes of livelihood. Other classes owning property were affected by the French laws of succession which required a more even division than in English law of a dead man's property among his children. There was also a desire in an old and settled country, with fewer opportunities than in more industrialized states of getting rich, to maintain a family in a certain status. The custom that all daughters must have a dowry survived longer among wider sections of the population than in Great Britain.

None the less the fact that there were fewer Frenchmen in 1914 than in 1815 in relation to the rest of Europe had political as well as economic consequences. The French had neither the advantages nor the disadvantages of emigration. Near at hand their North African possessions, which were counted as metropolitan territory, gave Frenchmen economic opportunities which they could not find at home. Outside North Africa most of the French colonies in the nineteenth century were unsuited for permanent European settlement. Few Frenchmen chose to go to them; the French colonial service, admirable in many ways, did not attract the high average of ability secured by the British Indian and colonial services and, especially in the Far Eastern colonies, the changes in personnel were too rapid. Few Frenchmen emigrated to the Americas; there is no 'French' vote in the United States.[1] The French-speaking population in Canada has brought problems which

[1] The number of French-speaking people in Louisiana, and their use of the French language, diminished rapidly, though it is not yet extinct.

have not yet been solved, but there has been no important French immigration to add to the difficulties.

The population question has been more relevant to national defence and through national defence to foreign policy. After 1871 French foreign policy became largely a search for security against a more powerful Germany. The German motives for annexing Alsace and a large part of Lorraine were partly sentimental, but mainly military; the economic value of the Lorraine ores was not fully recognized by either side until after the annexation. From 1871 to 1918 the French north-east frontier was as near to Paris as London is to Birmingham and the key fortress of Metz was in German hands. In 1870 the number of Frenchmen capable of bearing arms was almost equal to the number of Germans; forty years later there were four Germans to every three Frenchmen.

The study of nineteenth-century France is thus in many respects an exercise in population statistics. I have not yet done with this exercise. France throughout the century remained primarily an agricultural country. In 1850 large-scale industry employed only about 1,500,000 men and women. Many industries which might have been organized for mass production continued almost on domestic lines. There was, for example, in the nineteenth century a very large output of wooden shoes (associated traditionally in England with Frenchmen and popery), but the average shoemaker had only two assistants.[1] In 1870 the French export of corn was eight times as valuable as the export of engines and machinery. In 1872 the industrial workers and their families formed about 8·4 million or 23 per cent of the population. Seventy years later the figures had increased only to 27 per cent. If Frenchmen living in communes (the smallest unit of local government) with a *chef-lieu* or centre containing less than 2,000 inhabitants are counted as rural, 67·6 per cent of the population was in this category in 1876, and 55 per cent in 1911. The number of

---

[1] In 1866 the average ratio between workers and employers (*patrons*) in all French industrial establishments was 2:1. This ratio (leaving out the mining and transport industries) had not much changed forty years later. See below, p. 103.

peasant proprietors – persons working on land owned by themselves or their families – in France has been exaggerated and the number of landless workers – about a third of the agricultural population – underestimated. There were about 9 million peasant proprietors in 1870. Small landowners might be a better term for them, but most of them were peasants in the sense that they did not produce, or produced only in-incidentally, for a market. It is dangerous to generalize about them owing to the differences in the size of holdings and the mode of tenure, but on the whole one may speak of the backwardness of French agriculture throughout the nineteenth century. The subsistence farmers were ignorant, lacking capital, and very often in debt; the holdings were in general too small,[1] and communications for large markets were inadequate. As for the labourers, at the end of the century they were still unprotected by legislation against excessive hours of work or by inspection of their conditions of labour.

Obviously these agriculturists have had an important influence on French politics. They have supported the institution of private property; they have had something tangible to defend, their own land, or land which they hoped their children would own. They might vote for the radical left, but they would not support attacks on private ownership. Their stabilizing influence was, however, negative. The agricultural vote did not stand for any general constructive programme. They wanted local advantages; they had little interest in education or in social legislation which put up the taxes for the benefit, as they argued, of townspeople. Fortunately they cared nothing for the 'substitute' aggrandizement – national power – which attracted, for example, the German middle class: French agricultural voters were unmoved by the thought of the French colonial empire.

The peasants in the first revolution had seized land for themselves, or rather they had got rid of the landlords' feudal rights

[1] The peasants were buying more land, but in 1929 the land occupied by 54 per cent of peasant farms amounted only to 10 per cent of the cultivated land of France. In such conditions there was little mechanization of peasant agriculture.

over it. They did little else, except in the west where many of them fought for church and king, other than to endure the Napoleonic conscription when they could not escape it. The revolutionary transformation of France was carried out by the towns and, above all, by Paris. The centralizing policy of the monarchy had given Paris before 1789 an overwhelming importance which even London as a capital has held only at certain times in English history. Paris between 1789 and 1871 meant more to France than London to Great Britain after 1832. Lyons, Marseilles, Bordeaux, Toulouse counted for a good deal, but there was no provincial city in France during the nineteenth century to which one could apply the saying: 'What Lancashire thinks today, England will think tomorrow.' The first set-back to this immense political predominance of the capital came with the suppression of the left-wing insurrection after the closing of the National Workshops in 1848.[1] The construction under Napoleon III of the 'grands boulevards' on which it was less easy than in the old, narrow streets to set up barricades (the traditional revolutionary expression of resistance), the building of railways by which troops could be moved quickly from the provinces to the capital, the electric telegraph which gave a more rapid circulation of news and therefore greater scope for provincial newspapers, all these factors reduced the power of the Paris mob. The defeat of the Commune in 1871[2] marked another decline, but the centralization of authority in Paris was still a leading factor in French political life.

These frequent changes of regime, initiated by outbreaks of Parisian revolution, were due in part to a continuous reference in politics to first principles. One difference between London and Paris is that a good many prominent Parisian streets and squares are named after dates, e.g. the 14th July, the 4th September. These dates commemorate successful revolutions and most people have some idea why they are so commemorated. The only 'political' date which might mean anything to the ordinary citizen if applied to a London street is 5th November and this date would commemorate, not a successful revolution,

[1] See below, p. 76.
[2] See below, p. 90.

but the detection of a conspiracy against the Government. French politics since 1789 have been dominated too much by ideas of attack – '*à bas*' someone or something. Over a century ago a French minister said that, if he lost the thread of a speech and wanted a moment to put his ideas in order, all he had to do was to mention the word 'Jésuites' and a storm of catcalls gave him time to recover his argument. If all political divisions are about first principles, every crisis becomes a major crisis, an instance of the evils of a particular form of government. Compromise meant selling the pass, allowing the opposite principle to gain a foothold in the citadel of power. Since compromise is a practical necessity of party government, the lack of it meant a splintering of French parties into groups, each reluctant to merge its identity for long in a larger unit. The splits tended to be more serious on the left than on the right (though for a long time the monarchists disagreed about the candidate for the French throne), not because left-wing politicians are more quarrelsome – they may be to the extent that they include more social 'misfits' – but because it is easier to agree about not changing things than about the direction in which they should be changed.

The reference to first principles and the series of constitutional experiments were caused by the desire of most Frenchmen to find a way of keeping and extending, without the violence of revolutionary practice, the changes brought about by the first revolution. This dual purpose appeared to have been achieved, none too easily, by the end of the century, but the chances of success did not seem at first very great. The victorious allies brought back the old reigning house of Bourbon twice, in 1814, and again after Waterloo, but without much confidence in the ability of either of the brothers of Louis XVI to maintain himself as a constitutional monarch. Louis XVIII, the elder of the two brothers, was indolent and narrow-minded, but, like Charles II of England, determined 'not to go on his travels again'. He promised his subjects an indemnity for acts done 'during the first nineteen years of our reign', in other words, for everything which had happened in France since the death in prison in 1795 of the young son of Louis

XVI. None the less Louis XVIII recognized the revolutionary land settlement, the revolutionary principles of equality before the law, liberty of conscience, speech and writing. He accepted the organization of local government and the legal system established by Napoleon. He also 'granted' his subjects a parliament of two houses.

The greatest danger to the monarchy came from its own extreme supporters, the returned *émigrés* and the Church; the saying that the Bourbons had 'learned nothing and forgotten nothing' applied more to his over-zealous supporters than to Louis XVIII himself. The philosophy of the Counter Revolution was superficial, slightly absurd and not in the French tradition of the eighteenth century. Joseph de Maistre, the most popular writer on the conservative side (if one does not take the romantic prose of Châteaubriand as seriously as he took it himself), came, not from the old kingdom of France, but from the kingdom of Savoy-Piedmont.[1] The revolutionary armies drove him from Chambéry, or rather he left Savoy on their approach, and his most important book *Considérations sur la Révolution française* was written in exile at Lausanne. De Maistre described the revolution as 'purely satanic', without a single element of good. This type of judgement which lumped together the atrocities of the Terror and the introduction of the metric system, and regarded the creation of the French Départements as the work of the Devil, was typical of much of the 'thought' on the counter-revolutionary side. Bonald, another writer of the extreme right, and also not a French citizen by birth – he came from near Milan – justified the introduction of the death penalty for sacrilege (in fact no one was put to death under the law) with the argument that such a punishment was merely sending the criminal before his natural Judge.

Louis XVIII's brother and successor to the throne in 1824, was an elderly rake who had turned pious; he had neither good judgement nor common sense. He alarmed public opinion by a number of measures, tactless rather than sinister, and, after he had stirred up the people of Paris to a dangerous pitch of anger, took no steps to guard against a revolutionary outbreak. When

[1] Actually the Kingdom of Sardinia. See below, p. 148.

this outbreak occurred in July 1830, he merely ran away from Paris and took ship for England. No attempt was made to stop him. The moderate politicians, who did not want a republican revolution, persuaded the Paris revolutionaries to accept Louis Philippe, duke of Orleans, son of the odious 'Philippe Égalité' of the first Revolution, and head of a younger branch of the royal house, as a constitutional king without any farrago about divine right. Louis Philippe regarded himself as chosen in order to close an age of revolution, not, as the republicans hoped, to re-open it. If he kept his bargain with the bourgeois politicians who had put him forward, and if he acted constitutionally as the defender of property and order, he expected the throne to be safe for himself and his children. He overdid the part of a bourgeois king – walking about with an umbrella – and made himself ridiculous, a dangerous thing in France. A little more magnificence and a little less avarice in money matters might have given him some popularity. His greatest mistake, however, was to think that the middle class, or rather the 240,000 electors under the restricted French franchise, were the only people whose support was necessary to him. The Monarchy of July, as it was called, was served by abler ministers than any other nineteenth-century regime in France; Thiers, for example, who survived to be largely responsible for the consolidation of the Third Republic after the fall of Napoleon III, and Guizot who was totally repudiated in 1848.[1] Guizot, especially in his later years, was much too rigid in his view that the comfortable middle class was alone capable of providing France with a good government. Guizot himself had a high sense of personal duty, but he held to the full extent the prevailing ideas of economic *laissez-faire* and his only remedy for the current misery of the working class was one of self-help aided by private charity. For Louis Philippe and Guizot, the sons of men who had been guillotined during the first revolution, an extension of the franchise

---

[1] The historian Sir Charles Firth once told the writer that he had been present at a discussion between Lord Acton and John Morley on the question who was the greatest 'all-round' figure of the nineteenth century. Both had agreed on Guizot.

(something like the English Reform Act of 1832) seemed likely to result in control of the Government by doctrinaire radicals who would themselves be overthrown by a return of revolutionary disorder. The refusal even of a moderate franchise extension – doubling the electorate – lost Louis Philippe the support of a large section of the unenfranchised middle class. Consequently, when the middle-class battalions of the citizen National Guard appeared to be supporting popular demonstrations against the Government (not a planned revolution, which was the last thing the middle classes wanted), the king lost confidence and thought that the basis of his authority had collapsed. He abdicated in favour of his grandson and left Paris for England saying, so it was reported, 'Comme Charles X, comme Charles X'.

France was now without a government. The rest of the country accepted the initiative of Paris; there was no attempt at a counter-revolution and, almost as a matter of course, a republic was proclaimed in Paris. The republicans, however, were divided between those who wanted no greater political change than a moderate increase in the franchise, and those who were agitating for large-scale social and economic reforms. The latter meant by economic reforms an attack on the existing order of capitalist production. The most thoroughgoing reformers after about 1832 called themselves 'socialists', a term possibly borrowed from English writers.[1] At this time the comte de Saint-Simon, who might be called the founder of French socialism, had died in 1825. Saint-Simon, a more interesting though less powerful character than Marx, had gone to America as a young man to fight in the revolution, but had done nothing except to get himself imprisoned for a time as a suspect and to make a fortune in land speculation. He always believed himself destined for something great,[2] but here also

[1] The term was applied in English about 1826 to the followers of Robert Owen.

[2] Saint-Simon's valet had orders to call him every morning with the words: 'Souvenez-vous, M. le comte, vous avez des grandes choses à faire.' He also believed that Charlemagne, from whom he claimed descent, had appeared to him in a dream, and forecast a great future for him. He lost all his money in his own bank project and died in poverty.

he merely formulated great schemes, such as a canal from the Atlantic to the Pacific, and a bank of which the profits would go to works of public utility.

A man of this type was unlikely to be a systematic thinker (indeed Saint-Simon seems at times to be a less balanced and less ingenious imitation of Bentham). His schemes were systematized and popularized only after his death. He did not argue in terms of capital and labour, and was not a revolutionary; he appealed to Louis XVIII, of all people, to introduce his plans for the reorganization of society. Saint-Simon's originality lay in his early recognition of the political importance of technical change. Traditional ideas of government were out of date; government had passed through the stage of dominion over persons and had become the administration of things. This administration did not require feudal aristocracies; it needed scientifically instructed, technically competent chiefs to direct production to social ends. In this way society would get rid of the proletarian class which had evolved through slavery and serfdom. Saint-Simon proposed that high executive power should be given to a chamber of deputies recruited from manufacturing and commercial magnates who would accept or reject projects submitted to them by two chambers of savants, artists and engineers.

The Saint-Simonians in the 1830s attracted to themselves a number of interesting figures who were in some respects unpractical dreamers and in others far ahead of their time. One of their proposals was for a canal through the isthmus of Suez. Enfantin, who became later a director of the P.L.M. railway, an enterprise not outside the Saint-Simonian notion of works of public utility, did the movement no good by his absurd pontification and advocacy of free love. Saint-Simon himself invented a number of phrases with a future, 'the exploitation of man by man', 'the right to work'. His followers developed an attack on private property and the private ownership of land; the next stage in the evolution of property would be, in their words, the removal of the hazards of birth.

The attack on property, the very foundation of bourgeois

society, was not limited to the Saint-Simonians. F. M. L. Fourier (1772–1837) had written in 1808 an odd, wild book, the *Théorie des Quatre Mouvements*, a theory of 'four harmonies' – organic life, animal life, society, the material universe. The motive which led Fourier to these excogitations and to his proposals for phalansteries, or units of 1,500–2,000 workers (working to the sound of grand pianos) was a reaction from the sharp practice of the competitive system, not, incidentally, the factory system, though Fourier lived and wrote in Lyons, but in ordinary trade and commerce. Fourier, like Saint-Simon, believed that his plans had only to be understood to be generally accepted; he hoped that a rich capitalist would supply the funds for putting the plans into effect. One such capitalist did so; the plan collapsed, but Fourier went on hoping for more rich capitalists.

There were other, fiercer critics whose destructive or corrosive influence from a bourgeois point of view was greater. Proudhon's book published in 1840 gave a simple answer to the question in its title *Qu'est-ce que la propriété?* The answer was 'la propriété, c'est le vol' – property is theft. P. S. Proudhon (1809–65) began life in a poor household but, again, not in the proletariat of machine industry; his father was a cooper at Besançon. Proudhon himself at nineteen became a printer's compositor and then a proof reader. His first book was a worthless *Essai de grammaire générale*. He was really a moralist, and his attitude to economics was like that of Ruskin; he held to a crude version of the labour theory of value – one day's labour by one man was equivalent to one day's labour by another man, so all should be paid equally, no matter what they were producing or doing. Proudhon wrote *Qu'est-ce que la propriété?* while he was living on what would now be called a research grant for three years from the Academy of Besançon. He published the book in the second year of his grant. Such was the large and often forgotten measure of intellectual toleration under the regime of Louis Philippe.

There was in fact little danger to the Government from the utopias of the Saint-Simonians or the Fourierists who, for that matter, excommunicated one another, though they still held to the eighteenth-century belief that their reforms could be carried out by the existing authorities if only these authorities could be persuaded of their reasonableness. The threat to the Government was a more general one, the increasing volume of discontent with the social and economic order, the loss of respect for the family, for religion, property, social conventions and the possibility that some popular writer would bring forward remedies for economic evils and a plan of improvement which did not seem utopian. The general mood of dissatisfaction with the immobility of the regime, the actual and grim misery of early industrialism prepared the ground for any plan which looked plausible. As evidence of the way in which men, especially young men, were thinking, it may be noticed that Louis Napoleon (of whom more later) published in 1844 a book on the extinction of pauperism. Louis Napoleon had a genuine interest in the social question (Louis Philippe, a grand seigneur at heart in spite of his bourgeois allure, had no such interest) and also a flair for guessing what people wanted. His plan was to plant agricultural colonies in France; there was something, not much, in the idea and it associated the name of Napoleon with social reform.

The plan which caught on and did much to upset the monarchy of July and, very soon afterwards, the Second French Republic, was the work of a journalist, Louis Blanc. Louis was born of a Corsican mother at Madrid in 1811. His father was a legitimist who had become reconciled with Napoleon I. The Bourbons gave him a pension; the Government of Louis Philippe cut it off; Louis Blanc therefore had no reason for liking the regime. He was a vain man, ambitious and superficial. He busied himself with economic theory and especially with the question of unemployment; he was hardly more than a dabbler and anyhow was writing before the theory of a trade cycle had been fully explored. Louis Blanc published in 1840 an article, reprinted as a small book or rather pamphlet, on unemployment and its cure. The title of the book, *L'Organisation du Travail*, was borrowed from the Saint-Simonians. The book was not just wool-gathering. Louis Blanc, like Engels, pointed to the evils of the Industrial

Revolution (the actual term had not yet been invented) in England. He said that France ought to be warned by the English example, since she was taking the same disastrous road.

There was no doubt about the facts. In 1846, for example, out of 10,000 conscripts called up from manufacturing areas 9,000 were rejected as unfit; out of 10,000 called up from agricultural areas only 4,000 were unfit. Louis Blanc's remedy was to get rid of the capitalist exploitation of labour by the establishment of 'social workshops' (*ateliers sociaux*) on a co-operative basis. The State, that is to say, the capitalist taxpayers would supply the money to start the workshops; once started they would become self-supporting. The State would nominate the first directors; their successors, like the officers of the citizen National Guard, would be elected by the workers. Everyone would receive equal pay; no one would mind this equality, since a new education would bring a general levelling up. Louis Blanc thought that such a revolution could be peaceful: 'cette révolution, si nécessaire, il est possible, facile même de l'accomplir pacifiquement.'

The shortcomings of this co-operative plan, which Louis Blanc also wanted to apply to literature (*librairies sociaux* on the same basis as the *ateliers sociaux*) are obvious. The plan ignored the problem of fluctuations in demand; there was no general control of these independent co-operative units which might go on producing without selling their products. The plan did not meet the problem of exports and was based on the conception of a society of craftsmen and small workshops, the old French economy, whereas the worst social malaise was being caused by the transition – very much slower in France than in England – to great industry.[1] Nevertheless Louis Blanc's ideas had a large following, especially in Paris, whose economy was much more of the old than of the new kind. The problem of unemployment was particularly severe in 1846 and 1847 owing to bad harvests and a general industrial and financial slump, due partly to over-investment in railways.

[1] In 1848 one half of 64,000 master-employers (*patrons*) in Paris were either self-employed or had only one workman.

In the general confusion following the sudden overthrow not only of the ministers but of the regime of Louis Philippe, two 'provisional' governments were set up, both of them republican. One at least had a semblance of legality, since it was proclaimed, or rather acclaimed, in the Chamber of Deputies by a noisy mob to whom the names of the new ministers were read out; at the head of the list was Dupont de l'Eure who had been twenty-one in 1789 and was now chosen as a symbol of the continuity of the revolutionary tradition because he had sat in the first revolutionary assembly. The other 'provisional' government was set up, without reference to legality, by a crowd at the offices of a left-wing newspaper. The 'ministers' included Louis Blanc and a workman named Albert who was said to be connected with secret revolutionary societies.

A compromise was arranged between the two 'provisional' governments; the ministers accepted in the Chamber of Deputies agreed to take Louis Blanc and Albert into their number as 'secretaries' without departmental offices, but with a ministerial vote. Within a short time, after pressure from the crowds which kept on gathering outside the meeting-place of the ministers, Louis Blanc was empowered to draw up a proclamation on the right to work. Inevitably he put his own ideas into the proclamation and thus committed the provisional government to his plan of co-operative workshops, in which the workers would get the profits of their work. As no machinery existed for giving effect to these plans. Louis Blanc was made head of a commission to study the question.

The moderate ministers, supported by middle-class opinion, thought Louis Blanc's plans impracticable. Even if they had wanted to try the experiment, the Government could not have done so at once and without much study and organization, but the statistical basis for such a study hardly existed. These fundamental changes were put forward at a time of political and economic crisis when government stock was falling rapidly and the Exchequer was in difficulties. The economic depression was not confined to France; it was common to all Europe. Louis Blanc had no idea of the reasons for it.

Louis Blanc's plan was not and could not have been given a fair trial. The Minister of Public Works merely set up relief works, mostly digging; one of them was the construction of an embankment for the new western railway terminus at Montparnasse. The number of workers increased rapidly: unemployed men came in from the provinces where there was no system of relief for them. Only a few large cities, Lyons, Marseilles, Lille, Rouen, Nantes, set up Ateliers Nationaux on the lines of those in Paris. In mid-March over 6,000 men, in mid-April nearly 40,000 were being maintained in Paris. When there was no more digging to be done on the railway embankment, the men moved to the Champs de Mars, where they were given a dole. In the third week of May the numbers rose to 80,000 and early in June to 100,000. Most of the men were in the building and carpentry trades hit by the slump and the political uncertainty. Louis Blanc and his followers complained that the experiment of co-operative workshops under State supervision was not being attempted. Since it was not within the power of the Government, even if they had the will, to attempt it, the only alternative was to abandon the plan and to send the workers from the provinces back to their homes. The younger men were invited to join the army. The result was, almost immediately, an insurrection of the Parisian working class.[1]

This time the bourgeois did not side with the rebels. The elections, held in April, at which 84 per cent of the electorate cast their votes, had given the moderates a large majority outside Paris. The Government had 50,000 men, 30,000 of them regular troops, to deal with this armed insurrection and the rebels had not allowed for the new fact in Parisian outbreaks that troops could be brought quickly into the capital by train. After three days the Government forces were in complete control of the city. Nine hundred regular and reserve troops were killed. The number of dead on the side of the rebels is not known. After the fighting was over few of the rebels were put to death; some 4,000 were sent out of France, most of them

[1] Only a minority of the men from the Ateliers Nationaux joined the insurrection.

to Algeria.[1] The Government now had nothing to fear from the leaders of the working class.

The June days lost the Second Republic the support of the urban working class. This loss was the more serious because the republic was actually in danger from one man whose importance and conspiratorial ability the professional politicians naïvely ignored for too long. Louis Napoleon, nephew of Napoleon I, had the ambition to revive in his person the regime of his uncle, a strong government resting at least nominally on popular support. The nephew, however, had made himself ridiculous by two futile attempts at a *coup d'etat;* at the second attempt, in 1840, he took with him a tame eagle, the Napoleonic emblem. The Government of Louis Philippe sent the eagle to the Paris zoo and Louis Napoleon to imprisonment in a fortress from which, in 1846, with some skill and courage he managed to escape. Before the failure of his second *coup* he had written a book, *Les Idées Napoléoniennes,* in which he popularized the legend which Napoleon I had tried to build up in exile. He thus identified himself for thousands who had never seen him with the idea of authority based upon universal suffrage, strong government without royal absolutism, ultimate control of the executive by the sovereign people without the intrigues and wasteful talk of a parliamentary regime.

Louis Napoleon came back to France after the 1848 revolution. He stood as a candidate for the Constituent Assembly and was elected, but his first attempt at a speech was another fiasco; he sat down without saying anything. The regular politicians regarded him with contempt. Thiers said of him, 'C'est un cretin qu'on menera.' The new republican constitution however, provided for the election of a president by universal suffrage. Louis Napoleon put himself forward as a candidate and, to the astonishment of the politicians of Paris, was elected by a large majority. He owed his election to the general fear of disorder and further attacks on property, the suspicion

[1] It was decided at first to deport these men to the more distant French colonies, from which it would be less easy for them to return to France. This plan was given up, characteristically, because it was too expensive.

and jealousy of Paris felt by the provincial towns and the peasants, the dislike of the taxation imposed by the Assembly (the State was almost bankrupt) and, not least, to the skill of his own propaganda.

Once elected, Louis Napoleon showed great astuteness in overthrowing the constitution which he had sworn to defend. Within three years he had broken up the opposition and persuaded the country, outside the great cities, that a return to the Napoleonic dictatorship based upon plebiscite was the best guarantee of peace, order and prosperity. Until too late the politicians misread his intentions and underrated his ability and boldness as a political gambler. The assembly, nervous about electoral losses to the left, introduced what was in practice a property qualification disfranchising about three million voters; most of the disfranchised were working-class voters in the towns, since they were least able to prove a three years residence. Louis Napoleon could therefore pose as the defender of universal suffrage against the Assembly.[1]

He courted the goodwill of the Church and had little to fear from the royalist opposition. They too had underrated his skill as a conspirator and anyhow they were divided between the supporters of the grandson of Charles X and supporters of the grandson of Louis Philippe;[2] both groups preferred the candidature of Louis Napoleon to that of a good republican because they thought that after about ten years he might give way to a royalist restoration. He used his presidential powers to favour the army and to put his own supporters into key positions, such as the command of the Paris garrison, for an eventual *coup d'état*. Here again the Assembly did what he wanted by refusing to bring into the city a strong military force for their protection, because they were more afraid of a possible Orleanist *coup* than of one by Louis Napoleon.

[1] His own view of universal suffrage was expressed later in the words: 'Je veux être baptisé avec l'eau du suffrage universal, mais je n'entends pas vivre les pieds dans l'eau.'

[2] A plan for the 'fusion' of the two royalist parties – and families – on the basis that Charles X's grandson (who had no children) should be succeeded by the grandson of Louis Philippe broke down at this time. Thiers called it a plan 'for the fusion of foolscap and blotting-paper'.

Louis Napoleon carried out his *coup d'état* on 2 December 1851, an auspicious day for a Bonaparte since it was the anniversary of the battle of Austerlitz. There was little resistance and little popular support. He made one great error which was never forgotten, though it did him little harm at the time owing to the general fear of disorder and acceptance of 'strong' action by authority. In a mistaken belief that the republicans demonstrating in the streets of Paris were intending armed resistance, he sent out troops on the day after the *coup d'état* to teach the crowds a lesson. The lesson cost the lives of about 300 among the demonstrators and 27 soldiers. A plebiscite on 14 December gave Louis Napoleon a huge majority. A year later another popular vote, with an even larger majority, approved the change of title which transformed the Prince President, as he had called himself after the *coup d'état*, into the the Emperor Napoleon III.

It would be a mistake to think of this regime based upon plebiscite as an anticipation of the European dictatorships of the twentieth century. There were certain obvious resemblances; the 'double talk', the contempt for parliamentary government, the clever propaganda, the emphasis on a 'nationalist' foreign policy, the underlying corruption and jobbery of the regime, the drift towards war, the final collapse in military defeat; but the Second Empire was not a lunatic nightmare like that of Hitler, a piece of braggart play-acting like that of Mussolini or a ruthless drive for power like that of Stalin. The system of government was authoritarian, not despotic. It never had its concentration camps or its labour camps. After the *coup d'état* over 200 people were indeed deported to the dreaded prison settlement of Cayenne (which was not a creation of Napoleon III). Within five years all the prisoners who would accept the regime were released and three years later there was a general amnesty. A newspaper was fined for copying a joke in a comic journal that torture was to be reintroduced into political trials; there was no suggestion of any truth behind the joke. The freedom of the Press was restricted, but not to the extent of repressing all criticism. The French Academy was left free to elect royalists and liberals and to offer prizes for dissertations on subjects such as 'parliamentary eloquence in England'. Criticism of the Government meant exclusion from employment by it, not a risk to personal liberty. Furthermore Napoleon allowed after 1860 a gradual transformation of the regime in the direction of parliamentary control. Fear of disorder grew less; there was no likelihood of a royalist or a republican *coup*. The country was prosperous, the working class less harassed by misery and unemployment.

The political changes grew in importance until in 1869 they came near to the restoration of parliamentary government, with a great deal of administrative decentralization and almost complete freedom of the Press. The last plebiscite of the regime was held in May 1870. Nearly seven and a half million voters supported 'l'Empire libéral' and only one and a half million were against it, though there were nearly two million abstentions. As always, the great cities, Paris, Lyons, Marseilles, Toulouse, Bordeaux, had a majority of 'no', but the Emperor could feel that there was a very good chance for the succession of his son. The vote showed, however, more acquiescence than positive loyalty and the one thing which this regime could not survive would be military defeat.

Within a little more than two months of this last plebiscite the Franco-Prussian War had broken out. This war was the final stage in the German movement for national unification, a movement of which Napoleon had misunderstood the significance until too late. Napoleon III had none of the intense will to power of Napoleon I. He was too lazy, too hesitant and, one might add, too humane to be a conqueror. His career had been one of private rather than public daring. He had no 'great design', only a number of ingenious plans. People found him 'impenetrable', but only in the sense that it was impossible to know which way his mind would jump; a critic described him as 'a sphinx without a riddle'. The failure of the Vienna settlement to satisfy nationalist hopes had given Napoleon I the chance to interpret his own career as an attempt to settle Europe on liberal and nationalist principles which had failed owing to the selfishness of reactionaries. Napoleon III had made his career out of the Napoleonic legend; he had taken part in an unsuccessful revolt of 1831 in the Papal States, and by his antecedents was committed to do what he could to support the Italian nationalist cause. Moreover, if he supported this cause, while at the same time maintaining the temporal power of the papacy in the city of Rome against the Italian revolutionaries who wanted to destroy it, he would satisfy both liberal and catholic opinion in France. He might also, as the price of his support, and as the corollary of recognizing Italian claims to political unity, secure for France the French-speaking territories of the house of Savoy.

Napoleon III never thought out clearly what he meant by the 'doctrine of nationality'. Sometimes he meant by it nothing more than the vague conception of 'natural' frontiers, or, more concretely, linguistic frontiers, though this idea, like President Wilson's later doctrine of self-determination, could not easily be applied to the mixed areas of eastern and south-eastern Europe and might lead to dangerous consequences if it were applied, for example, to Alsace. At other times Napoleon seems to have had in mind what he called 'great agglomerations', a new balance of European power to be obtained through the union of peoples divided politically by historical accident. This idea, also very vague, took no account of small nations and might work out unfavourably for France. Napoleon III might have manipulated the unification of Italy to suit French interests – in fact he failed to do so – but the political unification of Germany was much more likely to be a danger to France especially if it were brought about by Prussia. Napoleon saw only too late that in weakening the position of Austria – which he did by opposing her in Italy – he was destroying her conservative and pacific influence among the German States.

He was tricked by Cavour in Italy before he was tricked by Bismarck in Germany. He had agreed to provide a French army to assist the Piedmontese in expelling the Austrians from Lombardy and Venetia, but he could not stop the Italians from political action beyond the point where he hoped to satisfy them, that is to say, a federated Italy under the nominal presidency of the Pope which would not be a military danger to

France and would not abolish, though it would limit, the temporal power of the papacy.[1]

He himself did not fulfil his promise to the Italians. He made peace after the Austrian defeats in Lombardy and without obtaining the cession of Venetia. The Italians showed no gratitude for what Napoleon had done for them and the Emperor's Italian plans vanished when Cavour arranged plebiscites in Tuscany, Modena and Parma in favour of annexation to Piedmont, and Garibaldi, after his rapid 'conquest' of Sicily and Naples, handed over the Bourbon kingdom of the Two Sicilies not to the family of Murat,[2] but to Victor Emmanuel.

Napoleon could not prevent Italy from obtaining Venetia as the reward for her alliance with Prussia in 1866. He was, however, still embarrassed because catholic opinion in France made it impossible for him to allow the Italians to take Rome as their capital. He would willingly have done so, but he would have lost the important catholic vote in France; the French garrison in Rome, taken away for a time, went back there in 1866 when Garibaldi led another expedition for the 'liberation' of the city.

Meanwhile he added to his failures by a fantastic attempt to establish an Empire under French protection in Mexico. Even if sufficient Mexican politicians had been willing to accept the Austrian archduke whom the French tried to force upon them as sovereign, the United States would not have allowed permanent control of the country by France or indeed any European Power. The United States, at the end of the Civil War, was fully armed and the Northerners already angry at Napoleon's open support of the South. United States intervention was

[1] For more details, see below, Chapter 3.

[2] Joachim Murat, one of Napoleon I's marshals, had married Napoleon's younger sister Caroline and had been given in 1808 the kingdom of the Two Sicilies by the Emperor. Murat had been popular in his kingdom and had introduced a number of reforms. After Napoleon's return from Elba, Murat tried to win back his kingdom from the restored Bourbons. He was defeated, taken prisoner and shot. Napoleon III's plans for Italy had included the substitution of the family of Murat for the Neapolitan Bourbons.

not necessary; the Mexicans themselves captured and shot the archduke.

The worst political mistake of Napoleon III, though the consequences were not seen at once, was not over the wars he fought but over one which he did not fight. The long-standing dispute about the duchies of Slesvig and Holstein[1] was not directly a matter of French concern, but if France and Great Britain had prevented Austria and Prussia from going to war with Denmark in order to detach these duchies from the Danish Crown, the career of Bismarck might have come to an abrupt end. Bismarck, however, was able to use the fate of the duchies, after Denmark had been despoiled of them, to bring on the war with Austria which he thought necessary for the attainment of German unity under Prussian hegemony. When the outbreak of this war was practically certain, Napoleon again missed his chance. He expected the war to be long and costly; at the right moment he would come in as mediator and, as the price of his mediation, secure Venetia for Italy from Austria and some 'compensation' on the western frontier of Germany for France. He would thus regain enough goodwill in Italy to enable him to hold off the Italians for a time from the seizure of Rome. He was so sure of his plan that he did not settle the 'compensation' before it was too late; the longer he waited, the higher price could he ask. The Austro–Prussian War lasted seven weeks and was decided after three weeks by the Prussian victory at Königgrätz. After this battle Napoleon had to decide at once whether he would mobilize the French army and threaten armed mediation if he did not get the compensation he wanted in return for accepting Bismarck's plans for Germany. Napoleon neither mobilized the French Army nor stated, as Bismarck had expected, what he would require for France. He did not even object to Bismarck's maximum demands, the extrusion of Austria from all influence in Germany and the formation of a North German Confederation extending as far south as the river Main. The compensation to France for the establishment of this strong military state dominated by Prussia would be settled later.

[1] See below, note to Chapter 2.

Bismarck of course did not wish to pay any compensation. Napoleon had no legal claim and the Prussians believed that they could defeat France if the French demands were pushed as far as war. Napoleon now made several successive demands. The first was for the Rhineland territories lost by France in 1815 – the Palatinate and Hessian territory west of the Rhine. Bismarck refused with a threat that, if France asked for these territories, Prussia would go to war, defeat France and take Alsace. Napoleon suggested a buffer-state in the Rhineland. Bismarck would not even discuss any cession of German territory. Napoleon then made the foolish proposal that Prussia might agree to the French annexation of Belgium and Luxembourg in return for French agreement to a federal union between the North German Confederation and the south German states. The plan was foolish because Great Britain would never have allowed France to take Belgium and Bismarck had no intention of going to war with the English on behalf of Napoleon III. The plan was dishonourable because France was one of the guarantors of Belgian independence. Bismarck did not reject the plan outright; he took care to get Benedetti, the French Ambassador, to put the terms in a letter which he (Bismarck) kept and published at the outbreak of the Franco-Prussian War in order to convince Great Britain of French designs. There remained only Luxembourg, at this time a personal possession of the King of the Netherlands. The King was not unwilling to dispose of it, but took the precaution of letting the proposed transactions be known. The result was an angry outburst in Germany; the King of the Netherlands then backed down and the outcome was not the acquisition of Luxembourg by France but its neutralization.

Napoleon had thus failed in every direction. He now tried to get Austrian and, if possible, Italian help in preventing what he knew to be Bismarck's next move, the merging of the south German states with the North German Confederation. The Germans in Austria and, still more, the Magyars in Hungary did not favour a French alliance; the Magyars were less hostile to Prussia than to Russia (who might oppose gains by Austria-Hungary in south-east Europe as compensation for the territory and influence lost in Italy and Germany). The Emperor Francis Joseph went as far as discussing the proposal, but could not accept Napoleon's terms, since they involved the surrender of German territory to France. As for Italy, while French catholic opinion still opposed the withdrawal of the French garrison from Rome, there could be no chance of an Italian alliance with France. Napoleon's efforts to get allies confirmed Bismarck in his view that his plan for German unity could not be secured without war with the French. From the Prussian point of view the sooner the war came, the greater the chances of victory. Prussia was ready for war; France was unprepared. On the other hand, Prussia could not undertake an aggressive war against France without alienating south German opinion and, possibly, giving Austria an occasion to interfere.

A military revolution of the familiar Spanish type in the autumn of 1868 deprived Queen Isabella of her throne and set the Spaniards looking outside Spain for a monarch. These events gave Bismarck an opportunity to provoke France. Bismarck did not initiate the so-called Hohenzollern candidature for the crown of Spain. An approach was made privately from the Spanish side early in 1869 to a son of Prince Leopold of Hohenzollern-Sigmaringen, a catholic branch of the house of Hohenzollern. Acceptance of the Spanish throne by a German prince would mean an extension of German influence worth, in Bismarck's words, two army corps. For this reason France would certainly oppose it. Bismarck could not give the candidature public support because he could not allow the south German states to think that he was risking a war with France in which they would almost certainly be involved. Privately Bismarck sent money to Spain to bribe Spanish politicians to favour the candidature; he also did his best to persuade the candidate, who might well have doubts about the permanence of his welcome to Spain, to accept the offer. Bismarck, however, made one mistake. He did not allow for the possibility that, through carelessness or deliberate policy, the Spanish politicians would let the offer become public before it had been approved by the Spanish Cortes.

The French Government, when they heard about the offer, at once took the sensible step of inquiring, not in Madrid, but in Berlin, that is to say, they assumed the complicity of Bismarck. The Prussian Government disclaimed responsibility; they said that they were not concerned in the matter. Hence the French could only appeal directly to the King of Prussia as head of the Hohenzollern family. The French Ambassador was instructed to ask the King (who was taking the waters at Ems) that the acceptance should be revoked. There was nothing incorrect about this request; according to nineteenth-century usage a member of a reigning family could not accept the offer of a throne in another country without the approval of the Great Powers.

To Bismarck's discomfiture the King gave way and sent one of his staff to the Hohenzollern-Sigmaringen household recommending the withdrawal of the candidature. The candidature was withdrawn and Napoleon III, if he had been content with this climb-down, would have won a considerable diplomatic victory. Unluckily for himself and for France, Napoleon decided to ask the King of Prussia for a promise that the candidature would not be brought up again. Obviously the candidature could not have been brought forward again without taking the form of a direct provocation of France, which, as I have pointed out, Bismarck had to avoid. On the other hand, the King of Prussia, having agreed to the French demand for withdrawal, could not bind himself for the future without undue humiliation. The king refused the second French request in formal and correct terms and told Bismarck what he had done. Bismarck sent to the Press a misleading account of the interview with the ambassador which gave the impression that Benedetti had been heavily snubbed. Bismarck also instructed the Prussian representatives at certain European courts to give out the news of the King's refusal.

Even at this point the French could have recovered their position if they had waited before taking action until they had received a full report from Benedetti of his second interview with the King. If they had published this report, Bismarck's distortion of it would have been made clear and the King would have had either to disavow Bismarck's version or to take the responsibility for an act of provocation. Instead, in a moment of foolish excitement over the supposed insult to French honour, the French, as Thiers objected, treated a Press telegram as though it were an official document. The French Chamber considered the King's refusal as equivalent to a declaration of war and voted for the call up of reservists.

After Benedetti's telegraphic account of the interview[1] had been decyphered, the news of Bismarck's instructions to the Prussian diplomatic representatives again inflamed French opinion. On 15 July Emile Ollivier, the French Prime Minister, explained to the Chamber that the Prussian 'insult' was not the King's refusal but the publication of the alleged facts about it. Gambetta now asked that the text of the announcement to the European courts should be read in full to the Chamber, but the ministers would not wait and the Chamber voted the war credits for which the Government asked. France declared war on 19 July and thus made it easy for Bismarck to get the support of the south German states.

Napoleon III was not Napoleon I. The French army was not in a condition to fight the Prussians, though the Emperor did not know it. Napoleon himself was too vague and, in fact, too ill to make clear decisions. At the end of the first week of August the Prussians were in Alsace-Lorraine. On 2 September a French army 80,000 strong surrendered at Sedan.[2] Another army of some 150,000 was shut up in Metz. The Prussians were able to march to Paris and to begin the siege of the capital on 19 September.

The Second Empire did not outlive military defeat. The immensity of the catastrophe at Sedan was not generally known in Paris until the afternoon of 3 September. On the following day, while the deputies were discussing a formula for the dissolution of the Empire, a mob, following the pattern of Parisian revolutions, invaded the Chamber and clamoured for the

[1] It is a matter of speculative interest whether war might have been avoided if the telephone had existed at this time between Ems and Paris.
[2] 20,000 had surrendered earlier.

establishment of a republic. Then, again following tradition, they went to the Hotel de Ville where they set up a Government of National Defence. This government had no legal basis, but it continued throughout the siege of Paris and delegated some of its members to establishing themselves at Tours. In October Gambetta left Paris by balloon to take control of the delegation at Tours. Gambetta tried to raise more troops and to organize resistance south of Loire,[1] but the Germans were too strong and too well organized to be much troubled by improvised opposition. After the surrender of the army of Bazaine in Metz (Bazaine was later court-martialled and sentenced to a long term of imprisonment)[2] at the end of October the end was inevitable. The capitulation of Paris came on 26 January 1871, when the city was almost without food, An armistice was signed during which a French National Assembly would be elected to consider the German terms of peace.

The National Assembly met at Bordeaux on 12 February. At least 400 of its 675 members were anti-republican; they were divided, as usual, between Orleanists and supporters of the elder Bourbon line. Their election showed the fear of Frenchmen that a republican government would mean disorder, an attack on property and a surrender to the mobs of Paris and a few other large cities. Thiers persuaded the deputies to leave undecided the future form of government: he was himself chosen to preside over a provisional ministry with the non-committal title of 'Chef du Pouvoir Exécutif de la République'.

The Assembly ratified the peace terms on 1 March; these terms included the surrender of Alsace (except Belfort) and

[1] Léon Gambetta (1832–82) was partly of Jewish–Italian origin. He was born at Cahors, studied law in Paris and almost at once after 1860 came into prominence as a member of the extreme left of the Liberal opposition to Napoleon III. Gambetta's outstanding oratorical powers enabled him to transmit his own enthusiasm to large masses of his countrymen, but he was not a first-class administrator and had no real understanding of the military situation and no carefully worked out plans for a practical recovery of the initiative against the Germans.

[2] Bazaine was condemned to death; the sentence was commuted to one of twenty years imprisonment from which he escaped after about a year. He died in exile.

about a third of Lorraine, with Metz, and an indemnity of five milliard francs. The acceptance of such terms seemed to the Parisian left wing an outrage, an act of betrayal by the bourgeois and an insolent disregard of the traditional sovereignty of the capital. Anger against the Assembly was increased by their decision to establish themselves, not in Paris, but in Versailles, where they would be less accessible to Parisian pressure. There were 350,000 citizen National Guards and only 30,000 regular troops in Paris. Most of the bourgeois battalions of the National Guard had disbanded themselves since there was nothing left for them to do; the battalions which remained were nearly all from the working class. They too had no duties to perform, but there were being paid 30 sous a day. The last act of the Assembly at Bordeaux was to suppress this payment except in cases where recipients could prove their need for it. Finally, the National Guard had 227 guns parked in the western suburbs which were occupied temporarily by the Germans.[1] The battalions of the Guard moved these guns to the high ground of Montmartre and Belleville where they threatened the city. Attempts by regular troops to get possession of the guns failed. Thiers then ordered the withdrawal of the garrison of Paris; the troops would return only when they had been sufficiently reinforced to put down all resistance.

The battalions of the National Guard, left to themselves and to the desperate assertion of the will of the Parisian extremists against nearly all the rest of France, now set up the Commune of Paris. The word 'Commune' had nothing to do with communism as it was then understood; it was the usual revival of historic memories of the first Revolution, the Paris Commune of 1793. Much argument has been wasted in trying to demonstrate whether the Commune of 1871 was or was not in intention and fact a proletarian revolution in the modern

[1] Bismarck had given the French the alternatives of surrendering Belfort or of allowing a German occupation of Paris from 1 March to the ratification by the Assembly of the preliminaries of peace. The Germans expected the Assembly to debate the terms for about a week, but the French brought back the ratification on the morning of 2 March. To his disappointment William I, who had been proclaimed German Emperor at Versailles a few days earlier, was thus unable to make a triumphal entry into the city.

sense of the term. Certain things are obvious. The revolution was not a long planned attempt by a group of conspirators or foreign exiles to transform by force the social and political regime of France; it began as the angry reaction of a populace over-excited and exhausted by the events of the siege – too little food and too much alcohol – and regarding themselves as having been betrayed by the comfortable classes outside the capital. The Commune was largely, not entirely, a working-class movement, if only because the better educated classes realized that the deputies at Bordeaux were not traitors and that there was no practical alternative to accepting the German peace terms. The working class had real economic grievances; if they set up a government of their own they would expect it to remedy these grievances. The men who controlled the Commune annulled legislations by the Assembly to enforce the immediate payment of debts (such debts were owed more by small shopkeepers than by working men); they did not touch the bullion in the Bank of France. The 'professional' revolutionaries who wanted the destruction of bourgeois society obviously tried to direct the Commune towards their own ends. It is impossible to say how far they would have succeeded, because the Commune itself was overthrown before there was any real attack on private property. If the French themselves had not overthrown it, the Germans would have done so.[1]

The fighting which ended in the complete defeat of the rebels had all the horrors of civil war. After attempts at a compromise had failed, the regular troops – about 130,000 – controlled by the National Assembly began a systematic reduction of the outer defences of Paris. The Communard troops (they did not use this term; they called themselves *fédérés* – the Republican federation of the National Guard)

---

[1] Marx's *Address to the Commune* was an *ex post facto* attempt to treat the insurrection as a movement on the lines of his own ideas of a proletarian revolution. At the time Marx admired the courage of the rebels; neither he nor Engels thought much of their ideology. Marx's own writings were not much known in France at this time. A French translation of *Das Kapital* was published about 1875.

had only about 30,000 fully trained men, and few good officers with combat experience; the attempt, again based upon memories of 1792, at a *levée en masse* was useless. As they were driven into the centre of Paris the Communard leaders lost control of their maddened and desperate followers; the last stages were outbreaks of savagery, the murder of nearly 500 hostages, the burning of buildings and, as usual in such cases, the reprisals by the victors were hardly less barbarous. The number of deaths on the side of the revolutionaries was not less and probably more than 17,000 The number of regular soldiers killed was about a thousand.

The Civil War of 1871 had a lasting effect on France. There were other reasons for the decline in the predominance of Paris; the decline itself must not be exaggerated, but Paris has never again asserted itself with such violence against nearly all the rest of France. On the other hand, the mutual distrust – one might well use a stronger term – between the urban workers and the propertied classes was wider than ever. The Assembly gave little attention to measures of social reform; for a long time security and the form of government were the main themes of politics. The fear of revolution turned to the advantage of the parliamentary republicans. The royalists were indeed put in an impossible position because the comte de Chambord, the legitimist candidate for the throne, refused to give up the Bourbon white flag, which he regarded as a symbol of royal authority, for the republican tricolour.[1] Most of the support, however, for a monarchical restoration at and after the election of the National Assembly was really a demand for a strong government. When the *de facto* republican government was seen to be exercising this authority, there was no need to insist upon a monarchical cover for it. Hence the long debate

[1] The white flag with the *fleur de lys* which played such a symbolic part in the comte de Chambord's decision was not in fact a traditional flag of the Bourbons, but merely that of the count's grandfather and great-uncle between 1815 and 1830. There was no recognized monarchical flag before 1789, though certain units of the royal guard used the white flag with a *fleur de lys*. The comment of Pope Pius IX on this palaver about the flag was 'Et tout ça pour une serviette'.

about the political regime ended in 1875 with the creation of the constitution under which the Third Republic lasted for the next sixty-five years. The solution of 1875 was provisional only in the sense that the republicans in the country were divided, as under earlier regimes, between those who regarded the existing constitution as a barrier against further change and those who took it as the beginning of a new era.

The temporary popularity between 1886 and 1889 of General Boulanger, a flashy soldier with vague hopes for his own dictatorship, actually showed the fundamental strength of the republic. Boulanger, prancing about Paris on a black horse, tried to give the impression that under his leadership France would fight and win a war of revenge against Germany. This did not worry Bismarck, but he used the occasion to get the Reichstag to renew the military budget for a seven-year period.

In 1887 the Government removed Boulanger from Paris by appointing him to a command at Clermont-Ferrand. He was retired from the army in the spring of 1888 and therefore free to engage in an electoral campaign. He was elected in Paris in January 1889 with a large majority; his supporters wanted him to go at once to the Elysée and carry out a *coup d'état*. It is unlikely that, if he had done so, he could have maintained himself in power, but he did not risk the attempt. He left France when the Government decided to prosecute him. His popularity, built up, as his enemies said, on the black horse, soon disappeared. In 1891 he committed suicide at the tomb of his mistress in Brussels.

One aspect of the French political divisions was that each side had powerful allies. The conservatives, and especially the royalists, could count on the Church, the republican left on the support of French freemasonry. The support of the Church was of much less value than it might have been owing to the maladroitness of high ecclesiastical authority inside and outside France. The French Church never recovered from the dislocation caused by the anti-religious policy of the first Revolution. The Napoleonic Concordat with the papacy, which reduced the clergy to the level of paid servants of the State, brought peace to the countryside but no real religious revival.

There is a story, typical of large areas of France, of a country gentleman asking his gardener, on the first Sunday when the church bells rang again for Mass, whether he was going to church. The gardener answered, 'Moi, je n'y vais pas, mais je suis content qu'on peut y aller.' Among the upper and middle classes there was a revival of religious conformism rather than of religious devotion. The *dévots* indeed were the bane of the Church, since they tended to be fundamentalist in religion and absolutist in politics. I have already mentioned the absurdities of the catholic theorists of the counter-revolution. The higher clergy, chosen mainly, though not entirely, for their subservience to authority, were too easily on the side of divine right. One archbishop of Paris described Jesus Christ as 'l'héritier légitime du trône de Judée'. The prince of Polignac, the last and most foolish Prime Minister of Charles X, believed that the Blessed Virgin had appeared to him and promised help in the measures which in fact brought about the Paris revolution of 1830. This revolution taught the high church authorities little; during the next two generations the unwisdom of papal policy in its opposition to liberalism everywhere, because liberals in Italy were attacking the temporal power of the papacy, widened the gulf between catholicism and modern society.

The monarchy of July had been careful not to associate itself with the political aims of the hierarchy. Catholicism was not described as the religion of the State, but the Concordat was maintained. The Church kept also its control of primary education; no other institution could provide the teaching personnel. Higher education, that is to say, education above secondary school level, remained under the direction of the University of France to which in 1806 Napoleon had given a monopoly. For obvious reasons catholics in general did not support the Second Republic. They accepted the favours shown to them by Napoleon III, including a certain modification of the University control of higher education, but most of the clergy still hoped for a Bourbon restoration.

In the later stages of the Empire the catholics opposed an increase in the lay control of free, compulsory primary education. Napoleon III's fateful and foolish Italian policy was largely due to his political need of keeping the catholic vote at a time when the rest of French opinion was turning against him.

The Communard revolution, during which the Archbishop of Paris and many other priests were killed by the rebels, confirmed the Church in its opposition to a republican regime and in its belief that safety lay only in a return to the monarchy. The republicans were equally confirmed in their distrust of the clergy and after 1875 began to introduce anti-clerical measures. They took their first steps against the religious orders and especially 'foreign' orders outside French episcopal control. The Jesuits were at the head of the list; 250 other religious houses were closed down, and with the establishment of free, compulsory primary education in 1881 religious instruction was disallowed in all State schools. In 1886 teaching members of religious organizations were excluded from these schools, but, owing to the shortage of teachers, the exclusion was not operative for five years.

The election of Leo XIII as Pope in 1878 at least brought a less rigid attitude on the side of the papacy; Leo XIII, however, was as active as Pius IX, though more subtle, in trying to get the catholic Powers to bring about the restoration of the temporal power of the papacy. On the other hand, he saw more clearly than Pius IX the folly of the French Church in committing itself to the cause of the royalists whose chance of a return to power grew less as the years passed. After earlier encyclicals pointing out that catholic doctrine was not concerned with any particular form of secular government, the Pope in 1890 instructed Cardinal Lavigerie[1] to make a public statement in favour of a *rapprochement* between the Church and the Republic. The statement brought strong opposition from the royalists and also from the more determined anti-clericals.

[1] Cardinal Lavigerie, archbishop of Algiers and Carthage, was widely known for his missionary and charitable work and his activities in suppressing the African slave trade. He had been a legitimist, but had become convinced of the permanency of a republican regime in France and futility of opposing it.

In February 1892 the Pope gave an interview to a French journalist in which he said that, while individual citizens might have their own preferences, they should unite under the government chosen for their country by all Frenchmen. Again the monarchists, whose money was more important to the Church after the anti-clerical measures of the 1880s, refused to accept the Pope's pronouncements on political matters, while the anti-clericals claimed to be strong enough to do without catholic support. Moreover, against the organized power of the church in politics, the anti-clericals possessed a counter-organization in French freemasonry. Freemasons' lodges had taken over, or at all events succeeded, the secret revolutionary societies of the early part of the century. After 1870 the number of freemasons increased rapidly and included most of the republican leaders. In 1877 the Masonic Assembly of the Grand Orient, to which the French lodges belonged, struck out from its rules the obligation of freemasons to accept a belief in God and in the immortality of the soul.

The attitude of the Church over the Dreyfus case destroyed any chance of success which the papal policy of *ralliement* might have had. Some of the details of this case are still obscure, but the main fact is beyond doubt. Captain Dreyfus, a Jewish officer, was not guilty of the offence – a betrayal of secret information to the German military attaché in Paris – for which he was convicted in December 1894. The 'key document' which was alleged to be in his handwriting was written by another officer; other important evidence brought against him was forged by an officer in the French intelligence service. If Captain Dreyfus had been given a fair trial, the truth would have come out at once. In the light of history the remarkable fact is that, to the credit of France, and owing to the persistence of a few men, the truth did eventually come out; Captain Dreyfus was restored at long last in 1906 to the army which had treated him with such shameful disregard of justice.[1]

[1] In 1899 a military court at Rennes had upheld Captain Dreyfus' conviction, but had declared, illegally and rather absurdly, that there were extenuating circumstances in the case. Captain Dreyfus was then released

The repercussions of the Dreyfus case went far beyond the wrongs done to one man. The whole of 'political' France became involved in it, and for a time the republic, which had been considerably tarnished by previous financial scandals, was seriously shaken. The monarchists and the clergy, with few exceptions, took Dreyfus' guilt for granted and regarded the case as another example of the inherent corruption of the republican regime and the sinister influence of Jews in the higher regions of the administration. Anti-semitism hardly existed in France, except in Alsace, before 1870. The number of French Jews was small; most of them were assimilated Portuguese Jews in the south. There was a considerable Jewish influx from Alsace in 1871 and a larger immigration of eastern European Jews after the Russian persecution and organized pogroms of Jews in the 1880s. Even so the total Jewish population about 1900 was only some 200,000. Anti-Jewish feeling was directed chiefly against a few very rich capitalists. The collapse of the Union Générale bank in 1882 had stirred up this resentment. The Union Générale, like the Crédit Foncier over twenty years earlier, had been founded largely by catholics to break the Jewish and protestant quasi-monopoly of high finance. The shares of 500 francs (125 paid up) had risen above 3,000 francs, but within a very short time the enterprise collapsed; the Rothschilds were said to be responsible for bringing about the collapse. The socialist leader Jules Guesde had attacked the supposed Rothschild domination, but the first anti-semitic book in France with a really large circulation was *La France juive,* published in 1886 by a clever, unscrupulous journalist named Drumont. The attack was continued in certain newspapers, notably in the catholic *La Croix* controlled by the Assumptionist order. The failure of the Panama Company, in which many small investors lost their

---

from prison. In 1903 with the agreement of the Minister of War, he asked for a consideration of his case by the Court of Appeal. In 1906 he was pronounced innocent. One of the many odd facts about the original sentence is that Captain Dreyfus could not be charged convincingly of selling his country for money. His family, though not of great wealth, was comfortably off and he was not in any financial trouble.

money, had already added to the discredit of Jewish financial adventurers.[1]

After the truth about the Dreyfus case became known, the Republicans directed their vengeance – one can use no lighter term – on the anti-Dreyfusards primarily against the Church. The Government wanted as far as was possible to spare the high military chiefs who were ultimately responsible for the scandal; the easiest way of diverting public indignation from the army was to turn it against the catholics and primarily against the already unpopular religious congregations. The Assumptionists, whose journalistic activities made them an obvious target, were dissolved in January 1900. The attack might have stopped at this point or after the suppression of the Jesuits, but the parliamentary majority was determined to get rid of the clerical control of secondary education. In a law of April 1901 dealing generally with associations, all the so-called 'non-authorized' religious congregations, i.e. orders or religious congregations existing before 1815, were required to obtain authorization from the State; even those which received this authorization were put under strict control and could be dissolved by official decree. Over 600 out of some 753 congregations applied for authorization; some of the most ancient religious houses in France, for example, the Benedictines of Solesmes, knew that their applications were unlikely to be granted and left the country.

[1] F. de Lesseps, whose enthusiasm had been responsible for the construction of the Suez canal, had founded in 1880 (he was seventy-five in that year) a company for the construction of a canal across the isthmus of Panama. Lesseps was not himself an engineer, and from a technical point of view the project was totally ill-considered. The company soon ran out of money; it secured additional funds until in 1889 it was compelled to go into liquidation. In its later stages the company had employed three Jews as publicity agents in money-raising; a certain Jacques de Reinach (who had acquired the title of baron in Italy) and two greater rogues, Cornelius Hertz, born in Bavaria of French parents, and one Aaron, alias Arton. These men had distributed money among politicians, journalists and society figures who might 'boost' the company. They also pocketed large sums for themselves. The 'revelation' of the scandals associated with this distribution of money affected a whole generation of politicians, including Clemenceau who disappeared from the Chamber until 1902.

The long list of applications had not been fully examined when the anti-clerical majority was increased at a general election. Emile Combes, the new Prime Minister, was a former seminarist who had begun his career with a thesis on St Thomas Aquinas. He had become violently hostile to the Church and attacked it with a certain high-minded fanaticism, oddly combined with methods of petty, underhand persecution. He refused authorization to a number of congregations and then proposed to deprive the old congregations of the right to teach; in other words, he planned to shut down some 8,200 catholic schools and teaching establishments. In spite of a good deal of opposition from his own supporters and some popular violence when the closures were enforced, the anti-clerical majority accepted these measures.

The logical conclusion was the denunciation of the Concordat and the complete separation of Church and State. The left-wing republicans had long demanded this separation, but there was considerable opposition to it even among anti-clericals owing to the unpopularity which it would bring to the Government in catholic areas and because it would deprive the State of its control over the clergy. Combes himself wanted to keep this control while cutting off the clergy from their obedience to the Holy See. It is possible, though unlikely, that a compromise might have been reached, but Pope Pius X, who succeeded Leo XIII in 1903, was as tactless and narrow as Combes and, although Combes had resigned (mainly over the discovery that the freemason's lodges were sending the Minister of War secret dossiers on the political opinions of officers),[1] the Concordat was officially denounced and payments to the bishops and clergy discontinued. There was still a chance that the catholics, like the protestants and Jews who accepted the conditions laid down for all cultural associations, might have kept their churches, furnishings, seminaries and other properties. Many catholics would have agreed to the new conditions under protest, but Pius X rejected them on grounds

[1] The Minister of Marine had also occupied himself with anti-clerical pin-pricks such as suppressing the Good Friday fast day on ships and giving tendentious names to cruisers, e.g. *Ernest Renan* and *Démocratie*.

of principle and through fear that the governments of other catholic countries might follow the French example. Finally, in spite of the obstinate refusal of Pope Pius X to ask for any concessions, the Government decided to allow the catholics the use of the churches; all other ecclesiastical buildings were taken over by the State.[1]

For the first thirty years of the Third Republic politicians had been concerned primarily with consolidating the regime against opposition from the extreme left and right and with 'decatholicizing' France. The successful establishment of the non-religious state now left the bourgeois republicans with another kind of opposition. Until about 1900 the social question though it had long needed attention, hardly existed as a political issue outside the field of education. The small, divided socialist groups were regarded as enemies not of the republic but of society – property-owning society – in general.

After 1900 the republican politicians could no longer satisfy the working class with a few, almost casual reforms. There had been, for example, no measure until 1876 for authorizing the appointment of inspectors to ensure compliance with the regulations for the employment of children in factories, and until 1892 no proscription on the employment of women in mines or of children between the ages of 8 and 10 in factories. A new working-class generation, educated in a secular environment by teachers without religion, would no longer be put off by the promise of consolation in an after-life. In the well-known words of the socialist Jaurès to the radical deputies in November 1893, human misery was awake and could no longer be quieted by the old lullaby of religion.[2]

On the side of labour there was also nothing until late in the nineteenth century to compare with the organization which had

---

[1] The occupation of a presbytery by a French curé as a rent-paying tenant thus depended upon the goodwill of a possibly anti-clerical municipality.

[2] Viviani used an equally memorable phrase in the Chamber in 1906: 'Nous avons éteint dans le ciel des lumières qu'on ne rallumera pas' – 'We have put out in the heavens lights which will never be relit.'

developed in Great Britain, and there were few Frenchmen like the remarkable group of men who built up English and Scottish unions after 1850. Trade unions, though they existed in France,[1] were not fully legalized until 1884 and even then their activities were carefully circumscribed. Strikes took place but workers had no legal right to strike until 1883.

The facts I have already mentioned about French industry go far to explain this backwardness; smaller urban agglomerations, smaller units of industry, an export trade of high quality goods with high standards of individual workmanship. Large-scale industry – mining, transport, textiles, etc. – was expanding but the workers were less well organized than in Great Britain. In 1892 only a third of the miners, iron, steel and engineering workers, and about 3 per cent of the textile workers belonged to unions; the total number of trade unionists about this time was about 400,000. In 1906 the figure had risen only to 836,000; it did not reach beyond a million until 1912. The number of strikes in 1893 was 634, affecting 170,000 workers. In 1906 there were just over 1,300 strikes in which nearly 440,000 workers were involved.

The absence of large and solidly built unions itself had restrictive effects; workpeople disliked paying dues to unions which, being small and poor, could not do much for them. Furthermore the French tradition of revolutionary violence tended to reject the quieter and ultimately more effective English methods, while the bourgeois politicians and voters were afraid that associations of workpeople might lead to disorder. Hence the unions, when they slowly began to gain strength, continued to distrust the politicians and the value of collaborating with them in carrying reforms through the Chamber. The working-class leaders were themselves divided about the best means of ousting the bourgeois from the control of the State, whether by 'gradualism',[2] in this case action by a parliamentary socialist party, or by direct action, pre-eminently through the strategy of the general strike. There was a further

---

[1] There was no national union of miners before 1883.

[2] 'Gradualism' is an English term originally applied in the 1830s to modes of emancipating Negro slaves.

division between those who wanted to get rid of the bourgeois in order to control the State and the anarchists who opposed all centralized governmental apparatus. The trade unionist in general were thus separated from the parliamentary socialists, most of whom came from the middle class. After bitter controversy lasting over ten years, the Confédération Générale du Travail was founded in 1895, with a clause in its constitution blocking collaboration with the bourgeois political parties. The controversy, however, was not settled. In 1901 there were two socialist parties in France, one of them rejecting and the other allowing parliamentary collaboration. They united in 1905 after the Congress of the Second International at Amsterdam in the previous autumn had finally condemned socialist support of a bourgeois government. Even so, a dissenting group remained outside the Parti Socialiste Unifié.

Without a 'clearer sense of the possible' which the C.G.T. might have gained from close contact with a parliamentary party, and without the practical experience of administering large benefit funds, French unionists were more open to the influence of sharp and extreme theories. Jaurès[1] realized that an attempt to break bourgeois society by shock tactics – the revolutionary general strike – would fail. The working class had not enough unity of purpose; the state was too powerful and the structure of French society too solid. Moreover the anti-patriotism and anti-militarism of the extreme left were out of touch with the temper of the country. Frenchmen in general did not associate the army with ideas of aggression. The parliamentary socialists did not want war for the recovery of Alsace-Lorraine, still less in the interest of Russian expansion

[1] Jean Jaurès (1859–1914), the ablest of the French parliamentary socialists, came of a bourgeois family (his brother was an admiral). Until the Amsterdam congress Jaurès was willing to collaborate with the bourgeois parliamentary parties. Jaurès greatly feared in the years before 1914 that capitalist greed and folly would lead to a European war in which the working class would be the victims. He supported the general strike as a means of stopping the outbreak of such a war. On 16 July he proposed a resolution at a socialist conference in Paris in favour of a general strike (which would not be confined to France). Fifteen days later Jaurès was killed by an assassin for his supposed treachery.

in south-east Europe, but they realized that the weakness of France before a militant Germany might lead to the defeat of French socialism, just as the majority of German socialists believed that a defeat of Germany by Russia could have a similar consequence for German social democracy.

Jaurès' forecast of the failure of a movement for change by violence was correct. For a few years such a movement towards violence was encouraged by the popularization of certain anti-intellectual theories such as those expounded in Georges Sorel's[1] *Réflexions sur la violence* (1906) and by a contemporary literary and artistic movement which might be described as 'action for action's sake'. The much canvassed philosophy of Bergson, which appeared to subordinate reason to instinct – an 'élan vital' – had as great an influence upon uninstructed intellects as the theories of Freud a decade and more later upon scientifically untrained literary men and artists. The importance of this 'revolt against reason' (which was not confined to France) can be exaggerated. Bergson never went to the extremes of his popularizers; the revolt against reason was in fact a more exact and subtler use of reason. The publicists who claimed scientific justification for their paper extravagances about violence were no less unscientific than many of their nineteenth-century predecessors with their popular versions of the Darwinian hypothesis. The logical conclusion of 'action for action's sake' was power for power's sake, as Sorel later showed in his approval of Mussolini and Italian fascism.[2]

Between 1906 and 1909 there were strikes in France leading to serious violence. After a stoppage of work in the Department of Seine et Oise had led to fighting, the C.G.T. ordered a general protest strike of one day in Paris. The number of trade unionists was still too small to bring about a complete stoppage, but again there was rioting in which four people were

[1] Georges Sorel (1847–1922) began his career as a civil engineer in government service. He gave up his post in 1892 and published a series of books of which *Réflexions sur la violence* had the widest circulation. He advocated revolutionary syndicalism, but even before 1914 he was veering to the right-wing neo-royalism of the *Action française* group. After the war of 1914–18 he supported both communism and fascism.

[2] See also below, p. 267.

killed. The test of the employment of the general strike as a political instrument came in October 1909, when the railway workers called a strike. The Government regarded this interference with a public service as illegal; they arrested the strike committee, issued a decree mobilizing all the railwaymen and dismissed the strikers who did not obey the mobilization order.

Thus in 1914, although the international situation was becoming increasingly dangerous, the most remarkable feature of French society appeared to be its stability. Agriculture still employed more Frenchmen than industry, especially 'great' industry; only 10,000 out of 100,000 industrial establishments in France had more than fifty workpeople.[1] On the land there was still a majority of owner-occupiers and the small businesses which served them; they might vote on the left, but not for revolutionary change. The large middle class was continually being reinforced with ability from the lower ranges. The currency was stable and general standards of living were rising; the consumption of sugar for example. rose between 20 and 25 per cent between 1906 and 1913.[2] The number of small savings accounts went up. If France was behind her neighbours in large-scale industry, she remained prosperous on traditional lines and was developing new sources of power – water-power, of which she had an abundant supply, for generating electricity. The old political problems seemed to have been solved. The republic was in less real danger from extremists of left and right than at any time in its history. There were new domestic problems for France, but the century-old task of reconciling liberty and order seemed to have been accomplished under the regime which, as Thiers had said long ago, divided Frenchmen least.

[1] The larger establishments, however, accounted for a much higher percentage of the total number of workpeople in industry. See p. 64.
[2] The price of refined sugar had fallen by about a half in the fifty years before 1914. The takings of Paris theatres increased almost five-fold during the same period and the consumption of tobacco by more than a half.

2. Germany

The *Encyclopaedia Britannica* of 1878, in an article on Germany, has as its second sentence: 'If by the designation "Germany" is meant the territory inhabited by Germans, this is considerably larger than the German Empire constituted in 1871; the former having an area of about 340,000, the latter of 208,000 English square miles.' Over sixty years later a British survey of Germany compiled for official purposes, began with the words: 'since the political frontiers of Germany do not coincide with geographical regions, a geographical description of that country cannot be made without including others.' Nothing like these two sentences could have been written of the nation-states of Great Britain and France at any time in the nineteenth century. The sentences thus sum up the political backwardness of Germany in 1815 and the fundamental problem of unification which Germans had to solve. The German Confederation established at the Congress of Vienna was, by definition, not a single sovereignty; the second Reich was founded after the exclusion of Austria, but never extricated itself from the destiny of the Habsburg Empire. It is indeed possible to regard the collapse of this second Reich as an indirect consequence of the failure of the Germans in Austria to solve the problems of their multi-national state.

The frontiers of the Reich, except for those on the North Sea and the Baltic, have little physical significance. North Germany stretched across the north European plain from the mouth of the Ems to Memel. Memel itself was Lithuanian rather than German; the territory along the Vistula above Danzig, and the Prussian province of Posen were mainly Polish in language (or dialect); a large Danish population was included in the part of Slesvig annexed to Prussia. The western frontier, with or without Alsace-Lorraine, had no very definite boundary except the Rhine between Strasbourg and Bâle. The clearest 'natural' frontier was in the south-west where it did not divide German-speaking from non-German-speaking populations. The Rhine has its source in Switzerland and its estuary in the Netherlands; the Elbe flows through Bohemia before reaching Saxony, the Oder also rises in Bohemia before flowing through Silesia, and the Danube and Vistula run mainly through non-German territory.

This wide area of some 800 miles from Memel to the south-west corner of Baden was not ideally suited for a great nation-state. It was not united around one capital city; the Hansa towns looked north, the Rhineland cities west and those of south Germany towards Italy. Berlin was of no account before the end of the seventeenth century; its population in 1815 was still under 200,000.

The Holy Roman Empire – the full title dates from 1254 – was, in Voltaire's well-known words, in the eighteenth century neither Holy nor Roman nor an Empire; it had become hardly more than a titular dignity belonging to the house of Habsburg. The Habsburgs were not strong enough to bring about German unity and too strong to permit it to be brought about to their despite. Before the French Revolution there was indeed little desire for a political consolidation of this kind. Something which could be called a German culture certainly existed and was based on the courts of the larger and medium-sized and even smaller German political units (Saxe-Weimar in its various positions amounted only to 1,000 square miles in area, less than the East Riding of Yorkshire). The higher ranks of German society imitated the culture of France; Frederick the Great habitually spoke and wrote in French. One of the most remarkable features of the country was its twenty-six universities,[1] already in the eighteenth century beginning those studies which were to give German scholarship so outstanding a reputation in Europe; they were state

---

[1] England had only two universities, but a higher proportion of the English population was literate and, in view of the predominantly legal character of the German universities, the English Inns of Court should be included in any comparison.

institutions encouraged by the princes because they provided lawyers, judges and civil servants. The mass of the population consisted of peasants whose status and condition grew worse as one travelled eastwards from the Rhineland. Prussia alone, owing to able, persistent and unscrupulous rulers, had greatly increased in territory and power, but in 1789 its institutions were a long way from those of a modern state. Frederick William I, who spent over half of the State revenues on the army, had in 1719 freed the peasants on the royal domains from serfdom; he could not risk the opposition of the landowning class by ordering them to follow his example.

The French Revolution had an awakening political effect upon the Germans. The ideas of the Revolution were more welcome than the French armies which soon followed them, but the administrative reforms and not least the high-handed treatment by Napoleon of the German sovereignties, large and small, brought a new outlook. The obvious aim was to keep the French reforms without the French. Prussia, which was first and last a military state, realized the need for drastic reform even before her military defeat in 1806. After this defeat a number of administrative reforms were set in hand at once. These reforms necessarily came from above; they were not directed towards a realization of popular sovereignty, but primarily to a strengthening of the army; financial reform because the rebuilding of the army needed money, educational reform to provide the administrators. It is typically Prussian that the Royal University of Berlin founded in 1809 should have been located next to the Royal Guard-House and the Arsenal. For a long time Prussia had attracted able men from other German states. Few of the leading figures in the revival of the State were Prussian-born; Stein came from Nassau, Hardenberg and Scharnhorst were Hanoverians, Niebuhr the son of a Holsteiner who had settled at Copenhagen.[1]

---

[1] Stein was responsible for the abolition of serfdom and other administrative reforms, Hardenberg for administrative reforms and foreign policy, Scharnhorst for the reorganization of the army. Niebuhr entered the Prussian service in 1806 when he was thirty. He was professor at Berlin from 1810 to 1816 and Prussian Ambassador to the Vatican from 1816 to 1823.

Napoleon had abolished the Holy Roman Empire in 1806 and after his defeat there was no question of restoring it; it was indeed impossible to bring back the three hundred and more separate units which had existed before 1789 and had since been absorbed in Napoleon's various political arrangements. It was equally impossible to set up a single, territorially consolidated German state (though certain Germans, including Stein, wanted to do so) or even a strong federal state. Considerable areas of Germany were ruled by sovereigns who held more important kingdoms outside their German possessions. The King of England was Elector and after 1815 King of Hanover; the King of Denmark was Duke of Slesvig and Holstein; the King of the Netherlands was Grand Duke of Luxembourg; the reigning family of Oldenburg was closely related to the Russian imperial house. These potentates would not give up their sovereign rights to a unified German state. In any case who would have been head of such a state? A republic was unthinkable in 1815, or rather thinkable only by Jacobins. Prussia would not agree to a Habsburg ruler, Austria and the south German states would not accept the Hohenzollern King of Prussia. The position was complicated by the multi-national character of the Habsburg dominions. A German state which did not include Austria hardly seemed possible in 1815, but, if Austria were to be merged in a German state, she would have to be dismembered or bring with her masses of non-Germans.

The maximum possible attainment therefore was the creation of a Germanic Confederation. This measure was itself a simplification, since the minimal sovereignties disappeared; only 38 (later 39) units remained and of these not more than a dozen had any real importance. The Emperor of Austria was President of the Confederation and Austria could count upon a majority of votes in the Diet. Each state kept its separate existence, its own army (if it had one), its own institutions; the Diet of the Confederation was not a parliament, but rather a conference of ambassadors. A vague clause in the act of confederation mentioned the establishment of representative assemblies in each of the constituent states, but no sanction was attached to the clause and only the south-western states, that is to say, those most affected by French influence, paid attention to it.

For thirty years the Confederation remained under Austrian control. The Austrian Government did not want to change it, since a change, especially on liberal lines, would raise the question of the relationship of Austria to a German national state as well as causing trouble in the other Habsburg dominions. Prussia was as conservative as Austria in domestic policy and as unwilling to surrender her separate existence to a German national state which she did not control, or to allow a free Press and other dangerous incitements to criticism of authority which might lead to revolution of a Jacobin type. Austria and Prussia in 1819 persuaded the Diet of the Confederation to accept decrees which sharply restricted freedom of publication and put officials into the universities – the centres of liberal agitation – to get rid of professors and students of radical opinions. For some time German intellectual life was cut off at least from open political activity. The French revolution of 1830 had considerable effect on Italy but hardly touched Germany or German Austria.

Economic growth was equally slow. Berlin and Vienna were the only German cities with a population over 200,000; neither came near to the 300,000 inhabitants of Naples, and after them Hamburg alone reached 100,000. The population, however, was increasing quickly; Germany had about five million people fewer than France in 1800 and had become equal to her in numbers between 1830 and 1840. The formation of a Common Customs Union (*Zollverein*) in North Germany between 1819 and 1834 was a necessary step towards providing a domestic market large enough to allow specialization in industry. Even so, except in textiles, Prussia and Austria exported few manufactured goods and made far less rapid industrial progress than Belgium.

Thus when a second revolutionary wave passed over Europe about the year 1848, the questions at issue in Germany were about matters which had been settled long ago in Great Britain and France, the formation of a national state and the introduction of constitutional forms of government approved by a majority of the electorate. There could be no parliamentary reform bill in Prussia because there was no parliament in the modern sense of the term, no accusation that the King of Prussia had broken a constitutional charter with his subjects because he had never signed one. When Napoleon III overthrew the second French republic, at least he submitted himself and his new regime to a plebiscite; he did not claim to rule by divine right.

Almost at once after the fall of Louis Philippe in Paris, revolution in Vienna drove Metternich, the leading figure of European conservatism (and now in his seventy-fifth year), from office and compelled the Emperor Ferdinand of Austria to call an assembly to draw up a constitution for his empire. The revolutionary outbreaks spread to Berlin and other cities in Germany. King Frederick William IV announced to his Prussian subjects constitutional reforms; his real opinion about constitutions had been shown in an earlier statement (April 1847) that he would 'never allow a piece of parchment to come, like a second Providence, between Almighty God and this country and rule us with its paragraphs'. He now told an excited crowd that henceforth Prussia would be merged into Germany. In other words, Germany would become a federal state with representative institutions, not a mere confederation of states.

With the seeming approval of the German sovereigns and with a certain legality for their action secured by a resolution of the Diet of the Confederation asking the governments to call a national assembly in order to discuss a constitution for Germany, the German liberals initiated a preliminary meeting at Frankfurt. This so-called *Vorparlament* in turn took care to get the assent of the Diet to their proposals for the composition of the German National Assembly.

For a time the liberals seemed to have won a complete victory over political reaction and absolutism. Their first anxiety was not about opposition in their own country but about a possible intervention by Nicholas I of Russia, the archenemy of liberalism everywhere. The German liberals were predominantly a middle-class body, hardly less distrustful than the conservatives of a real popular revolution; they were on the side of order against riots which broke out in Frankfurt in September 1848. These and other working-class outbreaks were protests against harsh economic conditions, the high price of food, the severe unemployment which was common to most of Europe in the years 1846–8. The middle-class action brought no remedy for this misery and even politically did not go much beyond demonstrations made, 'not to oust governments, but to change their persons and their policy'.[1]

In any case the urban middle class was unable to dictate to the rest of the country. The peasants in Austria were bought off at once by the abolition of what remained of feudal rights. In Germany they had no interest in political nationalism. The liberals had no armed force behind them; neither the Austrian nor the Prussian Army was likely to side with them. Their success in Berlin had been due to official mismanagement which had withdrawn the troops from the city and left the King defenceless. If the Habsburgs recovered their position, they would not support constitutional government in Germany or accept any plan which might lead to the disappearance of Austrian influence, still less the exclusion of Austria from a united Germany. The King of Prussia would not use the Prussian Army in the interest of the liberals since their political demands were incompatible with the continuance of the conservative regime of the Prussian state. Whatever he might say about the merging of Prussia into Germany, the King's real wish was in the opposite direction – the control of Germany by Prussia – but this solution seemed unattainable and was certainly not something for which he would risk war with Austria.

The second assembly, which in accordance with the decisions of the *Vorparlament* met at Frankfurt on 18 May 1848 to constitute the new Germany, showed its middle-class character in its composition; over one half of the members were State officials, legal or administrative; fifty were professors with the

[1] A. Ramm, *Germany, 1789–1919*.

German academic tendency to over-elaborate theory. There were no working-class representatives and only one peasant. The officials and professors also manifested the particular weakness of German middle-class nationalism; an exaggerated view of the mission of Germany in the world and a disregard of the equally valid nationalist aspirations of their non-German neighbours.[1] The view of an enlightened Germany whose destiny was to lead humanity was in a sense a throw-back to the pre-nationalist cosmopolitanism of the eighteenth century. Disregard of the interests and rights of other nationalities if they stood in the way of the fulfilment of German destiny soon showed itself in the attitude of the German liberals towards the Poles. At first, and when they feared Russian intervention, the German liberals had welcomed the idea of Polish independence. Within a few weeks, after it was clear that there would be no Russian interference, the delegates at Frankfurt began to consider in more realist terms the consequences of an independent Poland. Four-fifths of them refused to support a resolution deploring the partitions of Poland and welcoming its restoration. They were equally opposed to the claims of the Czechs to a parliament and responsible government for Bohemia. On 20 June the Frankfurt parliament discussed a resolution asking the Federal Diet to send troops to suppress the Czech national movement; the resolution was not passed because the Austrians had already done the work by the bombardment of Prague. The Frankfurt liberals were even more eager to coerce the Danes of Slesvig.[2]

The Frankfurt Assembly, while it was asserting the intention of German nationalists to deny to others the right of self-determination, was getting into difficulties about its own status

---

[1] One of the projects generally approved by the Assembly was the creation of a German navy as a symbol of national unity and an instrument of national power. A navy would also provide careers for the sons of middle-class families who were not welcome in more aristocratic circles of army officers. It is typical of the lack of practical sense in the Assembly that they began to buy ships before they had made any financial arrangements to pay for them and before they had sufficient trained crews to man them.

[2] For the Slesvig–Holstein question see Note at end of this chapter.

and tasks. Was it to draft a constitution to be submitted to the German Governments for approval, or had it powers of final decision? What was its relationship to the assembly which Frederick William IV had called in Berlin? Who was to choose the head of the new German state? Was this state to exclude Austria, or to include only the German parts of the Habsburg dominions? The deputies discussed for three months the 'great German' and the 'little German' solutions – the inclusion or exclusion of Austria. During these long debates over fundamental rights, when the only hope of success was rapid action, the conservatives had been recovering their ascendancy in Austria and Prussia. In December 1848 the King of Prussia dissolved the Assembly which he had accepted in March. This Prussian Assembly had been as slow-moving and impractical as the Frankfurt Parliament. The deputies did not begin to discuss details of a constitution until mid-October. By the end of the month they had not got beyond the preamble and articles I to IV, but they had eliminated the notion of divine right from the monarchy (the words, 'by the grace of God' disappeared from the royal title).

The King now issued a proclamation guaranteeing as an act of his own sovereign power certain basic rights, and providing for a parliament of two houses, one of them to be elected by universal suffrage, but maintaining royal control of the executive, a right of veto and of issuing decrees when parliament was not sitting. In Austria the army had suppressed revolution in Prague, defeated the Italians, put down more troubles in Vienna and set Slavs against Magyars in Hungary. Before the end of the year the restored Austrian Government, under a new Emperor Francis Joseph and a determined Minister President, Prince Schwarzenberg, was working to reassert Austrian hegemony in Germany under a reformed constitution for the Confederation.

In March 1849 the Frankfurt Assembly, which had accepted the 'little German' solution, offered the crown of the proposed state to Frederick William IV. For obvious reasons the King rejected the offer. The Frankfurt Assembly now faded out. In Prussia a 'revision' of the constitution in May 1849 established a three-class franchise which, by grouping taxpayers according to their incomes and allowing each class special representation, weighted the system in favour of the rich and the well-to-do. The King of Prussia made some unsuccessful attempts to get a 'little German' solution based upon the consent of the princes, but Austria was too strong for him and, finally, in November 1850, compelled him to accept the restoration of the Confederation in its old form. Schwarzenberg wanted to bring the whole of the Habsburg dominions into the Confederation, but the opposition of Prussia and other German states at least prevented this step.

The failure of the German liberals in 1848–9 was disastrous not only for Germany but for Europe. The professors, lawyers and bureaucrats, for all their chauvinism and their failure in action, at least had the intention of establishing in their own country a form of parliamentary government responsible to a wide electorate and buttressed by measures guaranteeing the fundamental rights of subjects, including freedom of writing and association. If the liberals had succeeded, the tide of events might have carried them beyond their narrow conceptions and their neglect of the rights of other peoples. At least the unification of Germany would not have been the work of a man who hated and feared liberal ideas, a man of genius who imposed his masterful but antiquated notions on the constitution and policies of the second German Reich.

The liberals surrendered to this mastery partly owing to their failure to realize where Bismarck was leading them, but primarily because in their scale of values they put German unity above liberalism. They wanted a Germany possessing state power and after 1848 they could get it only by making use of the Prussian Army; Bismarck saw to it that the Prussian Army would be available only on terms and for purposes which safeguarded the predominance of conservative control over Prussia and Germany. Bismarck was logical in his own way. He attacked the liberals because they wanted to introduce into Prussia what he called 'foreign elements' and by foreign elements he meant parliamentary government in the English and French sense of the term. Prussia had been made by absolute sovereigns, not by parliaments; by war, not by trade; by state officials and state planning, not by private enterprise. There had been no Magna Carta in Prussian medieval history, no Bill of Rights, no Act of Settlement. For many years a standing army was regarded in Great Britain as a threat to the liberty of the subject. The existence of Prussia as a kingdom was due to the maintenance by her rulers of an army almost beyond their resources. The background of Prussian history was one of force, tenacity and ruse; the traditions which came out of it produced the militarist, oligarchic domination of Prussian Junkerdom. Nationalism could hardly be a tolerant, still less a debonair growth in the Prussian geographical environment. To the west there were Germans – more 'Germanic' indeed than the partially Wendish Prussians; to the east a limitless plain, an ocean if you like, of Slavs; any conquest had to be made and held by stark, narrowing energy. It is impossible to imagine Mr Gladstone, Bismarck's contemporary, trying to solve the Irish land question in the nineteenth century, not by recognizing at long last the claims of an Irish peasantry, but by trying to repeat the earlier methods of plantation and by settling English farmers on Irish land.

Prussian ideals were not altogether mean (Bismarck could act meanly, but he was not mean-spirited); they created a bleak sense of duty and self-sacrifice, an unshakeable loyalty, the care and precision of a people who had to build out of spareness. The trouble, fundamentally, was that these ideals were out of date. They belonged to a colonizing, not to an industrial age, an age of scarcity, not an age of increasing plenty, an age of fear, not an age of widening international co-operation. Hence the danger to the rest of Europe when these ideals were imposed with such thoroughness on the German people accustomed to obedience and the acceptance of authority from above. A modern state, becoming rapidly industrialized, was given the temper and institutions, the moral and even the aesthetic values[1] of a conquering, feudal aristocracy of a pre-

[1] The railway station built by the Germans at Metz in the early years of the twentieth century is a good example of these aesthetic values. The design is that of an immensely strong Romanesque fortress decorated

industrial age. The result was a misfit, a personality at war with itself.

Prussia and Austria were now face to face, the one anxious to secure, the other to regain the leadership of Germany. The chance of a workable, united German state lay in accepting the 'little German' solution, but this plan could be carried out only by compelling Austria to agree to it, in other words using force against her. Bismarck took this fact for granted. He also realized that, if he were also to preserve the conservative regime in Prussia, he must be prepared to act without the support and, if necessary, against the German and Prussian liberals. Bismarck could not foresee the means whereby he would attain his purpose, but his first step was to support reforms in the Prussian Army which would ensure a Prussian victory in the event of war with Austria.

Bismarck had been called to office in September 1862 owing to a deadlock between the King[1] and the liberals in the Prussian Landtag over the question of army reform. The War Minister, von Roon, had brought forward proposals, which had the strong support of King William I, for important changes in the organization of the army. The purpose of the changes was to increase the efficiency and size of the regular army by lengthening the period of compulsory military service from two years to three, and by abolishing the independent existence of the Landwehr, or militia, as a reserve; the younger members of the Landwehr would be incorporated on mobilization into the regular army and the older members would be employed mainly on garrison duties. The Landwehr, with its tradition (much exaggerated) of service in the War of Liberation against Napoleon, was favoured by the liberals as a citizen force. They therefore resisted its virtual abolition and refused to grant the necessary funds for the increase in the regular army. The dispute

[1] Since 1860 William I. He had become Regent in 1858 for Frederick William IV who had practically gone out of his mind.

with huge figures of medieval knights bearing two-handed swords! The statuary at the entrance included the Emperor William II in the guise of the prophet David.

between the King and the Landtag had lasted for two and a half years when the King was persuaded to make Bismarck Minister President. Bismarck was prepared to resist the Diet and indeed to impose the army reforms on it. There was at least a semblance of legality in his willingness to carry on the government without the approval of the budget by the Landtag; the constitution did not state who should give way if the King and either or both of the two houses disagreed about the taxes. It could be argued therefore that the existing taxes might be legally collected and spent irrespective of a vote in the Landtag for their continuance. Bismarck realized that, if in the near future the army was, as he expected, actually used, military victory would secure him an indemnity for any constitutional illegality, while the opponents of the army reform would be shown up as unpatriotic.

Bismarck saw to it that the army was used and with success. The opportunity came with the reopening of the Slesvig-Holstein question. In 1863 the King of Denmark announced the legal absorption of Slesvig into the Danish kingdom and the separation of Holstein; i.e. legislation applicable to Denmark would also be applied to Slesvig but not to Holstein. This measure, passed in order to satisfy the Danish nationalists in Denmark and the duchies, caused an uproar among the German nationalists. The son of the duke of Augustenburg who had renounced his claims to the duchies now came forward and began to organize a provisional government. Liberal opinion throughout Germany supported Augustenburg but neither Austria nor Prussia would have him. Austria thought that recognition of Augustenburg, that is to say, recognition of the right of the inhabitants of the duchies to secede from a sovereign whose rights were laid down in an international treaty, would be an awkward precedent for the case of Venetia, where the inhabitants wanted to get rid of Austrian sovereignty. Bismarck hoped to be able to annex the duchies to Prussia, though he could not say how he would manage to do so, or even mention his intention.

In the event, owing to Austrian folly, his own unscrupulousness and the preoccupation of the Great Powers, Bismarck succeeded in getting the duchies for Prussia. It was significant for the future that the German liberals cared as little as Bismarck for the rights of Denmark. The Diet of the Confederation proposed action in favour of Augustenburg. The proposal in the Prussian Landtag had the support of the historian Sybel and the great scientist Virchow. Sybel said that a victorious war would heal internal dissensions in Germany. Bismarck was not the only advocate of bringing about German unity by blood and iron. Lord Salisbury (at this time Lord Robert Cecil) commented in the *Quarterly Review* upon the 'curious indifference to morality' of the 'great mass of Prussian and Austrian radicals'.

Bismarck was now able to goad Austria into the war which seemed necessary not only to secure the annexation of the duchies but the expulsion of Austria from Germany, the formation of a separate North German confederation and ultimately the merging of all the German states in a federal Reich under the hegemony of Prussia. Again Bismarck could not be sure how he would carry out his plan, but he worked stage by stage with extreme dexterity and at every point took advantage of the weaknesses of his opponents. Already in 1863 he had pleased the liberals by suggesting that a special assembly should be chosen by universal suffrage to consider the reform of the Confederation. He repeated the proposal in April 1866, just before the outbreak of war with Austria. Bismarck in fact believed that universal suffrage would not work to the advantage of the liberals since they would be outvoted by the conservative rural voters. Furthermore he had no intention of doing away with the 'weighted' three-class franchise in the Prussian Landtag.

After the defeat of Denmark by the combined Austro-Prussian forces and the removal of Augustenberg by imposing on him impossible conditions, Bismarck reached a temporary agreement with Austria for the administration of the duchies on the basis that Austria should be responsible for Holstein and Prussia for Slesvig. Austria did not want Holstein and could not conveniently administer it; the Austrian Government hoped for an arrangement whereby Prussia would take the two duchies and compensate Austria by territorial concessions in Silesia. Bismarck refused a concession of this kind.

Each side complained that the other was breaking the agreement about joint action over the duchies and each began to look for allies. War finally broke out – there was no formal declaration – on 21 June 1866. The Prussian military reforms and expenditure on the army now showed their value and Moltke, the Prussian commander-in-chief,[1] took advantage of the Austrian military blunders as Bismarck had taken advantage of their political and diplomatic blunders. Within three weeks the Austrians had been completely defeated at Königgrätz and within seven weeks they had accepted the Prussian terms. Moltke later described the war as 'not fought out of necessity to meet a threat to our own existence, not called into being by public opinion and the voice of the people. It was a war recognized by the Government as necessary, a war long planned, quietly prepared for, and fought, not for acquisition of land or increase of territory, but for an ideal end – for predominance and power (für ein ideales Gut, für Machtstellung).'

The victory over Austria secured for Bismarck the first stage in the unification of Germany under Prussian control. A North German Confederation was formed, including as a matter of course the two duchies and excluding Austria. The Confederation was dominated, as Bismarck had planned, by Prussia. Prussia directly annexed Hanover, Hesse-Cassel – the two states had taken the Austrian side in the war – and Frankfurt and thus completed the extension of her own territory over North Germany from the Main to Memel. She also brought the southern states into a new Zollverein with the North German Confederation. The constitution of the Confederation provided for a Federal Council (Bundesrath) and a parliament (Bundestag), the latter to be elected by universal male suffrage. The liberals tried to get a proper federal ministry

---

[1] Moltke was not Prussian by birth. His father was a Mecklenburger who had settled in Holstein and had taken Danish nationality. Moltke as a young man joined the Danish Army and transferred to the Prussian Army in 1823.

responsible to the Bundestag, but failed to persuade Bismarck; there was only one federal minister, the Chancellor.

As Bismarck had anticipated, he easily obtained an indemnity from the Prussian Landtag for his unconstitutional acts before the war. The largest section of the liberals was won over by his success; a new National Liberal Party was formed and conveniently sacrificed or at any rate postponed the liberalization of the constitution until the unity of Germany should have been completed (when in fact the position of Bismarck would have become even less assailable). This final stage was reached within five years. As in the earlier stages, Bismarck could not act on a preconceived plan, but once again he was able to make use of the maladresse of his opponents. His own position in Germany was now assured. His main preoccupation was with the attitude of France and Russia to the creation of a strong military power on their frontiers. He could be fairly sure of Russia. Prussia had supported Russia during the tragically unsuccessful Polish rebellion of 1863; Russia had accepted the North German Confederation and was more concerned with freeing herself from the restrictions imposed after the Crimean War which kept her from maintaining a fleet in the Black Sea.

France was a more difficult problem. The speed and completeness of the Prussian victory over Austria had deprived Napoleon III of the opportunity of mediation – suitably rewarded by territorial 'compensation' on the French eastern frontier – which the Emperor had hoped to exercise. Bismarck still expected that he might have to give some compensation, but he would make it as small as possible and avoid it altogether if, as he thought likely, he had to go to war with France. In the latter case he must make it appear that France was the aggressor. The south German states would not be drawn into a war started by Prussia, and Austria might try to revenge herself for her defeat, whereas, in the event of a French attack on Prussia, Austria would lose all German support if she took the French side.

The Hohenzollern candidature for the throne of Spain, which Bismarck could not have foreseen in 1866, though, when he heard of it, he used every means (including bribery in Spain) to support it, and the folly of Napoleon III after the candidature had been withdrawn, gave Bismarck an opportunity of provoking France to war. The Prussian Army under Moltke was more than a match for the ill-prepared, badly led French whose mobilization plans fell into chaos even before the fighting began.

On 18 January 1871 William I of Prussia was acclaimed German Emperor by the rulers of the German states in the palace of Versailles.[1] The German Reich was thus a federation of princes, with whom sovereignty ultimately rested. There was no transfer of this sovereignty, as in France, from 'le roi' to 'la nation'. The King of Prussia still believed himself a ruler by divine right. The Reichstag, like the Bundestag of the North German Confederation, chosen by universal male suffrage, was without real power of government or control of the administration. The Reichstag had indeed certain negative powers, but found it difficult to exercise them. Its financial power was limited, for example, by the fact that the all-important army vote from 1871 to 1914 covered seven-year periods; the contributions of the members of the Reich towards federal expense were fixed by law on a population basis and the sums voted by the Reichstag came mainly from indirect taxation which could not be changed very much annually without economic dislocation. The ministers were not responsible to the Reichstag; the only federal minister was the Chancellor who was chosen by the Emperor without reference to a majority in the Reichstag. An assembly of federal members – the Bundestag – taken over from the North German Confederation was hardly more than a conference of ambassadors and had practically no share in determining policy; the other states never used their numerical power to outvote Prussia. The political parties or rather groups (the system of proportional representation tended to multiply small and sterile groups) in the Reichstag always 'faced' the Govern-

---

[1] A picture of the acclamation by A. von Werner which appears in many textbooks is of particular interest for its skilful placing of the principal figures so that no one of them could feel affronted.

ment; the members were not trained to take authority or to exercise power. The real power of decision rested with Prussia; Germany, in fact though not in theory, had been merged into Prussia. Sixty per cent of the population of the Reich were Prussian subjects, 65 per cent of the territory of the Reich was Prussian; this territory included the main centres of German heavy industry. The Prussian Minister of War controlled the military forces of the Reich in all important matters. The Foreign Office set up in 1871 under a secretary of state – a civil servant, not a minister in the English sense – was merely the Prussian Foreign Office under a different name; the office of Prussian Foreign Minister was continued until Bismarck's dismissal and held by Bismarck himself.

Above all Bismarck was Imperial Chancellor and also Minister President of Prussia. Until his dismissal in 1890 he controlled the unwieldy and illogical machinery of state. Bismarck was unscrupulous, domineering and narrowly conservative. He was not aggressive; his aim was to preserve the Reich which he had created. He underrated its internal cohesion and involved himself thereby unnecessarily in a dispute with the Catholic Church and later greatly exaggerated the disruptive effects of social democracy. In 1878 he persuaded the Reichstag to accept an anti-socialist law which, although less stringent than he had wished, banned Social Democratic, Socialist or Communist associations aiming at the overthrow of the existing social order. The administration of the act gave wide powers to the police. In the autumn of 1878 sixty-seven persons were expelled from Berlin; the police even forbade collections on behalf of their families. The act did not proscribe the Social Democratic party as such, but the vagueness of its terms (e.g. on the question whether this or that activity was a threat to the public peace or the existing order of society) certainly interfered with the rights of public meeting and criticism. The Social Democratic party continued its activities, at first in secret, and then by the ingenious device of making the Social Democratic members of the Reichstag, who had immunity from arrest, into the party committee for the time being.

Bismarck's main concern was to ward off changes in the international situation which might threaten the safety of the Reich. Here again he exaggerated the threats to German security from other European Powers and caused distrust by the harshness of his methods, but he had a sense of limits; his diplomatic moves and countermoves aimed at the preservation of peace, a peace in German interests, but not a policy of European adventure. On the other hand, in spite of his brilliant handling of international relations for nearly twenty years, he failed ultimately to give lasting security to the Reich.

Bismarck had shown moderation – against the wishes of the Prussian Army commanders – in dealing with Austria after her defeat in 1866. If he had been equally moderate in 1871, that is to say, if he had not permanently offended French national feeling by the annexation of Alsace-Lorraine (military defeat could have been forgotten; the loss of territory remained an outrage), he would have had greater freedom of action. As things were, he realized that the French would never be reconciled to the loss of Alsace-Lorraine, though they were unlikely to start a war for its recovery. Bismarck's policy therefore had to be one of preventing a European combination against Germany in which France would certainly take part. Bismarck once said that in a world of five Great Powers, Germany must be one of three, not of two. Lord Salisbury was even nearer the mark in describing Bismarck's policy as that of 'encouraging his neighbours to pull one another's teeth out'.

This policy with its counterbalancing treaties and agreements – not all of them mutually compatible – was breaking down even before Bismarck's fall owing to Great Power rivalries which he could not control. The keystone of his policy was a close alliance with Austria, the other great Germanic Power, and the maintenance, in a common conservative interest, of good relations with Russia. The difficulty, however, was in the rivalry between Austria and Russia over predominant influence in the Balkans. Bismarck might pretend in his forceful language that the Eastern Question was not worth the bones of a Pomeranian grenadier, but he knew that he could not allow Russia to assert herself completely against

Austrian, or rather Austro-Hungarian, interests in south-eastern Europe.

The test came in 1877–8 after the Russo-Turkish War, when Austria and Great Britain were unwilling to acquiesce in the treaty of San Stefano which created an enlarged Bulgaria more or less under Russian protection. In the revision of this treaty at the Congress of Berlin (1878) over which he presided, ostensibly as an 'honest broker', Bismarck had to choose between supporting Austria or Russia. From this time, in spite of Russian dislike of association with republican and anti-clerical France and of French fear of being drawn into war for Russian interest in the Balkans, a Franco-Russian alliance was a logical consequence of the course of events. For over ten years Bismarck avoided a direct choice. The Austro-German alliance of 1879 was supplemented by a triple agreement between Germany, Austria and Russia which checked Austrian and Russian aggression and kept both of the Powers from joining with France. Nevertheless in the middle 1880s Austro-Russian relations were strained over their respective interests in the Balkans and in 1887 Bismarck went to the edge of safety and, one might add, honesty by signing the so-called 'reinsurance treaty' with Russia which committed Germany to neutrality if Russia were attacked by Austria, and Russia to neutrality if Germany were attacked by France; both parties were to be free if Germany or Russia were the aggressors. The incompatibility of this treaty with Germany's other engagements and, above all, with the Austro-German alliance was increased because it recognized Russian influence as predominant in Bulgaria and gave a pledge of diplomatic support to Russia if she had to defend the entrance of the Black Sea. Since Bismarck was at the same time encouraging Austria and Italy to oppose Russian aims in the Straits, he could justify his pledges only as a means of convincing Russia that he could not support Austrian aggression. If Russia accepted this assurance, the treaty would never have to be implemented. In any case the recognition of a *casus belli* would ultimately depend upon the meaning which the parties gave to the term 'aggression'; Bismarck intended that he should be the judge in the matter.

Bismarck's successor as Chancellor did not feel able to continue this diplomatic juggling and the Emperor William II allowed the treaty to lapse. Meanwhile, partly to prevent Russia from getting a loan which might enable her to go to war, partly as a reprisal for a Russian decree fobidding foreigners to hold land in border areas of the Empire (the decree affected numbers of Germans in Russian Poland) Bismarck had forbidden the Reichsbank to accept Russian securities as collaterals for loans. The French at once took advantage of this measure and between 1888 and 1889 began a series of loans to Russia which ended by engulfing vast amounts of French investors' money in the collapse of the Tsarist regime.

The breach between Emperor and Chancellor which led to the latter's dismissal did not take place over matters of foreign policy. The change in Bismarck's position had come after the death of the Emperor William I in 1888. His son and successor, Frederick III, who was already on the worst terms with the Chancellor, died of cancer of the throat three months after he had become Emperor. Bismarck was seventy-three in the year 1888; too much alcohol (not drunkenness) and over-smoking had increased his nervous irritability; he had taken to spending much of his time at his country estate from which he delivered massive and generally acute oracles on policy. He was still over-afraid of the consequences of the growth of Social Democracy upon the stability of the Reich and, in particular, feared the result of giving way to the demand for a widening of the restricted Prussian franchise. William II had no more sympathy than Bismarck for Social Democracy; he maintained the Prussian franchise until the beginning of the collapse of the Reich in 1918.[1] He disagreed with Bismarck over the question of renewal of the anti-socialist law. The Emperor believed that the law was not necessary and that the danger from the Social Democrats could be removed or at least neutralized by adequate social legislation.

The decisive factor which made William II break with Bismarck was a temperamental difference between the two men.

[1] Even in November 1917 a bill to abolish the three-class franchise was defeated in the Landtag.

William II was clever and versatile in a superficial way, unstable and given to a noisy self-assertion which a psychiatrist would easily have diagnosed as due to lack of confidence. He had none of the qualities of a good military commander, but talked too often in terms of military braggadocio and inclined to push even reasonable German demands beyond the prudent limits which Bismarck always observed and to mistake perpetual bluster and interference for a foreign policy upholding German interests. In general the Emperor did not support the small but influential party in Germany which believed in the domination of Europe by German force, but too often he gave the impression that he had this aim. William II, as he once wrote apologetically of himself, was 'not a bad man (ich bin doch kein böser Mensch)'. If the constitution of the Reich had allowed real parliamentary control, the Emperor's faults would still have embarrassed his ministers; they need not have been disastrous. The well-being of the Reich depended upon the ability of the Emperor to work with the Chancellor and upon the ability of the Chancellor to establish a tradition which would outlast his own time in office. Bismarck did not develop such a tradition. He wanted subordinates, not colleagues, obedience rather than collaboration. The Emperor was a bad judge of character. He was too weak to choose people superior to himself and indeed such people had little inducement to serve him for long. The highest post in the German Reich, the office of Chancellor – giving the holder greater power than a British Prime Minister – could be held for nearly ten years by a vain, time-serving, dishonest creature like Prince von Bülow, and the determination of German foreign policy could be confused – to quote a small example – because the reports of the German Ambassador in London were set aside by the Emperor in favour of different information reaching him behind the Ambassador's back from the naval attaché, a comparatively junior officer.[1] An even more serious example was the acceptance about 1900 of the plan of General Count Schlieffen for German strategy in the event of war with

[1] The Ambassador complained to the German Foreign Office, but he and they could do nothing to prevent what was happening.

France and Russia. This plan, which was put into effect in a slightly modified form in 1914, was based on a German invasion of Belgium, the neutrality of which Germany was bound by treaty to respect.[1] The plan could not be changed at the last moment since all the German arrangements for mobilization and deployment of troops depended upon it. The decision to accept the plan was taken without consultation between the General Staff and the German Foreign Office on its likely political consequences and, as a matter of course, without reference to the Reichstag.

For a long time the immense and methodical advance of the Reich in wealth and productive power tended to hide the confusion and uncertainty of purpose at the highest levels of the German state. The advance was indeed astonishing. The population of the Reich increased from 41 to over 65 millions between 1871 and 1914; the production of wheat and other cereals was doubled, the output of coal went up eight-fold, the production of steel from about a third of a million to 14 million tons; German export trade was expanding far more rapidly than British trade and was being carried increasingly in German ships. In 1857 the North German Lloyd Company bought from Great Britain its first steamships for a transatlantic service; the Vulkan shipyards at Stettin did not get their first contract for a large ocean liner until 1887. Twenty-five years later the annual output of German shipbuilding yards was about 400,000 tons. Vast chemical and electrical industries were built up in the first decade of the reign of William II. German colonial expansion began after 1884 when Bismarck, who belonged to an older generation than the economic imperialists, gave way to the pressure of shipping and banking interests and indeed to the pressure of German middle-class opinion which was being taught to regard the possession of colonies as a

---

[1] Before Schlieffen's appointment in 1891 the German plan, in the event of a 'two front' war, was first to attack and defeat Russia. Schlieffen realized that, owing to the difficulty of preventing the Russian armies from retreating into the vast spaces of Russia, a quick victory over them was unlikely. Schlieffen's plan at first envisaged, not a German invasion of Belgium, but at attack on France through the Vosges.

status symbol of a Great Power. The acquisition of colonies, mainly in Africa, brought Germany into sharp controversies with Great Britain and later with France. Bismarck's methods were abrupt and there was an element of blackmail in them, notably in the refusal to support British attempts to secure financial reform in Egypt[1] unless Germany obtained all she wanted elsewhere. The German colonies, whatever use might have been made of them later, were of little economic value to the Reich and less important to it than economic expansion in Turkey. In the late 1880s the Sultan readily granted German railway concessions in order to counterbalance the influence of Great Britain and France; the Germans by 1900 had built about 600 miles of railway in Asia Minor and were trying to get agreement for an extension of their construction to Baghdad.

This remarkable material progress, following upon military success, and in the view of most Germans, resulting from military success, had certain dangers. The Germans as a nation acquired a good deal of the arrogance of *nouveaux riches*. I have already pointed out that in the days of their political impotence German intellectuals cherished, as a kind of compensation, a belief in the superiority of the German mind and of a German world mission of culture; this idea was carried on and popularized in the cruder form of manifestations of German power. The middle class in particular was affected by national arrogance; Germany was the only European country in which in the first years of the twentieth century the younger generation were less liberal-minded than their fathers and grandfathers. The Germans were not alone in the nineteenth century in showing symptoms of 'getting too rich too quickly'; the comment of the Socialist, Bebel, as he watched a crowd cheering a procession of troops at the Brandenburg gate in Berlin, 'The people are still drunk with victory (Das Volk ist noch siegesgetrunken)', could have been applied to the British crowds at the time of Queen Victoria's Diamond Jubilee in 1897, but most foreign observers in Germany before 1914 came away amazed at the limitless belief in German superiority,

[1] See below, p. 131.

an almost total lack of consideration for the legitimate interests of other nations and a childish assertion of military arrogance.[1]

There were indeed signs of a possible reaction. The attacks of the Social Democrats and the Centre (catholic) party on the abuses of German colonial administration and the cruelty with which native rebellion was put down in German south-west Africa had a very considerable effect on public opinion. The growth of the Social Democratic party, in spite of the hindrances put in its way even after the lapse of the anti-Socialist law, slowly began to have real political consequences. In 1903 the Social Democrats polled 3,000,000 votes and secured 81 seats in the Reichstag;[2] at the general election of 1912 the number rose to 110 in a house of just under 400 seats. They were now the largest single party and with other left-wing groups formed a majority of the Reichstag. It is impossible to say whether, if war had not broken out in 1914, the Social Democrats would have been able by sheer force of numbers to overthrow the German military and conservative regime during the lifetime of William II. German socialism had gained from the great increase in the numerical strength and organization of the trade unions; trade union membership reached over 1,600,000 in 1906. The Social Democrats were not in fact a revolutionary party. They aimed in theory at the overthrow of capitalism and the balance of opinion swung to and fro on the question of co-operating with the bourgeois parties, but in 1913 at a congress at Jena the moderates won a majority in favour of a gradual and 'piece by piece' replacement of the capitalist state by the proletarian society. A minority broke away to form the Independent Socialist Party; the rank and file were disinclined to violent action. The German working class was not driven by misery to revolution. They shared as subjects in the material prosperity of the Empire; they enjoyed the display of its power and long habits of submission

---

[1] It is difficult to imagine Gladstone, Salisbury or Asquith appearing in public, as Bismarck and Bethmann-Hollweg appeared, in military uniform.

[2] In 1903 the Social Democrats polled nearly 18 per cent of the votes in the elections for the Prussian Landtag, but owing to the three-class franchise they did not secure even one seat.

to authority had made them docile. At the height of the revolution in 1918, when the soldiers (with good reason) were mutinying against the regime which had led them into terrible defeat, one of their demands was that they should say 'sir' once only in addressing an officer! The introduction of social legislation, Bismarck's 'other weapon' against socialism, had put Germany far ahead of other Great Powers in the provision of welfare measures; insurance schemes against sickness and unemployment, with contributions from employers and employed, were begun in 1883 and were followed by similar contributory schemes to deal with accidents, in 1884, and in 1889 by old-age pensions.

The collapse of the Second Reich was due to mistakes in foreign policy; these mistakes were the result, partly of an overestimate of German strength, partly of the confusion of purpose and the absence of a sense of limits among those directing German policy. The Germans brought upon themselves the 'encirclement' (*Einkreisung*) of which they complained. William II, in spite of his bellicosity in words and continual harping on Germany's armed strength, never supposed except in his most exalted moods that he could conquer the world or even Europe, but he must bear a heavy responsibility since he chose the men who misjudged almost every critical situation and since he mirrored in his person the worst political faults of his fellow-countrymen.

One can mention four of the most damaging errors of German high policy. The first of these errors during the reign of William II was to assume that Great Britain in her own interest was bound to take the side of Germany after the formation of the Franco–Russian alliance. The Germans were inclined in any case to regard Great Britain as a declining Power because she wanted merely to hold what she had. The Franco–Russian alliance was primarily a defensive move against Germany and, as such, evidence of the failure of Bismarck's efforts to keep France isolated. The alliance, however, which was not completed by a military convention until 1893, appeared at this time more of a positive threat to Great Britain. Both France and Russia had interests and ambitions outside Europe which could be satisfied only at British expense and a possible combination of the French and Russian fleets could be a danger to British naval power in the Mediterranean. This danger was the main reason for a large British shipbuilding programme in 1894.[1]

In the last years of the nineteenth century therefore the German Government felt confident that Great Britain would have to look for German support and could be made to pay a high price for it. From 1898 to 1901 the British Government, realizing the hostility of the Continental Powers at a time of crisis and, later, war in South Africa, and being unable single-handed to prevent further Russian inroads into the independence and territorial integrity of China, had tried to reach an alliance with Germany, with particular application to the Far East. The Germans considered that they could wait until they had obtained a full British commitment to the Dual Alliance of Germany and Austria–Hungary. Lord Salisbury (a wiser man than Joseph Chamberlain who wanted the German alliance) opposed such a commitment on the ground that a British obligation to defend Germany against Russia would be a greater liability than that of undertaking a single-handed war against France.

In any case the Germans were almost ludicrously wrong in thinking that Great Britain had no alternative to an acceptance of the German condition – a full alliance or nothing. In January 1902 the British Government covered their position in the Far East by an alliance with Japan. Later in the same year Anglo–French discussions were begun for a general settlement of outstanding differences between the two Powers. This settlement, signed in April 1904 after much hard bargaining,[2] was not an alliance and did not commit Great Britain to the

[1] Another reason for the programme was the development of the cordite-firing gun which allowed important changes in the heavy ordnance of battleships. Mr Gladstone's opposition to this naval programme was one of the causes of his resignation.

[2] One of the most contested points was the relatively minor matter of French fishing rights, which went back to the Treaty of Utrecht almost two hundred years earlier, along part of the coast of Newfoundland.

military support of France in a continental war, but in removing the likely causes of dispute between the two countries it also made it improbable that either country would take sides against the other if a European war should break out. The main feature of the agreement was a French recognition of the British position in Egypt and a British recognition of French predominant influence in Morocco.[1]

[1] Ismail Pasha, Khedive of Egypt and a nominal vassal of the Sultan of Turkey, was a well-intentioned and not unenlightened man, but without practical sense and wildly extravagant. (He once ordered a quantity of textile machinery. The machinery needed coal, so he chartered a number of coal ships. The coal ships arrived at Alexandria, but there were no lighters for the transfer of their cargoes to the shore.) The Khedive became bankrupt in 1879. Most of his creditors were French, but the British Government had a special interest in the Suez Canal (opened in 1869). A joint Anglo–French control was established to bring order into Ismail's affairs, but the task was hopeless and, after Ismail had got rid of a constitutional ministry imposed upon him, the British and French persuaded the Sultan to depose him. They then increased their own control. A nationalist movement in the country opposed this control and began to attack the Europeans in Alexandria and elsewhere. Great Britain and France agreed to put an end to the dangerous situation in Alexandria, but the French would take no further action to suppress the Egyptian rebels. A British force easily defeated the rebels at the battle of Tel-el-Kebir, but the French Chamber vetoed a proposal by their own Government to join in an Anglo–French occupation of the canal zone. The British were therefore left with Egypt on their hands. They began a general reform and reorganization of the finances and administration of the country and announced that they would leave it as soon as they had completed this work. This was indeed their original intention, but the task took very much longer than they had expected and the French in particular refused to believe that the British had not in mind a permanent occupation. The French had gained by the return of Egypt to solvency and order, but they now regretted their mistake in refusing their co-operation. They still had important rights of interference on behalf of the creditors of Egypt; their exercise of these rights was a continual trouble to the British administration and compelled the British Government to rely on the support of Germany – a support for which the German Government exacted their own price. From the British point of view, therefore, the Anglo–French agreement had the very great advantage of getting rid of French opposition in Egypt. Lord Cromer, who had been the leading figure in the administrative and financial reforms in Egypt, was one of the chief advocates of the agreement. Since the French could embarrass the British administration in Egypt but could not force a British withdrawal, they too gained greatly

This agreement disconcerted the Germans. They had not been consulted about it. They could have no grievance in this respect since they did not consult other Powers about their own agreements. In any case consultation would only have resulted in an attempt by Germany to break the Anglo-French *entente*. A wiser policy for the Germans might have been to have accepted the Anglo-French *entente* and have tried to reach a similar agreement with Great Britain. The Germans might have contented themselves with assurances that France did not intend to secure exclusive commercial privileges for herself in Morocco; they would have had British support for an economic 'open door', since British trade with Morocco was four times greater than that of Germany. Instead they concentrated on political action in an attempt to demonstrate to the French that their *entente* with Great Britain was useless to them.

The moment for such action seemed favourable since Russia, France's military ally, was fighting a difficult and unsuccessful war with Japan. The German diplomatic campaign began suddenly with a visit by the Emperor William II to Tangier, where he ignored all French claims and promised the Sultan of Morocco German support in the event of an attack on his sovereign independence. Neither the Emperor nor the German Foreign Office said what Germany really wanted. By direct pressure on the French Government they secured the dismissal of the French Foreign Minister, Delcassé, who had been responsible on the French side for the negotiation of the Anglo-French *entente*. They also insisted upon a Conference of the Powers over Morocco and obtained the desired safeguards for their commercial interests, but their threats to the French had an effect directly contrary to their intentions. Although the British engagement to the French had not gone beyond a promise of diplomatic support, the French, in their alarm over German threats, asked the British Government to give official sanction to military and staff conversations between the two countries on possible arrangements for co-operation in war.

---

by giving up their opposition in return for British acceptance of the position which France expected to acquire in Morocco.

The sanction was given, though on the understanding that the talks were on a non-committal basis. If the Anglo–French *entente* had been worth making, it was worth keeping; the German threats therefore merely strengthened British support of the French and gave to the *entente* something of a defensive and protective character against Germany which had not been one of the British intentions in making it.

The Germans also had attempted to weaken the Anglo–French position by a closer approach to Russia. Six months after the announcement of the Anglo–French *entente*, Germany taking advantage of Russian resentment against Great Britain as the ally of Japan, proposed to Russia a secret treaty of mutual assistance in the event of either party becoming involved in war with a European Power. The Emperor William II was foolish enough to think that, if Germany faced France with a treaty of this kind, the French would be compelled to accept it. The Tsar wanted to show the treaty to the French before its signature. William II objected that the French would reveal the draft to the British and that Great Britain and France would at once attack Germany in Europe and the Far East. Nothing came of the proposal at the time, but in July 1905 the German Emperor, at a meeting with Nicholas II of Russia on their respective yachts at Bjorko in the Baltic, persuaded the Tsar to accept a treaty of mutual assistance with the limitation of the assistance to Europe. The Tsar accepted the treaty; the German Foreign Office, to the surprise of William II, regarded the treaty as of little value owing to this limitation, since what they wanted was a Russian promise to attack India. The Russian Foreign Office anyhow thought that the French would never allow Russia to agree to the treaty, because it would mean the end of the Franco–Russian alliance. The treaty therefore faded out.

In 1911 the Germans again brought on a European crisis over Morocco and again their action (which few German writers have subsequently tried to defend) had an effect contrary to their intentions. Early in the year a rebel pretender – one of many in the uneasy condition of Morocco – threatened to seize Fez, the capital, and depose the Sultan. The French sent troops to Fez to protect the Sultan and the French subjects in the city and neighbourhood. In accordance with the conventions of the time Germany would not have been doing anything unusual or aggressive if she had asked for 'compensation' elsewhere in return for what was obviously an increase in the French hold on Morocco. The German Government, however, did not say what they wanted, but took the dramatic step of sending a warship to the Moroccan port of Agadir, ostensibly to protect German subjects and German commercial interest in the place. There were in fact neither German interests nor subjects in Agadir and the conclusion suggested to other Powers by this sudden action was that the German aim might be to get a naval base on the Atlantic coast of Morocco. Grey told the German Ambassador that the British Government could not be indifferent to these Moroccan events, but the Germans made no reply. After nearly three weeks, when there was still no German answer about their intentions, Lloyd George (with Grey's approval) made a warning reference in a speech that Great Britain could not allow her vital interests to be disregarded.

The German Government made an angry protest and for a time there was a real danger of war.[1] The Germans did not want war, for all their bellicose language. They were making very large demands on the French for compensation and, incredible though it seems, the German Foreign Office believed that their action at Agadir would help them in getting their demands. In the end they obtained a considerable area of the French Congo, though much less than they had demanded, in return for giving the French a free hand in Morocco.

The main result of the five months' crisis – a Franco-German settlement was not concluded until November – was once again to strengthen the Anglo-French *entente*. Inevitably the Anglo-

[1] The Agadir crisis, while it lasted, caused much less public excitement in Great Britain than in Germany. Apart from the diversions of an unusually hot summer, the British public was occupied mainly with the controversy over the Parliament Act of 1911. A railway strike broke out in England at the height of the crisis. The strike leaders seem to have given no thought to, and indeed knew nothing about the danger of war. In Germany there was for a short time a run on the banks.

Germany 135

French staff conversations which had been held at the time of the first Moroccan crisis were resumed and, inevitably, the Anglo–French defensive action was interpreted in Germany as a new stage in a deliberate and sinister 'encirclement'.[1] Furthermore this worsening of Anglo–German relations made it less likely that the German Government would agree to a relaxation in the naval ship building competition between the two countries.

It is possible, in retrospect, to regard as another great error in German foreign policy the Emperor's decision, with the support of Admiral Tirpitz[2] and, obviously, of the representatives of German heavy industry, to build, on a twenty years' programme, a large German battle fleet. This decision did not violate any treaty or understanding signed by Germany. Germany, like every other Power, was free to build for herself as large a fleet as she might wish. The question was one of expediency and of realist calculation. A German battle fleet could not be other than a challenge to Great Britain, the dominant sea power. The Germans themselves did not interpret it in any other way except in statements to Great Britain. If there had been any doubt in the matter, the German programme of a fleet of battleships constructed solely for use in the North Sea and neighbouring areas was sufficient to show where the fleet would be employed. The Emperor and Admiral Tirpitz made their purpose clear in the propaganda – a new phenomenon of its kind – necessary to convince the German people that British naval power was a threat to the security of the Reich and the expansion of its overseas interests. Moreover, when the naval programme was officially announced in 1897 (the first naval law was passed in 1898; a second law, doubling the number of battleships, followed in 1900) Tirpitz produced

[1] See below, p. 139.
[2] Grand-Admiral A. von Tirpitz (1849–1930) came of a Prussian landowning family. He developed his ideas about a German navy about 1891. He was posted in 1892 to the naval Oberkommando in Berlin. Here he made a ready convert of the Emperor William II who appointed him Secretary of the Reichsmarineamt in 1897. Tirpitz, although he set out to challenge British naval superiority, was not personally Anglophobe; he sent his daughters to school at Cheltenham Ladies College.

an ingenious argument – the so-called 'risk theory' – that, in order to put political pressure on Great Britain, a German Navy need not be as strong as the British Navy; all that was needed was a fleet strong enough to inflict such damage on its adversary (the British fleet) that the latter would find itself inferior to the combined navies of France and Russia.

As I have said, the Germans were free to build a large navy on this or any other hypothesis; British naval predominance was not a law of nature, but it existed and Great Britain, if she thought it necessary for her safety, was equally free to maintain it. If Great Britain lost her predominance, she could be starved into total surrender, whereas, if she destroyed the German Navy, she would still have been unable to meet the German Army. No British Government therefore, however anxious they might be to cut down expenditure on armaments, could risk the loss of naval superiority.

The Anglo-French *entente*, the destruction of the greater part of the Russian Navy by the Japanese and, in 1907, the Anglo-Russian agreement[1] cut away the basis of Tirpitz's 'risk theory'. If Great Britain no longer had to fear a possible Franco-Russian combination against her, a weaker German fleet would be unable to exercise political pressure – most English writers used the plainer term 'blackmail' – against her. The question which William II and Tirpitz had to ask was whether it was worth while for Germany to engage in a competition in shipbuilding which Great Britain for elementary reasons of national safety could not risk losing and which she need not lose because she had the resources to win it, whereas Germany had to spend very large sums on her army.

The British Government, obviously, wanted an agreement between the two countries and a general diminution of expenditure on armaments by the European powers. If Germany had agreed to an understanding of this kind, she would not have lost by it. There would have been a lessening of European tension and, in the event of a clash of interest between France and Germany, the British Government would certainly not have supported any measure of French

[1] See below, p. 210.

aggression. On the other hand, every step by Germany to increase the tempo of naval competition was bound to increase British suspicion of German intentions and to drive her closer to the Franco-Russian side. The need for naval agreement was even more urgent after the introduction of a relatively new type of battleship – the *Dreadnought* class;[1] these ships were so much more powerful even than their immediate predecessors that they would soon render obsolete the capital ships which made up the existing margin of British superiority. The German reaction to this new factor was twofold. They regarded the British proposals for a limitation of capital ship construction as a hypocritical device for maintaining British supremacy in the new *Dreadnoughts* on the cheap. They also thought that they now had a good chance by persistent effort of equalling or even surpassing Great Britain in the building of *Dreadnoughts*.

The most dangerous years of this naval competition were between 1906 and 1913. Germany increased the size of her programme, the rate of construction of new ships and the rate of replacing older capital ships. The Emperor refused to accept an agreement with Great Britain except in return for a British promise not to intervene in any circumstances in a Franco-German War. An undertaking of this kind would have meant – as the Germans intended it to mean – the end of the Anglo-French *entente*. Once again, if the *entente* had been worth making, it was worth keeping; the persistent German attempts to destroy it only confirmed Great Britain and France in its value and in their suspicion of German intentions.

In spite of the British reply to German increases by British increases in capital ships, the Germans in 1913 had not given up hope of overtaking British superiority, but they were

[1] The *Dreadnought* was completed in October 1906. She could outpace in speed and outrange in armament any other battleship. It has been a matter of controversy whether the British Admiralty was wise to construct this new type (which every other naval Power would have to imitate) and thus to give up the comfortable margin which Great Britain possessed in capital ships. The answer is that the introduction of the new type was being discussed in other countries and the question for Great Britain was not whether she should build the ships, but whether she should get in first and establish a lead which other countries would be unable to overtake.

temporarily unable to maintain the pace of the competition. William II wanted to add to their building programme, but even Tirpitz had to warn the German naval attaché in London early in 1914 that 'the bow is overstrung here as much as in England'. The cost of capital ships was continually rising; 'super-*Dreadnoughts*' were superseding the *Dreadnoughts*. A new factor in armaments had appeared with the development of the airship and the military programme of France required a German answer in the form of higher army estimates. In 1913 Germany announced a capital levy of 1,000,000,000 marks (in modern equivalent, at least £300,000,000) for non-recurrent military expenditure. In 1914, at the outbreak of war with Germany, Great Britain had twenty *Dreadnoughts* in the North Sea area, Germany had thirteen; four more British and two more German *Dreadnoughts*, or rather super-*Dreadnoughts* were nearing completion. Despite vast German expenditure, Britain had kept a superiority which was decisive for the issue of the war. The German revolution began at Kiel on 4 November 1918 after the sailors of the German battle fleet had refused to sail their ships on a last desperate engagement against the British Grand Fleet.

The third German blunder was to drive Russia finally to the side of Great Britain and France by a threat which the Russians thought vital to their future in the Near and Middle East. Here again, as in their naval expansion, Germany was not acting contrary to international law or breaking any engagement. The matter was one of a balance of interests. I have mentioned the development of German interest – encouraged by Turkey – in railway construction in Turkey and generally in trade with the Turkish Empire. The so-called Baghdad railway plan – a proposal for a railway from the Bosphorus to the Persian Gulf – arose out of these earlier enterprises. The Sultan granted to a German financial group a concession for the Baghdad railway in 1899. The railway would run through Adana to Basra, with branches to Aleppo, the Persian frontier at Khanikin and a point on the Persian Gulf. The company would be given mining rights and other privileges in the areas which it covered.

Already in 1900 the Russians had obtained from Turkey an agreement that all railway concessions in northern Asia should be given to them. The German group tried to get British financial support for the Baghdad line, but there was much opposition within and outside parliament to a plan which might be described as international, but which aimed principally at serving German interests. The German chargé d'affaires in Constantinople had earlier been surprised that the British Ambassador thought an economic partnership with Germany in Turkey even a possibility. In 1903 Lord Lansdowne, then Foreign Secretary, announced in Parliament that Great Britain would resist action by a European Power to establish a naval or fortified port on the Persian Gulf.

If German plans for Middle Eastern expansion threatened long-standing British interests, the threat to Russia was much greater. These plans would put an end to Russian hopes of reaching the Mediterranean or the Persian Gulf across Near or Middle Eastern territory. In February 1907 the Baghdad railway was discussed at a special meeting of the Russian Ministerial Council. The construction of the railway now appeared certain. The line would do so much harm to Russian interests that no 'compensation' could make up for the damage. Russia had therefore to content herself with limiting its bad effects. The best way of doing so would be by getting British support. In order to secure this support she must give up her own plans for bringing all Persia under her control and building her own railway to a fortified station on the Gulf. Six months later Russia signed an agreement with Great Britain. The agreement had no secret or military clauses; the terms dealt only with matters outside Europe. The agreement did not threaten Germany; Russia in 1907 was in no position to threaten any Great Power. William II, however, and his advisers chose to regard an Anglo–Russian rapprochement, following the Anglo–French *entente*, as a further step in the encirclement of Germany with intent to destroy her. The idea of a deliberate plot was useful as propaganda for German shipbuilding, but an Anglo–German agreement to limit naval competition was now even less possible because the German

Government held that the price of a naval agreement must be a British promise of unconditional neutrality in a continental war.[1]

Within a year of the signature of the Anglo–Russian agreement, developments in the Balkans led to a worsening of Austro–Russian relations. Germany then made her fourth mistake by threatening and humiliating Russia rather than trying to get her own Austro–Hungarian ally to do something more positive than settling or attempting to settle by force the problems of the multi-national Austro–Hungarian state. In 1897, when Russia had become increasingly engaged in Far Eastern adventure, she had agreed with Austria–Hungary upon the maintenance of the *status quo* in the Balkans. After Japan had put an end to the Russian Far Eastern plans, Russia, as soon as she had recovered from the internal troubles following her defeat, was likely to take a more active interest in the future of south-east Europe. The Russians indeed tried to counter a railway concession by the Sultan which would have allowed Austria to link up communications (through the Sanjak of Novi Bazar) with the Turkish line from Mitrovista to Salonika; the Russians asked for a concession to construct a line from the Roumanian border to the Adriatic.[2]

The revolution of the so-called Young Turks in July 1908 against the miserable Sultan Abdul Hamid brought a possibility that Turkey might save herself from dissolution by a patriotic revival. In this case both Austrian and Russian interests would be affected. Russia hoped that, in the event of the break-up of the remaining Turkish Empire in Europe, she might be able to secure the opening of the Straits to Russian warships,[3] while

[1] William II attributed the weaving of the 'plot' against Germany to the devilish cunning of his uncle, Edward VII. In the last days of peace, on 29 July 1914, when he realized that Great Britain was likely to intervene in the European war which then appeared certain, William still held to the theory of a 'plot' and commented: 'So the dead Edward is stronger than I who am still living.'

[2] See also below, p. 204.

[3] The closing of the Straits to non-Turkish ships of war had been affirmed by international agreement in 1841 and reaffirmed in 1856 and

Austria wanted to acquire full sovereignty over the former Turkish provinces of Bosnia and Herzegovina which she had been administering, under the nominal suzerainty of the Sultan, since 1878. In the autumn of 1908 Aehrenthal, the Foreign Minister of Austria–Hungary, met Izvolsky, the Russian Foreign Minister, at a castle in Moravia. Neither of these two men was noted for his trustworthiness,[1] and there is no reason to believe in the subsequent statements of either of them about the meeting, but Izvolsky seems to have promised to support an Austrian annexation of Bosnia and Herzegovina in return for a promise from Aehrenthal that Austria would support a Russian demand for the opening of the Straits. Aehrenthal, apparently to the surprise of Izvolsky, announced the annexation of the two provinces before Russia approached the other Powers about the opening of the Straits. Russia had been acting behind the back of Great Britain – the British Government did not want Russian warships in the Mediterranean – and could not have been astonished when the British Government refused to accept a change in the regime of the Straits.[2]

The Austrian annexation of Bosnia–Herzegovina caused great anger in Serbia, which had hopes of an enlarged southern Slav state. The Serbs looked to Russia for support; without it they could not risk war with Austria. Russia, however, had still not recovered from defeat and revolution and could not

[1] The British Ambassador in Vienna once said to Aehrenthal: 'Your Excellency does not love the truth.' Ivolsky's own memoirs show that he had a similar dislike or indifference to it.

[2] The British Government, since they had been able to use Alexandria as a base, were less concerned about the question of the Straits, but Grey objected to what amounted to unilateral action by Russia; he was also much disquieted by the Russian disregard of their agreement with Great Britain about Persia.

1878. The question is often confused by the different meanings attached by Russia and the other interested Powers to the words 'opening' and 'closing'. Russia wanted the Straits to be open to her own warships and closed to those of other Powers. The other Powers wanted them to be closed to all except Turkish warships. Russia had found the closing of the Straits a handicap to her in the Russo–Japanese War. She could not move her fleet from the Black Sea or transport men or military material from south Russia through the port of Odessa.

fight a war with a Great Power. In March 1909 the German Government insisted upon an unconditional Russian acceptance of the Austrian annexation of Bosnia and Herzegovina and the Russians had to agree. Instead of assisting Austria to make this Russian climb-down easier, the Germans went out of their way to humiliate the Russians. William II had not in fact promised more than diplomatic support to Austria if she declared war on Serbia, though it was clear to the Austrians that Germany could not allow their defeat by Russia and, under the terms of the Austro-German alliance, they could claim German help in the event of a Russian attack. A year later, however, William II, in a speech while on a visit to Vienna, spoke of the preservation of peace in Europe because Germany had 'stood shoulder to shoulder' with Austria and had 'confronted the world in shining armour'.

From this time the problem of the future of the Habsburg Empire was an embarrassment to Germany. Francis Joseph, who had come to the throne in 1848, was eighty in the year 1910. The general view in Europe was that his empire would break up after his death. The southern Slavs – Serbs, Slovenes and Croatians – were hoping for this break-up. Austria therefore had either to conciliate them – a task almost impossible in itself and wholly beyond the political capacities of Austrian and Hungarian politicians and bureaucrats – or to bring about the total collapse of Serbia as an independent state. The vicissitudes of the Balkan wars in 1912–13 increased Serbian demands, particularly for a port on the Adriatic. The Austrian military authorities thought it essential for the Habsburg monarchy to deal with Serbia while there was time, that is to say, while Francis Joseph was still alive and before Russia had recovered her military strength sufficiently to intervene in favour of the southern Slavs. Germany, however, held back Austria from war and Great Britain and France held back Russia. William II none the less, and even more strongly his General Staff, believed that a war in support of Austria-Hungary was inevitable.

When on 28 June 1914 the Archduke Francis Ferdinand, heir to Francis Joseph, was assassinated by a Bosnian Serb belonging to one of the revolutionary societies which the Serbian Government had done nothing to suppress and a good deal to encourage, military opinion in Austria–Hungary and Germany thought that a favourable moment – perhaps the last favourable occasion – had come to settle once and for all with Serbia. Even at this critical time there was confusion in German calculations. William II, without consulting his Chancellor, gave Austria a free hand to do as she wished to Serbia – he knew well enough what Austrian intentions were; Bethmann-Hollweg made no objection. Both of them thought that Austrian action would be rapid and that the war could be localized and indeed over before the slow-moving Russian war machine could be set into operation. Neither Emperor nor Chancellor remembered Bismarck's maxim of being one of three and not one of two in a Europe of five Great Powers and, strange as it seems, neither took much notice of the evidence that, after her previous humiliations, Russia would certainly not allow the destruction of Serbia and the extrusion of Russian influence from the Balkans. The German General Staff had worked out the implications for Germany of a two-front war and were confident of victory if Russia (with French support) should decide upon intervention. The so-called Schlieffen plan was for a quick defeat of the French; the German armies, after overrunning Belgium, would make a great enveloping move through northern France and bring about a French surrender, or at least a complete French defeat, within about six weeks. The Germans could then turn against Russia. Count Moltke, the German Chief of Staff, was the nephew of the Moltke whose strategy had won the Prussian campaigns of 1866 and 1871. If the nephew had looked with his uncle's scrutiny at Schlieffen's plan, he might have seen the weak points in it which led to its failure and the ultimate German defeat. As for the intervention of Great Britain, the German authorities at first thought it most improbable. If Austria acted quickly and decisively, Russia would not intervene. If neither Russia nor France intervened, Great Britain would not go to war on behalf of the Serbs. In any case, if the war extended to the five Great Powers, British intervention would have no effect upon the issue. The German General Staff thought the British Army (whose unexpected appearance in the way of the German advance was in fact one of the main reasons for the defeat of the Schlieffen plan and the breakdown of the German timetable) too small to affect the decision in France; the Germans did not try to prevent or even to hamper the landing of the British Expeditionary Force, since they expected to capture it in the general French *débâcle*. The war would be over before British naval power could affect the issue.

A closer study of the last days of peace and of the German failure to win the expected early victory and, at the last, to avoid utter defeat, would bring out more clearly the extraordinary contrast between German efficiency in the middle and lower ranges of organization and the confusion of thought at the summit and the inability of the rulers of Germany to work out the likely response of others to their military and diplomatic moves. In a final analysis the collapse of the Second Reich revealed the weaknesses of the system of government set up by Bismarck, a system dependent upon a Chancellor of the highest ability and an Emperor willing to accept his guidance. The collapse showed also the danger to a great state in the nineteenth and early twentieth century which ignored or tried to suppress the new democratic forces and allowed a military caste the position retained by the General Staff and army commanders in Germany. Finally the German collapse was a deserved retribution for a policy of power followed without thought for the general interests or susceptibilities of other states.

Note to Chapter 2

THE SLESVIG–HOLSTEIN QUESTION

The two Elbe duchies of Slesvig (more commonly known under its German name of Schleswig) and Holstein provided endless opportunities for dispute in the half-century after the Congress of Vienna. The duchies were personal possessions of the King of Denmark; they were also legally united one with the other, but Holstein was and Slesvig was not a member of the Germanic Confederation. The population of Holstein was predominantly German, that of Slesvig mixed German and Danish, with a Danish preponderance in the north.

German nationalists wanted to incorporate Slesvig into Germany; Danish nationalists wanted to incorporate it into the kingdom of Denmark. In 1848 Frederick VII of Denmark, who was childless, issued a decree providing for a joint parliament for Denmark and the duchies; he did not interfere with the existing provincial Diets of the duchies or attempt to detach Holstein from the Germanic Confederation. The German nationalists, however, who wanted the recognition of the two duchies as a single German state, refused to accept Frederick's decree and supported a separate government for the duchies set up by the Duke of Augustenburg.[1]

In order to satisfy the nationalists of his own kingdom, the King of Denmark then announced the annexation of the duchies to Denmark. The Diet of the Confederation replied by recognizing the government of Augustenburg and taking Slesvig into the Confederation. Both Danes and Prussians sent troops

[1] The old Frankish custom, known as the 'Salic Law', prohibiting the inheritance of lands by or through females, had been abrogated for the crown of Denmark, but not for the two duchies. If the male line of the reigning Danish house died out, the succession in the duchies would pass, unless special arrangements were agreed, to the Duke of Augustenburg.

into the duchies to enforce their respective decisions. The European Powers then intervened in the interest of a northern balance of power (i.e. the entrance to the Baltic) and the King of Prussia agreed to an armistice. The liberal nationalists of the Frankfurt Assembly strongly opposed the armistice and demanded the coercion of the Danes, but had no armed force with which to support their demand. In 1852 the Great Powers guaranteed the integrity of the possessions of the Danish Crown. The Duke of Augustenburg renounced his claims and the duchies returned to their *status quo*.

Danes and Germans alike were dissatisfied with the treaty of 1852, but the Slesvig-Holstein question did not flare up again for the next decade. In 1863 Frederick VII of Denmark died. His heir, Prince Christian of Glücksburg, also succeeded to the duchies. Christian accepted a new constitution bringing Slesvig within the scope of legislation enacted for Denmark even if Holstein rejected it. The son of the Duke of Augustenburg who had resigned his claims in 1852 now came forward and, asserting that his father's renunciation was only personal, set up a government for the duchies. The German liberals and some of the princes recognized Augustenburg, and the Diet, under Prussian and Austrian leadership, refused to accept Christian's constitution unless he promised to give proper regard to the rights of Germans. Prussia and Austria carried a motion for federal intervention in the duchies, but disagreed with the majority of the Diet by rejecting Augustenburg. On Christian's refusal to modify his constitution, Prussia and Austria declared war on Denmark. They occupied Holstein, invaded Slesvig and went on into the kingdom of Denmark.

The Danes hoped for the intervention of the Powers in their favour. Palmerston at first wanted to go to the help of Denmark, but British opinion in the decade after the Crimean War refused to become involved in another continental war, whatever the larger issues might be. Napoleon III had been disappointed with the British rejection of his proposal for a European Congress (which, as Palmerston and Russell knew, would solve nothing) and hoped that, if he supported or at all events did not hinder Prussia, he might get territorial compensation elsewhere. Russia wanted Prussia, Austria and Great Britain to work together and leave no opportunity for the schemes of Napoleon III. Bismarck's aim was the annexation of the duchies to Prussia. At this stage he was unable to see how he could bring about this end to the crisis. He realized that at first he must continue co-operation with Austria. He delayed the opening of peace talks at a conference in London until the victory of the Austro-Prussian forces were assured. Even so the conference came to no decision. Prussia and Austria would not accept Augustenburg; the Danes would not agree to a complete separation of the duchies from the kingdom of Denmark and the maintenance only of a personal link through the Danish king. The war therefore went on until the Danes were forced to make a complete surrender.

Bismarck then argued that the results of the war had annulled the treaty of 1852; the Danes were therefore compelled to surrender all claims to the duchies to Prussia and Austria jointly. The Diet of the Confederation was merely informed of the new treaty with Denmark and Augustenburg was ignored. Bismarck now began to Prussianize Holstein and to extend Prussian influence into Slesvig. Austria objected and began to support Augustenburg. Bismarck then suggested that the Estates of the duchies should meet to declare their preference. The Augustenburg party could not reject this proposal, but Bismarck delayed the meeting and meanwhile came to an agreement with Austria that Prussia should take charge of Slesvig, and Austria Holstein. This arrangement was hardly practicable; Bismarck never intended that it should work. He continued the Prussianization of Slesvig and complained that Austria was breaking her agreement by supporting agitation on behalf of Augustenburg. On this pretext war finally broke out between Prussia and Austria. After the Prussian victory, Prussia annexed both duchies with the promise of a plebiscite in North Slesvig. This promise was not carried out until the Allies enforced its fulfilment after the war of 1914–18.

3. *Italy*

I have discussed the emergence of a nation-state out of the conglomeration of sovereignties which made up Germany in the eighteenth century. I turn now to Italy. Here also I have to deal with the formation of a nation-state, but in a setting very different from that of Germany. The German Reich was, and is, a state ill-defined by physical boundaries, and unification was achieved by the forcible exclusion of the nine to ten million Germans of Austria. Italy had well-defined natural boundaries. In the north-east of her only land frontier the crest-line of the Alps did not altogether correspond with ethnological or (more important) linguistic dividing lines, and in the north-west the expansion of the domains of the house of Savoy on either side of the Alps had made the kingdom of Savoy-Piedmont, or, as it was called, the kingdom of Sardinia, partly French, partly Italian-speaking.[1] There were pockets of Italians dispersed among the islands and coast of the eastern side of the Adriatic, and on the west of the gulf of Genoa Nice might be counted as Italian or French. None the less these exceptions were not of major importance; Savoy-Piedmont could easily be divided between France and Italy if Italy became a unified nation-state.

In general, Italy, a long peninsula enclosed by a semi-circle of the highest mountains in Europe, might seem to have been fitted geographically to be one of the earliest and not one of the last of the larger European nation-states.[2] At the outbreak of the French Revolution in 1789, however, the Italian peninsula was broken up into a number of separate political units; the

[1] See also below, p. 149.
[2] See below, p. 161 note.

kingdom of Sardinia in the north, the kingdom of the Two Sicilies[1] in the south, Lombardy, which was part of the Habsburg dominions, the central duchies, the States of the Church, the once powerful republics of Venice and Genoa and one or two minor survivals like the small republic of San Marino. The Grand Duchy of Tuscany itself had absorbed a number of city states, Florence, Lucca, Pisa, Siena.[2] Before 1789 Italians accepted these political divisions almost as part of the natural order of things. Italy in the middle years of the eighteenth century enjoyed an unusually long period of peace – over forty years – and no important body of opinion was agitating in favour of national unity. The strength and intensity of Italian city and provincial life precluded an effective movement for a state comprising all Italians. The Lombards were not dissatisfied with Austrian rule which was in fact better than that found in any other part of Italy except the Grand Duchy of Tuscany. Owing to differences in dialect, Italian could hardly be called a common spoken language. French was spoken in parts of Piedmont. Cavour talked Italian with a French accent; Garibaldi's native dialect was the Franco-Provençal speech of Nice. Written Italian was described as a dead language; the Milanese-born novelist, Manzoni (1785–1873), rewrote his well-known book *I Promessi Sposi* after he settled in Tuscany and came to know Italian as spoken in Florence.

The States of the Church, extending across Italy from the Mediterranean to the Adriatic, set an immense obstacle to

[1] The kingdoms of Naples and Sicily were united in 1504. After much warfare they had been included in the Spanish Empire. In 1759 Charles III of Spain, son of the Bourbon Duke of Anjou (the grandson of Louis XIV who had become King of Spain), on succeeding to the Spanish throne handed over Naples and Sicily to his son, Ferdinand. Ferdinand was turned out of his kingdom by Napoleon, but came back after Napoleon's fall and continued to misgovern his dominions, known as the kingdom of the Two Sicilies, until his death in 1825.

[2] Tuscany was also a possession of the house of Habsburg. Until 1765 it had been governed by lieutenants; from this time until 1790 it was ruled by a member of the imperial house as Grand Duke. This ruler, Leopold, who in 1790 succeeded Joseph II as Emperor, was an enlightened reformer.

Italian unity. The papacy might be, in Hobbes' phrase, 'the ghost of the Roman Empire sitting crowned upon the grave thereof'; it was also a localized Italian territorial sovereignty, older than any of the greater nation-states. The temporal power of the papacy might be an anachronism in principle and useless in fact as a protection of papal independence, but the ecclesiastics who exercised this power would not surrender their privileges and a college of cardinals, mainly Italian, would never elect a pope likely to give up or even secularize the administration of his possessions, while catholic opinion outside Italy would not accept their disappearance in the interest of an Italian state.

A change in Italian sentiment, a real discontent with political nullity in a world in which the exercise of power was being limited to larger units and control of this power extended to wider sections of the population, could come only from influences outside Italy. Such a change was brought about by the French Revolution and, above all, by the Napoleonic conquests in Italy. French ideas and the practical example of efficient French administration at least stirred up the town middle class. This middle class was still very small in a country which was almost entirely agricultural and in which the peasantry accepted, because they had no chance of resisting, whatever government might be imposed on them. The changes enforced by the French invaders between 1793 and 1815 had perhaps less immediate effect than might have been expected. A few enlightened reformers at first welcomed the ideas of the revolution, but the intrusion of French armies and officials was a different matter. Moreover the changes of regime were so rapid and so short-lived that only under Napoleon was there anything like stability. In spite of his later assertions in exile, when he was trying to create a legend about himself, Napoleon merely used Italy as a source of men, money and supplies; he subjected Italian interests to French domestic requirements and to the necessities of his war with England. On the other hand, the introduction of the Napoleonic system of law was bound to have lasting consequences. The Italians employed in the new bureaucracy, like the Germans, might well wish to keep French improvements and methods without the French tax collectors and the obligation to provide conscripts to fight in French campaigns.[1]

The arrangements of the Congress of Vienna for the return of the dispossessed Italian sovereigns – only the republics of Venice and Genoa were not restored – were accepted in the general desire for peace. Their return meant the reassertion of Austrian influence. Lombardy and Venetia were Austrian provinces; the Neapolitan Bourbons looked to Austria for protection against revolution. An Austrian army came to Naples in 1821 to put down a rebellion and stayed there for six years. Another Austrian army suppressed an equally mismanaged revolution in Piedmont.

This situation was unlikely to last, if only because of the narrow incapacity, and worse, of the restored princes. The Grand Duke of Tuscany was the one exception; the kingdom of the Two Sicilies and the Papal States were the worst governed sovereignties in Italy. In Piedmont King Victor Emmanuel I brought back much of the substance as well as the shadow of the *ancien régime*. He prescribed the court dress of his youth, dismissed clerks who wrote the letter 'R' in the French fashion and would not allow the new French road over the Mont Cenis pass to be used for ordinary traffic (with the result that it became a smugglers' highway). Austrian rule in Lombardy and Venetia was better, but unimaginative, cumbrous and too much centralized in Vienna. Thus among the small number of Italians who thought about politics, the place of Italy in the world and the desirability of careers open to talent as in constitutional states like England and France, there was growing discontent and a desire to bring to an end a regime of incompetent absolutism. The desire for constitutional reform led to a movement to get rid of direct or indirect control, since Austria intervened to prevent any disturbance of the existing state of things.

After the failure of sporadic outbreaks of revolution in 1830 middle-class discontent increased. Business men wanted the

[1] Some 50,000 Italians were with the Grand Army on Napoleon's expedition of 1812 to Russia. Few of them survived the campaign.

removal, on the lines of the German Zollverein, of the innumerable Italian customs frontiers, and improvements in communications – a good railway system could be devised only for Italy as a whole. A number of books appeared on the need for political unification and on the historic claims of Italy to liberation from foreign, that is to say, Austrian domination. The dramatist, Silvio Pellico, who had been imprisoned for ten years after the futile rebellion or rather conspiracy of 1821, wrote an account of his life in an Austrian fortress-prison – *Le mie Prigione*. Gioberti's book, *Del primato morale e civile degli Italiani* (1843), had a very large circulation. Above all Mazzini (1807–77), a Genoese citizen, founded in 1831 a society which he called *Giovane Italia*. Mazzini did more than any other of his countrymen to create an Italian patriotism. He had what one might call a religious belief that an association of nation-states, based upon a democratic foundation, was the only sure way to European peace. Mazzini was a republican with a theoretically clear plan for a united Italian republic. He did not know Italy well; for the greater part of his active life he was an exile and latterly he became at least as much interested in the general European as in the Italian aspect of his ideas for the future. The plan for an Italian republic had some support, but was unlikely to overcome Italian particularism, at all events between 1830 and 1848. Local and regional feeling was too strong for the Piedmontese to agree to unification under the Neapolitan Bourbons, even if these poor-minded sovereigns had been capable of bringing it about, while the South, discontented as its small educated minority was with Bourbon absolutism, would not merge its independence with the North; there was indeed always a considerable movement in Sicily for independence from Naples. Mazzini's republican solution therefore was unlikely to get general support. Union under the leadership of Piedmont was the ultimate solution, but there seemed little chance of it; the King, Charles Albert, would have liked to follow the tradition of his family in extending his kingdom, but he was weak, irresolute and fundamentally conservative. He introduced, or rather his ministers introduced for him, a few sensible reforms; otherwise he just waited on events.

The unexpected election of a supposedly liberal pope in 1846 changed the Italian situation. Pius IX, easy-going, not over-intelligent, and without much political judgement, was unlikely to satisfy the fundamental liberal demands. Anyhow a pope could not put himself at the head of a liberal political movement against catholic Austria, though for a time he seems to have believed it possible to do so. The revolutionary wave of 1848 at once affected Italy. Ferdinand of Naples had already been compelled by his Neapolitan and Sicilian subjects to promise them a constitution.[1] Revolution had broken out in Milan owing to a boycott by the population of tobacco from the Austrian state factories.[2] Another outbreak occurred in Venice. Charles Albert was now forced by events to attack the Austrians. Although he cannot have rated highly his chances of success against the Austrian Army, he could not allow the pope to take even the nominal headship of an Italian movement. In particular he was afraid of Mazzini's republican plans, and above all of possible intervention by the new French republic. Charles Albert's well-known phrase that Italy would do her own work (*in grado di fare da se*) was in fact a mixture of appeal and warning to the French that they were not wanted.

Charles Albert's troops were unprepared for war; they had not even maps of Lombardy which they were sent to invade. Instead of acting at once before the Austrians had time to recover, the Piedmontese advanced slowly. They were indeed doubtful of the support of the Lombards, and Charles Albert himself felt uneasy about encouraging subjects to rebel against their legitimate sovereign. The Austrians fully recovered their military position and the Piedmontese were finally defeated in March 1849. Charles Albert abdicated, but his son, Victor Emmanuel II, maintained (without enthusiasm) the constitution

[1] In 1832 John Henry Newman during a stay in Naples asked the donkey-driver whom he regularly hired why the Neapolitans wanted a constitution. 'The English have a constitution,' said the donkey-driver, 'and the English are rich.'

[2] A free issue of cigars was made to the Austrian troops who puffed their smoke into people's faces. At the same time bands of riotous youths in the streets knocked cigars out of the mouths of citizens who were not supporting the boycott.

which his father had given to Piedmont. Ferdinand of Naples withdrew the Neapolitan constitution; the Pope ran away from Rome before Mazzini's republican insurrection, but Louis Napoleon, who had become President of the French Republic and wanted to get catholic support for his intended overthrow of the French constitution, sent French troops to suppress the Roman republic. Pius IX came back and for the rest of his pontificate had no good word for liberalism.

With the return of Austrian domination, the Italian nationalist movement of 1848, such as it was, seemed to have failed. The demand for national unity, however, had grown stronger with the humiliation of failure, though it was still limited mainly to the towns and, in the towns, for the most part to the professional and business classes and the students. Moreover, although the latter might support Mazzini's semi-mystical republicanism, it was becoming clear that, if Piedmont could take the lead, north and central Italy was likely to accept this leadership. One of the publicists of the 1840s, Cesare Balbo, had forecast that Austria's interests would divert her more and more to the Balkans and that therein lay Italian opportunity. In the early and middle 1850s there was little sign of such opportunity.

Victor Emmanuel II was as ready as Charles Albert to extend his kingdom if he had the chance. His own intelligence and tastes did not rise much above the level of a loyal and competent non-commissioned officer,[1] and he was a superstitious, if not devout catholic, but he had courage and was shrewd enough to accept the advice of people abler than himself. To his good fortune, though not altogether to his personal liking, one of his

[1] In 1855 Victor Emmanuel paid a state visit to Queen Victoria. His ministers kept the king's mistress – the daughter of a drum-major – away from Windsor, but were nervous about the king's behaviour with his hosts. To their relief the visit went off well. One of the ministers wrote with a satisfied surprise that the king 'really had the air of a gentleman'. Cavour himself said of the court life at Windsor, 'non e divertente'. The English protestants, misinterpreting the anti-clerical measures of the Piedmontese Government (which gave the king an uneasy concern about his own future salvation), presented Victor Emmanuel with a Bible during his visit.

ministers, Count Camillo Cavour, was as remarkable a man in his way as Bismarck. In some respects indeed Cavour was even more remarkable since he had to do his work without the powerful support of instruments like the Prussian Army and bureaucracy. Cavour was born in 1810; he began his career in the army but soon left it and occupied himself with large-scale agriculture. He founded a newspaper, *Il Risorgimento*, in 1847, but the confusion and failure of the revolutionary movements turned him against complete democracy and strengthened his view that economic reform was a pre-condition of Italian unity.

Cavour became Prime Minister of Piedmont in 1852; he died in 1861. Before his death he had modernized the Piedmontese state, secured the expulsion of the Austrians from Lombardy and persuaded the other Italian principalities, including (with Garibaldi's help or rather, dangerously independent initiative) the kingdom of the Two Sicilies, to accept a united Italy under the house of Savoy. Cavour never won the support of Mazzini, who remained an irreconcilable republican and died in exile in London, but he managed to use, cajole and outwit Garibaldi. Cavour had to begin by bringing together moderate opinion in Piedmont in a centre party with a programme of economic reform. He continued to reassure this moderate opinion by his rejection of Mazzini's revolutionary methods and, at the same time, by putting into effect long necessary internal reforms. These reforms lost him the support of the Church. The attitude of Pius IX to all forms of liberalism made it almost impossible for Cavour or anyone else wanting sensible change not to be anti-clerical; the Pope's refusal to surrender his temporal sovereignty forced Italian nationalists into an absolute opposition. In any case the financial and political privileges of the Church in Piedmont were not compatible with the organization of a modern state. One in every 214 Piedmontese was an ecclesiastic (including the religious orders); the figure for catholic Austria and Belgium was about one in 500 or 600. The Church had its own courts and a total control of education. The archbishop of Turin, with full papal approval, refused to give up any of the privileges or endowments of the Church.

Cavour was not anti-catholic; to the end of his life he hoped that he might persuade the hierarchy to accept the principle of 'a free church in a free state', but no compromise could be reached with Pius IX and, after Cavour's death, clerical refusal to come to terms not only with Italian nationalism but with the ideas and assumptions of modern society reached its climax. A papal encyclical of 1864 laid down that the Church could not reconcile itself with progress, liberalism and modern civilization (*cum progressu, cum liberalismo et cum recenti civilitate*). No gloss by liberal-minded catholics could explain away these ignorant damnations and Pius IX at once disavowed attempts by liberal-minded catholics to do so.

Without the reforms introduced by Cavour, Piedmont would have been incapable of absorbing into a single kingdom the greater part of Italy. Without Cavour's adroit (and unscrupulous) diplomacy there would have been no opportunity for such absorption. Napoleon III – the victim and accomplice of this unscrupulousness – deserved to be tricked, since he was willing to provide a French army, that is to say, to sacrifice the lives of French conscripts, in order to help the Piedmontese expel the Austrians from north Italy; his motives were personal and dynastic, however much he might cover them by talk about the 'principle of nationality'. The difference between Napoleon III and Cavour was that the Emperor was vacillating, unable to think far ahead and oddly slow at detecting trickery in others, while Cavour, like Bismarck, knew what he wanted and took every occasion to get it. Cavour met Napoleon secretly at Plombières – a spa in the Vosges – in July 1868. Napoleon promised a French army of 200,000 to help drive the Austrians from Lombardy and Venetia in return for an Italian settlement in conformity with French, or at least the French Emperor's interests. Lombardy and Venetia, Piedmont, the northern duchies and part of the papal territory would form a kingdom of Upper Italy under Victor Emmanuel II with, roughly, the boundaries of the North Italian kingdom created by Napoleon I. Most of central Italy would be united in a new state under the Duchess of Parma. Nothing was agreed about the kingdom of Naples; Napoleon hoped that the Bourbons would be supplanted by the family of Murat. The three divisions of Italy would be joined in a federal union under the nominal presidency of the Pope, who would retain his rule over Rome and its immediate neighbourhood. Nice and Savoy would be ceded to France[1] and Victor Emmanuel's sixteen-year-old daughter would marry Napoleon's cousin, an elderly libertine. The pretext for war against Austria would be provided by stirring up the quarry workers of Carrara against their ruler, the Duke of Modena, the worst of the Italian princelets; the Austrians would intervene on behalf of the duke and the Piedmontese on behalf of the quarry workers.

At the last moment Napoleon nearly wrecked his own plan. He began to be afraid of German opposition to a French attack on Austria and of French catholic opposition to a scheme which would in fact deprive the Pope of most of his possessions. Austria, however, with the rashness which, fifty years later, destroyed the Habsburg Empire, refused a proposal suggested to the Tsar by Napoleon for a European Congress. A Congress of the Powers might have thought that the best way to meet Piedmontese allegations of threats from Austria would be to give to the country the neutral status of Belgium or Switzerland. Piedmont, as Cavour realized, would then have 'no political future'. Austria, hoping to teach the Piedmontese a lesson and fearing that a Congress might ask her to give up Lombardy, if not also Venetia, sent Piedmont an ultimatum.

In the war which followed Napoleon, to the consternation of the Piedmontese, agreed to an armistice after the two battles of Magenta and Solferino,[2] and before the Austrians had been compelled to surrender the key fortresses protecting the entrances to Lombardy from the north. Napoleon was alarmed at the beginnings of mobilization by Prussia in the Rhineland; the surrender of Alsace or Lorraine would have been a heavy

[1] When Cavour, during his talk with Napoleon, suggested that the cession of Nice to France would be contrary to the principle of nationality, 'Napoléon caressa à plusieurs reprises sa moustache'.

[2] The name 'magenta', oddly enough, was given to a scarlet aniline dye discovered shortly after the date of the battle. The heavy casualties at Solferino led to a movement by a Swiss doctor, Henri Dunant, which resulted in the foundation of the International Red Cross at Geneva.

price to pay for the acquisition of Nice and Savoy. The Emperor was alarmed also by the French casualties and the outbreak of typhus in the army (the doctors had instructions to call it by another name). His own health was bad; he could now see, as he should have guessed much earlier, that Cavour was not going to keep his word about the political reconstruction of central Italy. The Austrians gave up Lombardy, but not Venetia. Tuscany, Modena, Parma and the papal territory of the Romagna accepted annexation to Piedmont; only the presence of French troops in Rome preserved for the Pope what was left of his temporal sovereignty and kept out the Piedmontese whom Cavour would have sent, ostensibly to prevent the outbreak of a revolution in the city.[1]

There remained, with Rome and the rest of the papal states, the kingdom of Naples, where in 1859 Francis II, an even more feckless creature, had succeeded Ferdinand II. Almost at once a rebellion broke out against Francis. The rebellion, organized at a distance by Mazzini, was easily put down in Naples but the position was more difficult in Sicily, especially because the popular hero, Garibaldi, had promised to go to the help of the Sicilians if they made a serious attempt to free themselves from the Bourbons.

Garibaldi had been born in Nice. He took part in 1834 in one of Mazzini's insurrections and, after its failure, escaped to South America. He spent ten out of the next fourteen years fighting in revolutionary wars. He came back to Italy in 1848 with very real experience of guerrilla tactics. He was the leading figure in the republican defence of Rome after the Pope had left the city in 1848. When the republic collapsed, Garibaldi brought his followers in a daring retreat across the mountains to the Adriatic; he was arrested on reaching Piedmontese territory and exiled from Italy. He went to New York, became a sea-captain and, after saving enough money to buy for £360 part of the

---

[1] On 23 December 1860 the canons of St Peter's were so nervous of a liberal demonstration in the basilica that they decided not to sing the liturgical pre-Christmas sequence 'O Emmanuel, rex et legifer noster, veni ad salvandum nos (O Emmanuel, our king and lawgiver, come to save us)'.

small island of Caprera, settled down to farm his land and to await events.

Garibaldi had no liking for Cavour, especially after the latter had bargained away Nice to France. He also had no interest in diplomatic finesse and was indifferent to, if he even understood, the possible international consequences and the effect on Cavour's plans if a republic should take the place of the Neapolitan Bourbons. On the other hand, if Garibaldi intended to go to Sicily (and, obviously, if he succeeded there, to cross to the mainland), an attempt by Cavour to stop him might well lose him (Cavour) control of the nationalist movement. If Garibaldi were defeated – the Neapolitan Army was nearly 100,000 strong and holding good fortresses, while Garibaldi had only about a thousand volunteers – there would be a popular outcry. If Garibaldi were victorious in Naples, he would certainly try to march on Rome, where he would meet the French.

The matter passed out of Cavour's hands when Garibaldi and his volunteers landed in Sicily. Cavour still expected him to be defeated, but there was little opposition in Sicily. Within two months Garibaldi was able to move (August 1860) to the mainland. Cavour wanted to anticipate him by starting a revolution in Naples in favour of union with Piedmont, but for once the Neapolitans refused to rebel. The Neapolitan Army in the field, however, did little and within a week Garibaldi had occupied half of the kingdom; Francis telegraphed from Naples five times in one day for a special papal blessing.[1] Garibaldi entered Naples on 7 September. The King left the city almost unnoticed, but Garibaldi could not at once get to Rome, because Neapolitan troops still held the frontier fortresses of Capua and Gaeta. Cavour could try only to anticipate him again by starting a rebellion in Umbria and sending Piedmontese troops to put it down. This time the pretext served its purpose, though the 'rebellion' was a very small affair; anyhow a plebiscite in Umbria and the Marches voted in favour of union with the kingdom of Italy. Meanwhile in Naples, to Cavour's immense

[1] The last two benedictions were sent by the Cardinal Secretary of State on his own authority.

relief, Garibaldi was willing to hand over his conquests, as soldier to soldier, to Victor Emmanuel. A plebiscite was duly held in Naples and Sicily. Some pressure was put upon the voters; a Piedmontese observer wrote in his diary that he admired 'the civic courage of those who dared to vote "no"'. Only 31 out of the 106,000 voters in the city of Naples showed this courage; there was no doubt that most people thought themselves well rid of the Bourbons.

The kingdom of Italy now included nearly the whole of the peninsula, but it had no capital. Outside Piedmont there was no support for Turin as the capital; from a military point of view the city was dangerously near the French frontier. The Piedmontese would not agree to Naples; neither Piedmontese nor Neapolitans would accept Milan or Florence. Hence the urgency of a settlement with the papacy which would allow the obvious choice of Rome. Cavour spent the last months of his life in trying to get Pius IX to agree to the formula of a 'free church in a free state'; the Church would surrender its temporal power and receive a subsidy to compensate it for its lost property; the Italian state would guarantee the freedom of the Church to manage its own affairs. Pius IX refused the settlement, partly because he could not trust the Piedmontese to carry it out, partly through fear of the effect on the relations between Church and State in other catholic countries if he accepted the principle of separation in Italy and at the centre of the hierarchy.

In 1864 the Emperor Napoleon III, who wanted to get French troops away from Rome if he could find an excuse likely to satisfy the French catholics, suggested to the Italian Government privately an arrangement under which the Italian capital would be fixed at Florence; the French garrison would leave Rome and the Italian Government would undertake to protect the city and what was left of papal territory. Napoleon himself knew that this arrangement would not last long; the only attack on papal sovereignty in Rome was likely to come from the Italians themselves. The French conceded that the arrangement did not make provision against a 'spontaneous' outbreak of revolution in Rome; Napoleon could hardly object to a plebiscite. In 1867 Garibaldi made another wild raid on Rome. After much vacillation, orders and counter-orders to the French fleet of transports, and pressure from French catholics, Napoleon sent back French troops to the city. They defeated Garibaldi and stayed in Rome until the exigencies of the Franco-Prussian War compelled Napoleon to recall them to France. After they had gone, and two months after the Vatican Council had acclaimed the Pope's infallibility, Italian troops entered the city. Venice had been won, or rather obtained, four years earlier when Italy joined Prussia as an ally in the Austro-Prussian War. The Italian part in this was inglorious; the Austrians defeated them on land and sea. Nevertheless the Prussians kept their bargain and Austria was forced to cede Venetia.

In 1870, with a few Italian-speaking areas still 'unredeemed', Italy became one of the European Powers. What kind of Power? A Great Power or a minor Power? Much of Italian history for the last hundred years has turned upon this question. Italians who were 'nation-conscious' and who remembered classical tradition could not think of Italy as a minor Power. She had been mistress of the ancient world; she had civilized the barbarians of the north. Even in her cultural and political decline she had remained the centre of a universal church. On the other hand, she was not as well fitted economically as politically to be a Great Power in the nineteenth century and it could be said that even her political unity had come too soon and before her people were really prepared for it. There was perhaps something in the remark of the poet, Robert Browning (in spite of his affection for the country and its people), that 'Italy is stuff for the north and nothing more'. Italy, notwithstanding its great beauty, is less fertile than Great Britain. The northern plain is rich enough, though torrid in summer and very cold in winter; the mean temperature of Copenhagen in winter is higher than that of Turin. About a third of Italy is mountainous and one tenth is barren rock. At the time of the unification of the country large tracts of low-lying areas between mountains and sea had been abandoned or semi-abandoned owing to malaria. As late as the third decade of the twentieth century Aosta – close to the Alpine frontier – was notorious (as any tourist could observe) for the amount of cretinism among its inhabitants. Communications were bad; only one river of any size – the Po – was navigable even partially by small ships. Most of the country was unsuitable for canals and roads were few and bad. In 1848 there was no railway connecting Milan, Turin and Venice. There was no railway out of Genoa and no lines south of Leghorn and Florence. More lines had indeed been projected, but their construction was delayed by local jealousies and disputes over routes; Austria wanted to develop Trieste and not Genoa as a port for north Italy. As late as 1861 the only main line south of Naples was from Foggia to Brindisi. Italy had few good ports; there were only three on the Adriatic south of Venice – Ancona, Bari and Brindisi.

Large-scale industry hardly existed; there was not much to encourage industrial development in a country with very little coal; as late as 1913 the coal output was about 700,000 tons compared with the British figure of nearly 300,000,000 tons. Sulphur was the only important mineral product. In 1885 only 3·4 per cent of Italian steamships were Italian built.[1] In this mainly agricultural country the greater part of the population was illiterate – 59 per cent in the north, 84·1 per cent in the south. Most of the 400,000 peasants farming their own land lived north of Rome; about one half of the agricultural population were landless labourers. In the great estates of the south, owned largely by absentees, the peasants were desperately poor and, although legally free, still liable to labour services. Owing to the absence of a middle class in the south, other than the agents of the absentee landlords, there was an almost total gap between rich and poor; brigandage was the only remedy of the peasants against their misery and secret societies, such as the Mafia in western Sicily, interfered with law and order.[2] In

---

[1] In 1912 the figure was only 30 per cent.
[2] The Mafia existed, as a roughly organized brigandage, long before it was known under this name. The organized Mafia is said to have developed in Sicily during the disordered state of the island after King Ferdinand I had taken refuge there from the French armies which had

other parts of Italy standards of living were also low; a commentator in the late 1890s wrote that the Italian people had been accustomed for two centuries 'to live on half rations'. If they escaped the early horrors of industrialism, they did not improve their conditions of life very much during the second half of the nineteenth century. Agricultural depression largely cancelled out a slow rise in the national income during the first twenty years of the kingdom of Italy. The imposition of protective duties benefited certain industries and the great landlords of the south, but was of little use to the hungry land workers. Agricultural improvement brought gain to the wealthier landlords rather than to the peasants, while the incidence of high taxation for the appurtenances of a Great Power – an army, navy and armaments industry – was relatively heavier on the poor; the landlords in the south controlled local government and patronage. In 1893 the average income per head of the population of Great Britain was about four times as great, and that of the industrial areas of Saxony about two and a half times as great as the average income per head of the Italian people. Out of a group of 10,000 Italians paying the local 'family tax', nearly 8,000 had incomes under £40 a year and only three had over £2,000.

Statistics of average incomes must be taken with caution, since they are not tables of purchasing power; but lack of money had serious effects upon Italian economic life. The industrial progress of a society in the nineteenth century depended very much on education. The Italian state had little to spare for public education and anyhow most Italians could not afford to keep their children at school. Compulsory education for children between six and nine was not introduced until 1887; the bill had been postponed for three years owing to lack of money and for a long time was not strictly enforced. As late as 1895 a quarter of the children of school age did not

---

invaded his mainland kingdom of Naples. The British Government, who controlled Sicily, compelled Ferdinand to grant his Sicilian subjects a constitution, and the disbanded feudal retainers of the landlords took to brigandage.

go to school. Nearly one half of the Italians, and only 3 per cent of the Germans who emigrated to America were illiterate.[1]

In these circumstances the basis of a parliamentary democracy was lacking. The first franchise law of the kingdom required electors to be literate and to pay a minimum of 40 lire a year in direct taxation. In 1870 there were only 529,000 electors, or about 2 per cent of the population. In 1882 the property qualification was lowered and the age limit reduced from twenty-five to twenty-one, but the literacy test was maintained. A majority of the left, who would in principle have favoured universal suffrage, were afraid of it because the peasant vote might favour the conservatives and the clericals. The number of electors increased from about 600,000 to 2 million. Universal male suffrage was introduced in 1912 for literates at twenty-one, and even for illiterates at the age of thirty or after completing their military service; the electorate now rose to about $8\frac{1}{2}$ million.

The Italian electorate was thus hardly even semi-educated and, in order to maintain themselves in power, ministers used bribery on a large scale; in 1900 the price of a vote was said to vary between £1 and 6d. An ex-Minister of Justice described the Sicilian police as an 'excellent electioneering agency'. Political life tended to be a gamble for the spoils of office; in 1900 more than 200 of the deputies were, directly or indirectly, under government control. In the lower ranges of the administration the taking of bribes was an all too common result of paying officials inadequate salaries, but corruption was not limited to the humbler ranks of the bureaucracy. In 1893 the Banca Romana was found to have issued over £2½ million notes illegally; some of the money had been used in payments to ministers and officials. A Cabinet Minister and one of the personal friends of the Prime Minister were involved in the scandal.

There was less of this kind of thing in the decade before 1914, but public life was still at a low level. Some politicians might

---

[1] Illiteracy in the north fell from 54 to 41 per cent between 1861 and 1881; in the south the fall was from 86 to 79 per cent (the Sicilian figure was worse).

have a temporary popularity, but few won real respect. In the absence of a solid basis of principle, governments continued to win and keep majorities by satisfying interests, and official favours were 'the dividend which every member of the majority received for the investment of his vote in the service of the Government.... The needs of the country were satisfied, not through the clash of organized parties, but through individual deals. Politics became a series of business transactions with a recognized technique which could be learned.'[1]

Apart from the poverty which hampered Italian development, the greatest difficulty for her political leaders was that the Italian people as a whole were not enthusiastic about the union which had come to them less by their own efforts than by the help of other Powers and the Machiavellian tactics of a few very able men. The local and particularist interests which had divided Italy for centuries could not be abandoned or transformed in a generation. The ministers who now had to devise legislation for the whole of Italy themselves knew little about the kingdom outside their own principalities; Cavour himself had never been south of Florence. Italian politicians of the north were as little inclined to investigate at first hand the special problems of the south as English Ministers to travel in the south and west of Ireland. The obvious solution of administrative decentralization was impossible, since one of the main tasks was to get rid of regional particularism, but centralization, which for a long time meant, in fact 'Piedmontization', was equally unsatisfactory. The north treated the south almost as colonial territory, but ministers and officials had no understanding of colonial administration. Above all they thought in terms of politics rather than economics and did not realize that the problems of the south – its violence and unrest – were only made worse by giving voting power to a southern electorate consisting largely of landlords, their agents and their clients. This small minority received protection for their privileges and also for their illegalities and corruption, in return for their parliamentary votes; the deputies whom they elected obediently passed, for example, the fiscal measures which benefited the

[1] C. Seton-Watson, *Italy, from Liberalism to Fascism, 1870–1925*, p. 247.

northern manufacturers at the expense of the southern peasantry.

There was indeed some improvement in the conditions of the southern poor during the half-century before 1914, and especially in the last decade of the period; much of this improvement was due to money sent home by emigrants to America, but the gap between the development of the north and that of the south had increased. Illiteracy was still very much greater in Calabria than in Piedmont; Piedmont, with about the same population as Sicily, had about 9,000 schools and Sicily only 5,000. In 1911 the south, with just over a quarter of the population of Italy, had less than one tenth of the factories employing more than ten workpeople. More money was spent on land reclamation in the north; no capital was made available for dealing with the problem of the vast, poverty-stricken estates of the absentee landlords.

The agricultural workers of Italy had little reason to feel an 'Italian' patriotism. The only institution extending beyond their humble, local environment to which they felt a traditional loyalty was the Church, but for decades the Church was fighting, or rather losing, a political war with the secular state, and did little or nothing to alleviate popular misery beyond conventional works of charity, such as the maintenance of orphanages for foundlings without inquiry into the social and economic causes of illegitimacy. To catholics, and especially to the papal hierarchy, the kingdom of Italy was an impious usurpation, and the application to the rest of the kingdom of the Piedmontese laws confiscating church property (though it did something and should have done more to help the dismal finances of the State) added to the anger of the clergy. Neither Pius IX nor his successor Leo XIII would accept the Law of Guarantees by which the Government hoped to settle with the pope by recognizing him as a sovereign (without territory) and granting him as financial compensation $3\frac{1}{2}$ million lire (£130,000) a year. Pius IX and Leo XIII forbade catholics to vote in parliamentary elections, though they could and did take part in municipal affairs. The two popes tried, with complete lack of success, to get one or other of the catholic Powers to restore the temporal possessions of the Holy See, and catholics in Italy were encouraged to organize themselves in an anti-government organization styled Catholic Action.

Throughout the nineteenth century the public attitude of the Church towards the Italian state did not change. There was, however, a gradual drift away on each side from the absolute hostility of the early years of the kingdom, partly owing to the failure of the destructive political intrigues of the Vatican, partly because the State and, for that matter, the Church, began to see a more dangerous enemy in international socialism, partly also to the mere lapse of time. A new generation of catholics knew nothing of the days of papal rule over a part of Italy and did not see why they should debar themselves from taking part in the political life of their country owing to an outworn dispute over the temporal claims. The State had consolidated itself and was unlikely to be overthrown by catholic forces from outside Italy; the Italian laity and some at least of the clergy had come to realize that papal freedom was enhanced, not endangered, by the loss of temporal responsibilities. Leo XIII was a more important figure in Rome and in the world than the King of Italy. One direction in which the pope could use his freedom from entanglement in local Italian administration was by taking up the social question (which had a world-wide and not just an Italian significance) and using it as an instrument for reconciling the working class with the Church. Leo XIII's well-known Encyclical *Rerum Novarum* of 1891 aimed at something beyond the *laissez-faire* capitalism of Italy.[1]

Pius X, who succeeded Leo XIII in 1903, was indifferent to the question of the temporal power and more afraid of the danger to the Church, at least in Italy, from left-wing revolutionaries than from bourgeois anti-clericalism. In the 1904 Italian general election the ecclesiastical authorities allowed catholics in certain constituencies to vote in order to prevent a socialist victory; a papal encyclical in the following year gave formal

---

[1] The Encyclical enjoined governments to protect the interests of workers against exploitation and advocated the corporate organization of labour.

leave to bishops to permit catholics to vote where necessary in the interests of the Church; this permission was extended in the general election of 1913 to two-thirds of the Italian constituencies. Pius X, a conservative fundamentalist, had no wish to develop Leo XIII's far-reaching plans of catholic democracy; the danger to the Italian state now was that organized catholic activities would be too much of a buttress of political conservatism and, oddly for the Church, extreme nationalism.

The long abstention of the catholic laity from direct participation in the political life of their country deprived the Government of the services of many honest and able men. There was no strong moderate conservative party on the right, just as, without a large industrial proletariat, there was no strong working-class opposition party on the left.

A lack of imagination on the part of ministers and parliament, as well as lack of money, was responsible for the backwardness of Italy in social legislation. The first important social measures were a workmen's compensation law (on a voluntary basis) in 1883 and a law of 1886 regulating the employment of children. Trade unions began to spread after 1870, mainly in the north; they were not fully legalized until 1889. The first working-class political party, Partito Operaio Italiano, was founded in 1882 and officially suppressed four years later as a criminal conspiracy after the Government had been alarmed at the party's support of agricultural strikes. The party, however, continued to exist and in 1892 combined with the 'intellectual' middle-class socialists to form a United Workers Party (including agricultural workers). The united party had the usual socialist programme with the refusal to co-operate with the bourgeois parties.

Up to this time Italian revolutionists had been divided between Marxists and supporters of the anarchist, Bakunin. This division continued after 1892. The extreme left wing inherited and maintained a tradition of violent action, though most outbreaks of violence were due to sheer misery and despair of getting long-standing grievances remedied by peaceful means. In 1893 serious trouble broke out in Sicily. Here again the final cause was economic depression, a slump, intensified by a tariff war with France, in the three main exports – sulphur, wine and fruit – of the island. A number of socialists took the opportunity to unite the discontented elements under a socialist programme. The agitation, in the form of strikes, got out of hand and was not put down until January 1894; martial law was declared and 40,000 troops sent to restore order. The socialist leaders were heavily punished and the socialist party officially dissolved, but nothing was done to improve conditions in Sicily; a bill for breaking up large estates was defeated in parliament.

These repressive measures merely strengthened the socialists. At the end of 1896 a socialist newspaper *Avanti* began publication in Milan. There were more disturbances both in the north and south. Once again ministers and officials were almost panic-stricken, but parliamentary and public opinion was too strong for them. In June 1897 the Government was defeated in a general election. The most repressive measures were then abandoned and, on their side, the socialists realized that mob violence would not transform Italy into a socialist state. A Socialist Congress in Rome in September 1900 accepted a double programme, maximal and minimal; the former stated the ultimate aims of the party and the latter a list of immediate reforms which many liberals could support. Nevertheless the divergence between those who believed in the transformation of society by peaceful and parliamentary means and those who wanted violent action made it unlikely that the socialist party would remain united. Developments in Italy in the decade before the war were similar to and influenced by those in France. Revolutionary syndicalism, with its doctrine of the general strike, spread rapidly and in April 1904 obtained a majority at the annual congress of the socialist party. A general strike broke out in Milan in the following September and spread to the chief cities of the centre and south. This time the Government did not rush into panic measures. The strike collapsed, as Giolitti,[1] the Prime Minister, had expected.

[1] Giolitti (1842–1928) was a Piedmontese who became Prime Minister in 1892 and again in 1903. He resigned in 1905 but returned to office from 1906 to 1909 and from 1911 to 1914.

Giolitti then held a general election and won a large majority. Other strikes occurred under syndicalist influence, notably an agricultural strike in the province of Parma in 1908. This strike failed and the syndicalists began to lose popular support. Landlords and industrialists replied in kind to organized violence; they also had the strength of the State behind them. Most workers wanted a direct return for striking, an improvement in pay or conditions of work; they were not willing to be pioneers in the transformation of society and had no interest in revolution for revolution's sake. The formation of the Confederazione Generale del Lavoro in 1906 favoured the moderate 'reformist' socialists. In 1908 the syndicalists refused to attend the socialist party congress; the congress declared in their absence for co-operation with the moderate trade unions. By 1911 the C.G.L. had nearly 400,000 members. The 'breakaway' syndicalists formed their own party but never secured more than about 100,000 members. It was, however, easy for the left wing to point out that the moderate trade unionists and socialist leaders were just adapting themselves to the sordid bargaining of Italian politics and that they were getting concessions only for a privileged minority of the working class in the north. After the Libyan war this discontent came out in a general leftward move of the socialist party. For a time in 1913 there was a revival of revolutionary syndicalism. The number of strikes – 800, involving nearly 400,000 workers – was the highest for any single year. Mussolini, at this stage in his career of self-advancement a strident left-wing extremist, advocated in *Avanti* the 'psychological preparation of the proletariat for the use of violence'. In June 1914 the C.G.L. decided on a general strike as a protest against the shooting of some workers in a disturbance at Ancona. The strike was without plan or direction; the C.G.L. called it off after two days of rioting, but it lasted on in a good many places. The war brought a new situation in Italian political and economic life, but the underlying traditions of violence and contempt for legal, parliamentary action were as great a threat as ever for the future.

The Government of Italy, whose transformation into a nation-state had taken place without adequate preparation of her citizens or her economy for membership of the Concert of European Powers, had none the less to adopt an Italian foreign policy. They began with two great handicaps; Italy had been liberated to a large extent by foreign aid and had obtained much of this aid by diplomatic trickery. These facts were not lost on other countries. Prussia had achieved German unity after defeating two Great Powers; the only significant victories won by the Italians had been those of Garibaldi against other Italians. When the Italian delegation at the Congress of Berlin in 1878 put forward large claims, one of the Russian delegates asked, 'What, have they lost another battle?' Bismarck's even harsher comment a few years later was that the Italians had 'developed an appetite before cutting their teeth'.[1] The Italians themselves could not avoid a sense of inferiority for all their talk. The poet, Carducci, wrote bitterly that the heirs of Imperial Rome had crept into the Capitol like the ancient Gauls whose stealthy approach had once awakened the geese.

Hence the Italian desire (Mussolini is a case in point) to do something grand. The simplest and most necessary attribute of a Great Power is that it should exercise great power. Such exercise became increasingly expensive in the nineteenth century and Italy was poor. The Italians overspent themselves and starved their social services for years on end in order to build ships and train soldiers. Most of the soldiers were peasants who had no interest in a grand foreign policy and no wish to fight for it. In any case, even with her expenditure on armaments, Italy could not hope to match another Great Power on land or to challenge British or French sea-power. Colonies were also the marks of established grandeur. Italy therefore wanted colonies. She wanted them for other reasons than prestige. The country was over-populated and under-developed: Italians were going to work in neighbouring states, especially France, or emigrating to North and South America. Their emigration robbed Italy and gave France the advantage of labour which, with more capital, might have been employed at home. Most –

[1] An earlier French comment was 'les peuples affranchis n'ont pas de gratitude: ils ont des prétensions'.

not all – of the emigrants to America were lost for good and all. In 1900 about one eighth of the purely European population of Brazil and nearly a third of that of Argentina were of Italian birth. These working people were of sound stock and able to stand climatic conditions in which English or German emigrants could not do much manual labour. Italy thus needed colonies of settlement. Once again, however, her weakness prevented any assertion of imperial power. Tunis, with the potentially important naval base of Bizerta, was under a hundred miles from the south-west of Sicily and contained more Italian than French settlers, but France, not Italy, established a protectorate over it in 1881. For the first forty years of the Italian kingdom the other Powers would not allow Italy to seize Tripoli from the feeble sovereignty of Turkey. The Italians were left with a dangerous interest in Abyssinia and the Red Sea coast.

Italy was not strong enough to take an important diplomatic initiative, but in a Europe which after 1870 was moving towards a division into two armed camps, the old policy of 'balance' practised by the house of Savoy was an obvious if not a glorious expedient. Italy could divert a number of French troops from the Rhine in a Franco–German War; conversely the Italian Army could embarrass Austria in the event of a war between Austria and Russia. For about two decades the Italian Government was less concerned with the possible hostility of Austria than with the pressure of French catholic opinion in favour of the claims of the papacy and the efforts of France to extend her North African possessions. The acceptance of a French protectorate over Tunis inclined the Italians to give up at least for a time their hope of gaining the *terra irredenta*, as they called the Italian-inhabited lands still in Austrian possession; a more urgent need was to get an ally against France and at the same time to prevent the Austrian Government from listening to papal appeals. In May 1882 Italy joined Austria and Germany to form the Triple Alliance. Bismarck intended the alliance to be conservative, that is to say, it would safeguard Italy, assist Germany against France and strengthen Austria against Russia; the alliance would not encourage Italian expansionist claims.

When the alliance came up for renewal in 1887 Bismarck had to make more concessions to Italy because he was more afraid of a Franco–Russian *rapprochement*. Italy was now promised support in the event of a French threat to occupy Morocco or Tripoli and her right to 'compensation' was recognized if Austria were to take any Turkish territory in the Balkans. These clauses were included in later renewals of the alliance; Austria promised to give Italy notice of any advance she intended to make in the Balkans. The fact that Austria did not give this notice in 1914 provided Italy with a formal pretext for remaining neutral.

For obvious reasons the French wanted to break the Triple Alliance, especially after the conclusion in 1888 of an Italo–German military convention stipulating the dispatch of Italian troops to the Rhine in the event of a war between the Triple Alliance Powers and France and Russia. A Franco–Italian tariff war, which lasted for some years and damaged Italian trade, embittered relations on both sides. The Italians suffered more than the French and could ill meet the economic losses because they had begun colonial expansion on the coasts of the Red Sea as the only area open to them. Crispi, an extravagant, ebullient southerner, who had fought under Garibaldi in Sicily and Naples, described colonies when he was Prime Minister as 'a necessity of modern life'. Crispi also said that he 'did not understand moderate policies'. He established an Italian protectorate on the coastal areas of the Abyssinian Empire – a large tribal agglomeration – with the obvious intention of absorbing the whole of this Empire.

Crispi's general extravagance led to the fall of his government, but he came back to power in December 1893. Earlier in the year the Emperor Menelik of Abyssinia denounced the somewhat ambiguous treaty which he had signed with Italy. The Italians asserted that this treaty gave them a right to control Ethiopian relations with other Powers; Menelik claimed that the treaty allowed Italian advice, but did not compel him to take it.[1] France and Russia were supplying Menelik with

[1] According to the wording of the treaty, the Emperor 'consented' to use Italian assistance in managing Ethiopian foreign relations.

arms, and early in 1894 a French company, with French official backing, began a railway from Djibouti to Addis Ababa which would give Menelik access to the sea without going through Italian-controlled territory. In 1894 also the Italians used the opportunity of a local rebellion to advance well beyond their colony of Eritrea into Abyssinia. This advance, for which Crispi took the credit, excited Italian opinion; Crispi, without a careful study of the military situation, sanctioned a further move forward. The advance already made had united the tribal chiefs under Menelik, who defeated and drove back the Italians. Crispi might have come to terms with Menelik; his German advisers warned him against his more ambitious plans, but he refused to give up the territory which the Italians had occupied or to liberate Menelik from the conditions of his earlier treaty. He sent about 20,000 reinforcements to General Baratieri, the Italian commander, and persuaded the Italian parliament to vote an additional 20,000,000 lire for the war. Crispi, however, did not give Baratieri definite instructions what to do. He merely told him that he must win a victory. As Menelik's forces advanced towards him, Baratieri hesitated whether to attack him or to retire. He decided to advance in the hope of provoking the Abyssinians to attack the Italian prepared positions, but to retire, owing to shortage of supplies, if they failed to attack. His own dispositions were badly planned; the enemy caught his divided columns and destroyed them piecemeal. The Italians were utterly defeated; nearly 5,000 of them and 1,000 Eritreans were killed and 1,500 Italians captured.

This defeat of Adowa, which two years later seemed the more humiliating in view of Kitchener's overwhelming victory over the Mahdi at Omdurman, was considered by all Italians as a terrible national disgrace.[1] Once again they had been defeated and not by a European army but by a host of barbarians. Crispi

---

[1] The feeling of military inferiority was greater than the facts warranted. Baratieri had been pushed by the Italian politicians against his own judgement. The Abyssinian Army was 100,000 strong and well armed with Russian rifles and mountain guns. A Russian is said to have commanded the artillery. If Baratieri had retreated, as he had wished, the enemy might well have dispersed, since they too were short of supplies.

resigned and never returned to office. The plans for a colonial empire were set aside for almost a decade. The reaction at home was followed by a gradual reappraisal of Italy's position as a member of the Triple Alliance. This change came more from French than from Italian initiative. The French Foreign Minister, Delcassé, and Barrère, whom Delcassé sent as ambassador to Rome (Barrère stayed there until 1924), decided that France was more likely to detach Italy from the Triple Alliance by concessions than by attacks on Italian interests, just as Delcassé came also to think that France had more to gain by collaboration with Great Britain than by hostility. A Franco-Italian trade agreement in 1898 ended the tariff war; in 1900 France and Italy exchanged assurances of 'disinterestedness' respectively in Tripoli and Morocco. About the same time the worsening of Anglo–German relations over the South African War caused Italy a certain anxiety lest she might be involved as Germany's ally in a war with Great Britain. In March 1902 Italy obtained from Great Britain a guarded statement that, if (which Great Britain did not want to happen) a change took place in the status of Tripoli, such change should be in conformity with Italian interests or, in plain language, Italy might take Tripoli. In this same year Germany somewhat high-handedly refused the alterations which Italy wanted in the renewal of the Triple Alliance, that is to say, a new statement (to reassure France) that the alliance was defensive, a recognition of Italian claims to Tripoli and a new commercial treaty. The Italian Government then signed a secret agreement with France providing for the neutrality of either country if the other were attacked or forced to declare war by the actions of a third party.[1] Italy could thus feel free from the risk of an attack on her interests from France, though the double commitment to the Triple Alliance and to France (somewhat on the lines of Bismarck's Reinsurance Treaty) could mean the danger of alienation either from the Triple Alliance or from France, since all the parties would disclaim responsibility for the outbreak of a war.

[1] The fact of the agreement was generally known, though the text was not published until after the 1914–18 war.

The announcement of the Anglo-French agreement added to Italy's new sense of security. At the same time the links still binding Italy to the Triple Alliance were further strained by Austrian activities in the Balkans and, inevitably, as Italo-Austrian relations became cooler, by the revival of Italian claims to the *terra irredenta*. The Austrians signed a secret reinsurance treaty of their own with Russia guaranteeing Russian neutrality in the event of an Austro-Italian war. So far Italy had no direct conflict of interest with Germany, but the German use of Morocco as a means of breaking the Anglo-French *entente* put the Italians in a difficult position; they might have to choose between their obligations under the Triple Alliance and those under their secret agreement with France. At the Algeciras Conference of 1906 on the Moroccan question the Italians tried to pose, in Bismarck's earlier phrase, as 'honest brokers', but failed to satisfy the Germans. Two years later Aehrenthal's *coup* in annexing Bosnia and Herzegovina – without any 'compensation' for Italy – angered Italian feeling.

The Italian Government now went to the limit, or rather, beyond the limit of compatible 'reinsurances'. They made an agreement with Russia for the maintenance, if possible, of the *status quo* in the Balkans; any changes which might have to be made would recognize the 'principle of nationality'. Italy and Russia would take joint action against a Power (obviously Austria) violating this 'principle' and would come to no agreement with a third Power (again, obviously Austria) until after mutual consultation.[1] The Italians almost at once broke the terms of this agreement by exchanging undertakings with Austria not to make any agreement on the Balkans without mutual consultation. The sole Italian reason for putting themselves in this awkward and dishonourable position was their awareness that they were not strong enough to go to war with Austria.

It is politically a paradox, but psychologically explicable that, in

[1] The agreement was known as the Racconigi treaty because it was signed at a palace of this name near Turin during a visit of the Tsar to Victor Emmanuel.

spite of her weakness, Italy now became affected by a renewed outbreak of imperialist megalomania. A new generation chose to forget the disaster of Adowa and to develop a cult of violence in contrast with the drabness of Italian politics. The new movement was not limited to Italy and its intellectual origins were not in fact Italian, but Italian writers and artists gave it a certain life and colour. *Sacro egoismo*, the decadence of plutocratic democracy, the ultimate supremacy of the young and vigorous states, and most of the clichés of later fascism came into common use at this time.[1]

There were two possible outlets for this semi-hysterical fervour. One was to intensify the demand for the Italian *terra irredenta*. The Italian claims, like everything else in this supposed movement of regeneration, were much exaggerated. The Italian-speaking subjects of Austria–Hungary made up less than one-sixtieth of the population of the Habsburg Empire. There was an Italian majority only in the Trentino and Fiume; along the Adriatic coast the Italians were actually losing in numbers to the Slavs. Italian propaganda distorted the facts and built up a myth about the Adriatic as an Italian-bordered sea. The tension was greater owing to Austrian naval construction; the race in armaments between the two countries became ruinously expensive with the introduction of the *Dreadnought* type of ship. Austria, however, was too strong for the Italians, and in any case an opportunity for the display of Italian 'will to heroic action' came elsewhere and against a much weaker enemy.

The Italian Government had made careful preparation to ensure that no other Power would interfere if Italy seized Tripoli. After the Young Turk revolution and the Austrian annexation of Bosnia and Herzegovina, nationalist feeling in Italy brought a demand that the favourable moment should be used. The Franco–German agreement of 1911 over Morocco seemed to make an immediate move necessary. If Italy waited longer, France, having secured Morocco, might not be interested in Italian demands and Germany might even aim at getting at least a port in Tripoli for herself. At the end of September 1911

[1] See also below, pp. 267–268.

Italy sent a hastily prepared force to Tripoli and requested the Turkish Government to allow an Italian military occupation of the country.[1]

If the Tripoli war was not as inglorious as the Ethiopian campaigns, it can hardly be called a striking demonstration to the world of Italian power and vigour. The Italians acted with extreme caution, and also with considerable brutality. They easily overwhelmed the Turkish garrison, but were unable to suppress the local guerrillas and, although they eventually brought about 100,000 troops into Libya, the enemy might have held out for a long time if Turkish attention had not been distracted by war in the Balkans. In October 1912 Turkey gave up to Italy sovereignty over Tripoli; even so guerrilla resistance went on and in the summer of 1914 60,000 troops of the Italian regular army were still in Libya. The cost of the war was over 1,300 million lire; at the outbreak of the European war in 1914 the Italian Army had not recovered from its material losses.

The gyrations of Italian policy between the Tripoli war and the European war are of little importance. The Italians were concerned principally with preventing Austrian interference in the Balkans to Italian disadvantage. In the critical days after the assassination of the Archduke Francis Ferdinand, the attitude of the Italian Government was determined by their desire to get compensation from Austria in the event of a war which they expected Germany and Austria to win. If Austria had approached them with an adequate offer they might well have come into the war at once on her side. Austria, in spite of repeated German advice, made no such offer. The Italian Government then maintained that the Austrian attack on Serbia was an act of aggression which did not entitle her to Italian support under the treaty of the Triple Alliance. Italy therefore announced her neutrality. A policy of neutrality had its dangers. After the war neither side would feel an obligation to listen to Italian demands for 'compensation'. In May 1915, after Austria

---

[1] The pretext was that Turkish misrule was endangering Italian lives and interests. The Italian action was a violation of the treaties of Paris (1856) and Berlin (1878).

had again refused until too late to offer the Trentino to Italy, and when the Italians thought that the Entente Powers looked like winning the war, Italy, having exacted a very heavy price in the Treaty of London, joined in the attack on her former allies.

4. *Russia*

France, Germany and Italy differ from one another and from Great Britain in so many respects that it is easy to forget how much they have in common and how much more important, fundamentally, this common background is than the sum of their differences. The unity in diversity of western Europe stands out more remarkably in comparison with the character and history of the people of Russia. Russia has been a European Power for a long time and Russian culture is a part of European culture, even though the former Russian Empire extended and the present U.S.S.R. extends across Asia to the Pacific Ocean. Russia took her own distinctive culture overland to Vladivostok and Kamchatka and for a time there were Russian forts and traders on the west coast of North America, but Russian civilization has owed as little to this vast territorial expansion as Spanish civilization owed to the Aztecs.

Russia entered western European politics at a late date. Early Muscovy was occupied mainly with enemies to the east. Smolensk, only 200 miles west of Moscow, was not acquired permanently until 1667; Peter the Great founded St Petersburg in 1703 and Catherine the Great annexed the Crimea in 1783. The Russians received Christianity from Byzantium, with the concept of a semi-divine monarchy, but without the insistence of the western Church on the idea of law or limiting the power of temporal rulers. They had nothing like the intellectual life of the western universities, no development of representative institutions, no groups of city states. There was no Russian Reformation and therefore no Counter-Reformation. The Russian Church was seriously affected by schisms; most of the schismatics were illiterate peasants, more fundamentalist, in modern terminology, than the orthodox. The greatest schism of the seventeenth century, that of the Old Believers, was a reaction against the reforms of the patriarch, Nikon (the Moscow Patriarchate had been set up in 1589 to secure independence from the jurisdiction of the patriarchate of Constantinople and thus to increase the control of the Russian State over the Church). Nikon actually wanted to reform the liturgy and ritual of the Church. Church and State authorities alike failed to suppress the schismatics;[1] their attempts to do so only brought the Church more firmly under the domination of the State. Peter the Great, who cared nothing for religion, abolished the Moscow Patriarchate and set up a committee, the Holy Synod, with a lay Procurator, to govern the Church. In these circumstances the Church sunk into being merely a department of state. The bishops were chosen from monasteries and required to be celibate; the lower clergy were compelled to marry and were drawn almost entirely from the peasantry. The Church never attracted the sons of the nobility; the great mass of its ministers formed a hereditary class. A judgement on the value of this class to their fellow peasants must depend on a general view of the importance of institutional religion, even at the low level of a repetition of rites and ceremonies. In the attempts at the regeneration and reform of Russia, the Orthodox Church, manipulated by the Government, hardly affecting the minds and consciences of those who exercised power, and despised by the revolutionaries, was of little practical importance.

The only way in which Russia could be brought into closer touch with the more advanced political and administrative institutions of western Europe was through the initiative, driving force and, one must add, ruthlessness of an outstanding Tsar. Peter the Great (1682–1725) was such a figure; he introduced the Russians to western ideas and technology by methods

[1] The Old Believers thought either that they would defeat the attempts to suppress them or that their defeat would presage the victory of antiChrist and the end of the world. As in all Russian peasant movements until the twentieth century, opposition to the authorities of Church and State did not mean disloyalty to the Tsar. According to a peasant saying, 'The Tsar is gracious; not so his kennel-keeper.' B. H. Sumner, *Survey of Russian History*, p. 167.

which have been likened to those of 'a peasant hitting his horse with his fist'.¹ After Peter's time there was no permanent going-back, but the size of Russia and the social and economic structure of its people limited westernization to a very small minority.

Russia is enormously large. The Russian expansion into Asia was begun in the second half of the sixteenth century, mainly by hunters and outlaws, and was consolidated after a fashion by the State. The Urals were not a physical barrier and the frontier was fixed far to the east on the Amur river as early as 1689. There was very little local opposition to this advance; the Russians met only barbarians or savages until they reached the borders of China.² The later colonization was easy owing to the similarity of physical conditions with those of Russia in Europe. In 1713 there were more Russians in Siberia than American subjects of the British Crown in the thirteen colonies of North America.

The Russian Empire in 1914 had an area of some $8\frac{1}{2}$ million square miles, one sixth of the land surface of the world. To the north this empire reached nearly 1,000 miles beyond the Arctic circle; in the south the frontier near Mount Ararat was closer than Naples to the tropics. The inland lakes of European Russia covered an area not far short of the whole of Scotland. The borders of the Empire touched Norway, Sweden, Germany, Austria-Hungary, Rumania, Turkey, Afghanistan, Manchuria and Korea. Russian outposts on the Bering Sea were nearer to the Alaskan territory of the United States than Newhaven is to Dieppe and, although this confrontation counted for little until the middle years of the twentieth century, Russia faced Canada across the frozen Polar region.³

---

¹ Sumner, *op. cit.*, p. 102.

² It is an interesting fact (with much history behind it) that the Chinese delegation which signed the treaty of 1689 with Russia was accompanied by a Jesuit father and that Latin was one of the five languages inscribed on the boundary posts delimiting the frontier between China and Russia.

³ Russia agreed separately with Great Britain and the United States in 1825 to give up her claims along the Pacific coast south of lat. 54.40. In 1867 Russia sold the whole of Alaska to the United States for 7,200,000

Between the Pripet marshes and the Great Wall of China there has been no political entity large enough or sufficiently stamped with its own culture to resist russification. Russian imperialism (a fact hardly realized in Europe, and even less in the United States, by anti-imperialist critics) had absorbed the Moslem khanates of central Asia by 1885.

Within European Russia three great rivers, the Volga, Don and Dnieper, have made for internal uniformity. The course of each of these rivers in this monotonous country is slow and even. They and their interlacing tributaries have provided easy means of communication (with the drawback that, like all Russian waterways, they are frozen over for three months in the year). On the other hand the rivers have not led the Russians directly to open seas or oceans or brought them in touch with western Europe. The Dniester and Dnieper flow into the Black Sea, the Don into the Sea of Azov, the Volga into the Caspian. Similarly with Russian ports; St Petersburg, now Leningrad and for a short time Petrograd, lies at the end of a sea closed many miles away to the west by the Sound between Sweden and Denmark. Odessa and Batum can be reached by sea only through the Dardanelles and the Bosphorus. Archangel in the far north at the head of the White Sea is an immense distance from the world trade routes; in the Far East Vladivostok is shut off from the south by the Straits of Shimonoseki. Hence the aim of Russian foreign policy has been to look for 'warm water ports' and to try to control the narrow exits from the inland seas. This policy has brought Russia westwards as a conqueror of the mixed national groups – Finns, Estonians, Letts, Lithuanians – around the Baltic and its hinterland. A similar advance would have been made to the southern shores of the Black Sea and the Dardanelles if the other Powers had allowed it.

In the eighteenth century the Russian advance was contested first by Sweden and then by Poland. The partitions of Poland

---

dollars. The Russians were influenced by what they took to be the general tendency of the European Powers to give up overseas colonies as not worth their cost. (See also footnote p. 34.)

settled this earlier conflict for over a hundred years; the Eastern Question of the nineteenth century was no longer concerned with the northern or central European plain but with the future of Turkey and especially of the Turkish possessions in Europe. Towards the end of the century, as I shall have to explain, there was a shift or rather an extension of the conflict – a Middle Eastern and a Far Eastern question; the latter was settled for a time by the defeat of Russia in the war of 1904-5 against Japan. Russian policy then turned again to the Balkans where it had to meet the rival policy of Austria-Hungary supported by Germany.

If there was uniformity throughout these vast areas, except among the mixed population of the Russian western frontier districts, another series of lateral divisions must be kept in mind for understanding the problems of the Russian peasantry. One can name three, four or five great bands of Russian territory. The three main regions are the Arctic tundra, the forest area and the steppes. The second of these regions can be sub-divided into a northern area of coniferous forests and an area of mixed forest and clearing roughly a triangle from the south of Lake Ladoga to the Pripet marshes and Kazan. To the south of this region, between the Pripet marshes, the Carpathians and the Urals, is a wide strip of woodland and meadow grass land, with a fertile black soil; farther south are the treeless, feather grass steppes, and finally a narrower belt of arid steppe leading eastwards to the Central Asian deserts.

Russia everywhere was a country of peasants; until 1861 nearly all of them were serfs and over a half of the number was 'owned' by nobles. The serfs formed about 90 per cent of the population in 1800; they were clustered most thickly in the black earth areas. In 1833, outside Finland and the kingdom of Poland,[1] there were only nine towns in the Russian Empire

[1] Generally known as 'Congress Poland'. At the Congress of Vienna, Russia secured the former Grand Duchy of Warsaw with the exception of Posen, Danzig and Thorn. Alexander I treated these lands as a separate kingdom with its own constitution and full internal self-government. After the Polish rebellion of 1830 Poland was treated more as a conquered country, though the constitution was still separate from the rest of the Empire. After a second Polish rebellion in 1863, repression was more severe and russification enforced on a wider scale.

with a population of more than 30,000. Most of these towns were just marketing and administrative centres; there was little industry outside St Petersburg and Moscow and their immediate neighbourhood. Even in 1860 there were only about 500,000 industrial workers, of whom a tenth were serfs. In 1911 out of a population of some 167 million there were no more than nineteen cities in the Empire with a population over 100,000; two of these cities were in Poland, one in Finland, one in the Baltic provinces, two in the Caucasus, two in Siberia and two in central Asia. The number of factory workers had risen to about three million and there were about a million miners and about 800,000 railway workers.

Until the later part of the nineteenth century and the early years of the twentieth century Russia had only a very small middle class – nothing like the bourgeoisie of western Europe. The Russian merchant class was on the whole unenterprising and subservient, more like small shopkeepers than the industrialists, bankers and entrepreneurs of the west. The professional class was also small; as late as 1914 only 35,500 Russians were attending the state universities.[1] The cynical Polish saying that 'the human race begins with barons' could well have been applied to Russia. The all-powerful Tsar, with his bureaucracy and his army, towered above an ocean of illiterate peasants. Originally the nobility owed their status simply to their service; there was no ancient territorialized aristocracy. Peter the Great had issued a 'Table of Ranks' representing grades in the army and bureaucracy. Members of each grade were assigned a money salary; they were ennobled by their service and this service was still compulsory. The abolition of compulsory service from the nobility in 1762 did not bring an end to the tradition of service or to the conception that office, including commissioned rank in the army, conferred nobility,[2] but it cut

[1] About 40,000 students were attending other higher educational institutions. These figures exclude Poland and Finland, but include the Baltic provinces where the educational standard was much higher than in Russia proper.
[2] In 1858 some 600,000 persons in Russia were entitled to noble status.

away the *raison d'être* of serfdom since the landlords could no longer maintain that the services exacted by them from their peasantry were the necessary counterpart of their own compulsory duties to the state.

Serfdom, as it was in the century before its abolition, had been formalized not much later than 1600; in 1675 the right of the landowner to sell his serfs without their land had been legally recognized. This formalization was due to the peasants' indebtedness to the landowners,[1] to the need of the latter for labour and, above all, to the need of the Government for money. Peter the Great instituted a general poll tax which reduced free peasants approximately to the same conditions as the serfs of landowners and made it essential for landowners to keep their serfs from running away. The position of the 'private serfs' was made harsher by an edict of Catherine binding the serfs legally to their landlord, but not to their land, and thus putting them completely at the landlord's mercy. Catherine and Paul I made large grants of crown land, with the 'state peasants' attached to them, to the nobles. In 1834 30 per cent of the serfs belonged to 870 landowners and another 15 per cent to 1,459 landowners. The burdens of the serfs were getting heavier because both types of obligation laid on them – the *obruk*, a money payment, and the *barschina*, labour service – tended to increase. Meanwhile, owing to a dangerous number of serf revolts between 1772 and 1775, government and landowners alike had been frightened into greater severity.

The abolition of compulsory service by the nobles also began their gradual though never complete separation from the bureaucracy which thus, in the nineteenth century, became more isolated. The Government was in any case remote from the ordinary citizens, especially the peasants. The administration was reformed to some extent by Alexander I after 1800 but retained its arbitrary character. It is hardly possible to emphasize too much that Russian administrators had little of

---

[1] After the so-called 'Time of Troubles' – famine, invasion, civil war and anarchy – between 1601 and 1613 very many peasants in desperate need bound themselves, without a time-limit, to their landlords in return for loans in money or in kind.

the western respect for law or for the personal rights (if they existed) of subjects. In an age of bad communications and almost universal illiteracy, and with the absence of accurate statistical data, uniformity was the only principle by which so immense an entity as the Russian Empire could be governed.[1] Uniformity implied centralization and the central authority, which had to apply the same rules everywhere, had no substitute for coercion, no room for imagination and no thought of the possibility of associating rulers and ruled in the processes of government. Alexander I established a Council of Ministers, but the ministers were chosen by him and responsible individually to him; they had no collective responsibility.

The central administration was a federation of independent departments, often at war with one another, and represented in the provinces or 'governments' – there were forty-nine of them in European Russia – by a governor. The governor had great powers but was himself spied upon by the special secret police who were directly under the so-called 'third section' of the imperial chancery.[2] The imperial chancery and, in particular, the third section was developed under Nicholas I partly to increase his own powers of supervision and to deal with the paradox of all autocracies, the difficulty – for the autocrat – of finding out what is going on. Nicholas had a reputation for travelling at breakneck speed about his empire (before the building of railways) but it was his only means of taking his officials by surprise.

In different circumstances Alexander and Nicholas might have introduced more reforms. Alexander, though unstable,

[1] The principle of uniformity went right through the Russian system. Thus the planning of towns and their public buildings was strictly centralized. A *ukase* of 1806 to all provincial governments forbade such building except according to plans and designs coming from St Petersburg. Between 1810 and his death in 1832 a large number of towns were replanned by the Scottish architect, William Hasties (who in many cases – including his designs for towns in Siberia – never saw the sites). Hasties' plans included models for village houses, façades for warehouses, etc.

[2] This name was abolished by Alexander II, but the secret police remained.

indecisive and untrustworthy, had begun his reign with liberal ideas; Nicholas also wanted to continue the modernizing of Russian institutions. Neither Tsar thought it practicable, even if he had wished to do so, to surrender his absolute power in favour of constitutional rule in the western sense of the term. Alexander and Nicholas also realized the need to get rid of serfdom; neither was able to do so. They could not risk alienating the landowners, and indeed they would have found it impossible to provide enough officials to take over the administrative functions which the landowners, that is to say, the serf-owners performed. Nicholas made a beginning with measures to improve the condition of the state peasants. In 1833 he prohibited the public sale of serfs. He also brought forward other proposals affecting the private serfs but, owing to the opposition of landowners, could not make his proposals more than optional.

Alexander and Nicholas, and especially the latter, were afraid of the spread of revolutionary ideas which, to them, meant any kind of liberal notion. Alexander was alarmed in 1820 by a mutiny in one of his trusted Guards regiments. Nicholas never forgot the so-called Decembrist conspiracy at the very beginning of his reign. This conspiracy was mainly the work of young officers – all of them, owing to their military status, nobles – who had seen western European conditions for themselves during and after the last stages of the Napoleonic War and were discontented with the stagnation of their own country under autocratic rule. Like the rebels against autocracy elsewhere, they were compelled to form secret societies for conspiratorial action. There were two such main groups, one in the north, the other in the south of Russia. They had no effective organization and no common programme; one group was more radical than the other. They took no steps – they hardly could take any steps – to associate themselves with other classes. They did not even try to get the support of the rank and file of their own regiments. They started revolutionary, or more precisely, military mutinies – the so-called Decembrist rising of 26 December 1825 – in St Petersburg and elsewhere in the sudden confusion after the death of Alexander I. Alexander's successor would have been his brother, the Grand Duke Constantine,[1] viceroy of Poland, but Constantine did not want to leave Poland where he had married a Polish countess. Alexander appeared to have agreed that Constantine should resign his claims and that his younger brother, Nicholas, should succeed him as Tsar, but no definite statement had been made. On Alexander's death Nicholas at first assumed the succession of Constantine and only after the latter's refusal proclaimed himself Tsar. The conspirators thought they must strike at once and tried to raise the St Petersburg garrison. Their movement failed and was put down with considerable harshness.

Nicholas I thus began his reign with a complete distrust of any movement among the nobility for reform. The European revolutions of 1830, and especially the outbreak in Poland, increased his hostility to liberalism and with the renewal of revolutions in 1848 Nicholas regarded himself as a ruler designated by Providence to save not only Russia but the rest of Europe from anarchy. This over-confidence in the power of his army as well as the virtue of his absolutism led him into the Crimean War.

The immediate circumstances out of which the war developed were a dispute between France and Russia over the control of the Holy Places – the sacred Christian sites in Palestine. This minor dispute could have been, and indeed was settled, but Nicholas I then put forward claims to a general right to 'protect' the Christian subjects of the Sultan. The Sultan regarded this claim as incompatible with Turkish independence; Great Britain and France also refused to recognize it. Nicholas I had been trying to get British consent to a partition of Turkey (on the ground that the Ottoman Empire was anyhow on the point of collapse).[2] The Tsar did not realize that the British Government, however strongly Lord Aberdeen, the Prime

---

[1] It is said that during the disturbances at St Petersburg, when a peasant in a crowd shouting for a constitution asked his neighbour what a 'constitution' was, he was answered, 'Why, you fool, "constitution" is the wife of the Grand Duke Constantine.'

[2] See also below, p. 204.

Minister, wanted to avoid war,[1] suspected Russia of plans for undermining Turkey (and also Persia) in order to get control of the overland routes to India. Nicholas also failed to see that British opinion at this time regarded Turkey as genuinely attempting domestic reform, with some hope of success, while Russia remained an autocracy based upon serfdom and with a ruler who had shown himself everywhere totally opposed to liberal measures.

Within the area of combat the Crimean War was fought as grimly as other wars but it was limited in the sense that neither side attempted to bring about the total collapse of the other.[2] The western Allies did not encourage a Polish rebellion against Russia; the Russians did not encourage a Bulgarian revolt against Turkey or a Hungarian revolt against Austria (though Nicholas especially resented the 'ingratitude' of Austria, whose support would have been invaluable to him, for Russian assistance a few years earlier in putting down the Hungarian revolutionaries). Nevertheless Russia lost the immense military prestige she had kept for nearly half a century after the defeat of Napoleon; the brilliant defence of Sebastopol did not compensate for the manifest backwardness and breakdown of the Russian administrative services.[3]

Nicholas's death in 1855 was therefore likely to be the end of a period of almost complete negation in Russia. Nicholas's

---

[1] Aberdeen's feeling of responsibility for the fact that, as Prime Minister, he had involved his country in war had a sequel years later when he refused to rebuild a church on his Scottish estates. He left this work to his son, like King David who had left the building of the Temple at Jerusalem to his son, Solomon, because he (David) had made war and 'shed blood abundantly'.

[2] The incompetence of British military administration in the first period of the war caused the fall of Aberdeen's ministry. Similar incompetence had passed almost unnoticed by public opinion in earlier wars, but the Crimean War was the first in which a great newspaper – *The Times* – through its own correspondent published a full account of what was happening. One curious fact shows that the age of 'total war' had not yet come; it was a matter of public discussion whether English merchants should be allowed to continue their trade with Russia, so that the English economy should not suffer.

[3] See also below, p. 211.

son, Alexander II, was better educated than his father and had a better understanding of the urgent economic problems of the Russian Empire. He was no more inclined than Nicholas to surrender his autocracy, but more willing to use it to bring about limited reforms. The first of such reforms – without which economic progress was hardly possible – had to be the abolition of serfdom. Most serf-owners – there were over 260,000 of them – were now favourable to abolition on adequate terms of compensation, while the peasants were insisting more and more menacingly upon it; thirty bailiffs and a hundred and sixty-six landowners were murdered by their serfs between 1855 and 1861 and the number of local peasant risings was increasing.

The problem of compensation was not easy; two-thirds of the private serfs were already mortgaged to the State in return for loans to the landowners. Moreover, there were differences of interest in different parts of Russia. In the fertile 'black earth' zone the landowners, if they were allowed to retain ownership of the land, did not much mind liberating their serfs; owing to the steady growth of population, labour was plentiful and free labour was more productive than the compulsory services of serfs. Agricultural experiments requiring capital, and indeed most innovations, were blocked by the poverty and conservatism of the serfs. On the other hand, in the forest regions the landowners were more interested in the non-agricultural earnings of their serfs, that is to say, the dues paid by serfs who were allowed by their owners to work in towns. These landowners were ready to allow considerable allocations of land to the serfs, but they wanted compensation for the loss of their dues.

A further question divided the reformers in Russia down to the twentieth century. The peasants held to the belief that, although they might be owned by their masters, they owned the land. They did not own it individually, but as village communities. This communal organization (*mir*) was not universal and had not developed for the idealist reasons which Slavophil enthusiasts often assigned to it. It had two aspects. As an agricultural unit, the members of the village community held the land and reallocated it at intervals to individual households, while any improvements or enterprises were carried out in common. As a fiscal unit the *mir* was responsible for the payment of taxes, especially the poll tax, by its members. The system, within its narrow limits, was one of extreme democracy. Women, if widows, had a vote in the decisions of the *mir*. These decisions had to be unanimous – majority rule was never a Slav tradition. Moreover, the habit of communal action also affected the town workers, most of whom at least in the nineteenth century were closely connected with their villages; as late as 1900 a census of 2,600 workpeople in St Petersburg showed that nearly 70 per cent were still holders of communal land. Even if they worked in a factory, the workers formed so-called *artels* or co-operative units in which they lived together as households, hired themselves out as units and divided the proceeds of their labour.

The problem for the reformers was whether they should keep this system of communal ownership of the land and the periodical redistribution of holdings, or whether the Government should work for individual ownership and the consolidation of holdings. The Emancipation Edict of 1861 was a compromise between the interests of the different classes of landowners, the peasants who wanted the land (free of all dues and services) and the Government, which could not allow its tax-collectors to find empty villages or the peasants to drift into the individualism which Russian conservatives and many Russian revolutionaries thought to be destroying the western world and leaving the supremacy of civilization to Russia. Broadly, the peasant communities kept the allotments which they had held as serfs; the state advanced four-fifths of the compensation money to the landowners; the peasants paid the remaining fifth and were to repay the State in forty-nine annual instalments.[1] The land was not given to the peasants individually; if it had been so given it would soon have been mortgaged. The village community paid the peasants' share of the compensation money

---

[1] The landowners did not get off without loss. They found it difficult to get the one-fifth compensation money from the peasants and the government advance of four-fifths was paid in Treasury bonds which went down 20 per cent in value. Anyhow the compensation was less than the value of the labour services which the serf-owners lost.

and allocated the contributions of its members. The state peasants were treated slightly better than the private serfs in the matter of land allotments.

Thus for the most part the semi-communal system remained, but the settlement was not satisfactory. The compensation paid by the peasants was too high for their resources and the allotments of land too small for their needs. The stability of the village community was undermined in the next two generations owing to the accumulation of land by the more go-ahead peasants, the *kulaks* or *mir*-eaters, as they were called. In 1905 over a third of the peasant holdings in the communes were in the hands of a tenth of the peasantry. The desire of manufacturers and many landowners to get cheap labour also tended to the break-up of the communal system. The growth of the population intensified the wretchedness of the peasantry and their craving for more land. Between 1861 and 1905 the numbers of the peasants increased by more than 50 per cent. The Government did little to raise output by improving methods of farming. Emigration to Siberia, especially after the opening of the Trans-Siberian railway, brought a certain relief, and the more prosperous peasants were buying 'noble' land, but the majority were living in deep poverty. The Government was still divided on the vital question whether to encourage or discourage the maintenance of the communal system. The arguments cut across parties and even across ministries. The Ministry of Finance was against the system on economic grounds; the Minister of the Interior favoured it because at least it prevented the growth of a landless proletariat and because it worked for peasant loyalty to the State. Peasant loyalty was wearing thin in the early years of the twentieth century and peasant discontent was one of the causes of the revolution in 1905. Stolypin during his years of office between 1906 and his assassination in 1911 initiated far-reaching measures to get rid of the system of communal ownership,[1] but at the outbreak of war in 1914 the change had affected only about a tenth of the peasant population. The results of this official slowness and of the apparent indifference of the Tsar to the increasing poverty

[1] For Stolypin's reforms and the position in 1917, see below p. 214.

of the greatest section of his subjects were manifested in 1917.

After the abolition of serfdom Alexander II continued to introduce reforms within the limits of his conservative ideas. A measure of 1864 at last separated the judicial and administrative functions of government, but the change was much less complete than it might have been in political cases owing to the use of 'exceptional' authority, such as the holding of trials *in camera*, and to the arbitrary actions of the police. In 1864 also the Tsar set up provincial and district councils (*zemstvos*). The members were chosen by separate electoral colleges of nobles, townsmen and (by indirect election) peasants; election on a single poll would have put the peasants, in the words of the Government, 'in relationships unsuitable to their persons and habits'. Even so, the representation of the peasantry was almost entirely abolished in 1890. The *zemstvos* did useful work and, if he had paid more attention to their expression of liberal opinion, Nicholas II might perhaps have saved his throne, but in the long years of stagnation after the assassination of Alexander II their limited powers were closely controlled by the central government. In any case the *zemstvos* were no substitute for an elected national assembly. Alexander II and his two successors before 1905 refused such an assembly even on a narrow franchise, though just before his assassination Alexander II had agreed to the appointment of two commissions, administrative and financial, which would submit plans of reform for consideration by a General Commission including representatives chosen from the *zemstvos* and some of the chief cities. Free discussion could not, however, be harmonized with autocracy. Free discussion implied that 'authority' might be wrong. A police state could not admit 'doubt' or allow public, that is to say, dangerous criticism of itself in the press or at public meetings.

Nevertheless it was impossible to prevent the subjects of the Tsar from wanting widespread change. If the Tsar would not, like Peter the Great, impose reforms, and if there were no legal ways of advocating them, the supporters of change would have to use violent means and to plan them by underground methods. The results of driving would-be reformers into illegality were cumulatively disastrous. The character of public life was degraded on the one hand by police suppression and on the other hand by revolutionary terror. The authorities were as lacking in forbearance as their opponents. The police who forced the supporters of radical change underground had to follow them there; espionage reached an astonishing degree of finesse. Even today it is often difficult to decide whether this or that figure in the 1880s and 1890s was a police spy posing as a revolutionary or a revolutionary getting inside information by working with the police. If the authorities acted outside the processes of law, the revolutionaries replied by the murder of individuals. The reformers who at first had shown enthusiasm for Alexander II assassinated him when they saw the narrow limits of his concessions.

Terrorism was as futile as persecution and never produced the results for which the terrorists hoped and for which they often sacrificed their own lives as well as those of their victims. The assassination of Alexander II put an end to any likelihood that his successor would go on with his plans of reform; nearly all the group responsible for the Tsar's murder were detected and punished by the police. The police did everything possible to lighten their task by keeping the Tsar out of harm's way. They could do this most easily by isolating him in honourable seclusion from his subjects. The ideal form of seclusion was a palace in a large park, away from the capital, walled around and patrolled by sentries. Alexander III rarely left the grounds of his palace of Gatchina near St Petersburg. Nicholas II lived after 1905 almost entirely in the palace of Tsarskoe Seloe and took his holidays on a yacht at sea. The Tsar was thus cut off from his subjects and left at the mercy of a court camarilla. If the police did not want the Tsar to go out of his palace, the court camarilla did not want people hostile to themselves to come into it. The fatal refusals of Nicholas II to introduce political changes before it was too late were partly due to his weakness of character but almost as much to his unawareness of what his subjects thought – and knew – about the condition of his Empire.

The revolutionaries themselves were divided and subject to

changes of intellectual fashion. After the failure of the Decembrist conspiracy, a movement developed among the students and the Russian intelligentsia to widen the basis of the revolutionary party. The term intelligentsia is itself Russian and denoted those who earned a living by their ideas in contrast with the well-to-do liberals of the noble class. Obviously not all of the so-called intelligentsia were revolutionary and not all revolutionaries belonged to the intelligentsia, but without this class there would have been no professional revolutionary party.

The Russian Government, for economic reasons and in order to get educated civil servants, had to do something about education, but its plans were always handicapped by the fear of training up an opposition to the established order. Alexander II went beyond Nicholas's bleak view that education ought not to encourage anyone to leave the social class into which he had been born, and therefore that the peasants should hardly be educated at all. The execution of Alexander's reforms, however, was affected by the reaction after his assassination. Secondary and university education was treated as politically dangerous; the Government fluctuated between the view that such education should be 'scientific', i.e. mainly technical, or based on the classics. There were less than 10,000 university students in the early 1880s.[1] Hence the intelligentsia was, and remained, a relatively small class. As for the great mass of Russians, peasants who learned to read and write did so mainly in the army.

From this small class of intellectuals about the year 1874 came the so-called Populist movement[2] to get the support of the peasantry. The Populist method was simple and direct; the young revolutionaries went out into the countryside to preach their doctrines to the peasants. These doctrines were confused and impractical, but the missionaries to the people agreed at least negatively in a total rejection of the Russian state machinery, the only form of government of which they had direct knowledge. They also rejected western capitalism and regarded the communal organization of the Russian village, the

---

[1] See above, p. 185.

[2] For an account of the Populist movement see F. Venturi, *The Roots of Revolution* (Eng. tr. 1960, with an introduction by Sir I. Berlin).

mir, as a basis for a society of co-operative producers; they differed about the amount of central co-ordination required by a society of this kind as large as the Russian Empire. They wanted to apply the principle of co-operative organization to industry; here again the *artel* already provided a foundation. Only a minority of these missionaries to the people had fears lest, in their attempts to remove the oppressive paraphernalia of the existing Russian administration, they might be substituting one tyranny for another. In any case the peasants failed to understand them; some were hostile, others suspicious and the great majority were merely apathetic. Nevertheless the Government was alarmed and, by tightening the regime of intellectual oppression, widened the gulf between the bureaucracy and the small body of enlightened public opinion.

The extreme left wing of the revolutionaries thought the appeal to a scattered and ignorant peasantry useless; they argued for concentrating on the small but growing industrial population, who in a still distant future might 'make' the revolution. In the last two decades of the nineteenth century Marxist ideas, spread through the agency of revolutionaries who had gone into exile, overshadowed the influence of the pre-Marxist French socialists and of Bakunin[1] and his anarchism. Lenin, the most remarkable of the younger exiles, had joined the Marxist revolutionaries in 1893; his brother had been executed in 1887 for complicity in an attempt to assassinate Alexander II. Lenin was arrested in 1895 and sent to Siberia for three years of not too uncomfortable exile.[2] Lenin knew very

[1] Mikhail Bakunin (1814–76), son of a nobleman of Tver. He resigned his commission in the Imperial Guard in 1846 and went to Paris where he met Proudhon. He was expelled from France in 1848, and, after being sentenced to death for complicity in revolutionary outbreaks in Germany (the sentence was commuted), was handed over to the Russian authorities who exiled him to Siberia. He escaped in 1861 and spent most of the rest of his life in Switzerland. His anarchist views were opposed by Marx and he was expelled from the Third International in 1872. For an interesting life of Bakunin, see E. H. Carr, *Michael Bakunin*, 1937.

[2] Vladimir Ilyich Ulianov, who took the pseudonym Lenin, was born in 1870 at Simbirsk, now Leninsk, south of Kazan. His father, a native of Astrakan, was an inspector of schools. Lenin was expelled from the University of Kazan during his first term owing to his violent political

early in his revolutionary career what he wanted. A pamphlet written by him in the winter of 1901–2, *What is to be done?*, laid down a plan from which in the main he never deviated. He saw more clearly than his fellow revolutionaries the difficulties in applying Marxist strategy to Russian conditions. As with most rigid orthodoxies, the sacred texts were themselves obscure, but their general tenor was that the social revolution would come about in two stages; the first stage would be the overthrow of the 'feudal' autocracy by the liberal capitalist bourgeoisie; in a second stage the proletariat would overthrow bourgeois capitalism. In Russia, however, the capitalist bourgeoisie, unlike that of western Europe, was too weak to play its allotted part and, even if it succeeded in getting radical reforms, would be too much afraid of the possible anarchic consequences to support a through-going destruction of the bureaucratic machinery of the autocratic state. The working class, if left to its own organizations, would never get beyond trade unionism, that is to say, the workers would fight to better their own conditions but not for a complete change in the 'system'. The peasants, once they had satisfied their demands for land, would also have little interest in further change and, as they formed the greater part of the rank and file of the Russian Army, would be loyal instruments in suppressing the second stage of the revolution, the destruction of the bourgeoisie. Lenin at first regarded the peasants merely as belonging to the petty bourgeoisie, but he could not do without them. His conclusion, which he also reached before 1905, was that they could be used to support the first stage of the revolution by the offer of land. At a later stage they could be divided by setting the landless and poorer majority against the richer and more prosperous minority.

Lenin's problem was how to bring over the industrial proletariat to his ideas. Obviously he would have nothing to do with

---

speeches. He went to the University of St Petersburg where he graduated in law in 1891 and formed a Militant Union for the Liberation of the Working Classes. After his return from Siberia he lived first in Munich and then in Switzerland.

'reformism'. Even in the first stage of revolution he wanted the workers to act as a separate class with their own organization. Lenin had no place for a revolutionary party in the ordinary sense of a body of supporters with many variations of opinion and differences of zeal. He wanted a small company of 'professional' revolutionaries, in total ideological agreement, and willing (like members of a religious order) to submit to strict discipline and obedience. He was so sure of himself that he did not hesitate to split the Russian Social Democratic Workmen's Party which had been founded in 1898. At a party congress held in London (most of the members who had not been arrested were in exile) in 1903, after the secession of a number of his opponents, Lenin obtained a majority for his views. This majority took for themselves the title of Bolsheviks (majority) and named the seceders Mensheviks (minority). For a time the two groups did not actually separate and the revolution of 1905 had spent its force before they could take effective action.[1] Lenin, however, maintained his strategy and ultimately had the opportunity in 1917 to carry it out in circumstances which he could not have foreseen.[2]

The Russian autocracy also applied its oppressive methods to the non-Russian nationalities within its borders. The greatest trouble for the Russian Government was Poland. Under Alexander I there was little attempt at russification and, as long as the Poles were content to give up ideas of independence, little interference in Polish domestic affairs. Poland at least had a constitution and the Catholic Church to which most Poles belonged was not persecuted. A small educated minority, however, was not content to give up hopes of complete independence; in 1830, five years after Alexander's death and in a year of revolution in Europe, a conspiracy in Warsaw developed almost accidentally into an insurrection and the insurrection into a rebellion largely because there were no Polish leaders sufficiently strong to prevent so hopeless an enterprise.

[1] See below, p. 213.
[2] See below, pp. 217–219.

The peasants, that is to say, the majority of the Polish people, gave the rebellion little support because they were not offered any land reform. Nicholas I was not unconciliatory after the rebellion had been suppressed, but made no concessions likely to satisfy the Polish radicals who wanted not reform but independence. The Poles indeed remained divided. The moderates thought in realist terms that at least for the time being co-operation with the Russian Government was necessary and that the position of the Poles in the Russian Empire might be satisfactory if they were given civil liberties. Prussia, as a more efficient country, seemed ultimately a greater obstacle to Polish hopes than Russia. There were also differences among the Poles about land reform. All parties accepted the need to abolish serfdom but the landowners wanted the conversion of services into money payments, while the more radical reformers proposed to give freeholds to the peasants in return for payments to the Government over a period of years.

In 1861 there were serious riots in Warsaw in which about 200 people were killed. Alexander II was in fact introducing reforms for Poland as well as for the rest of his dominions, but not to the extent of the radical programme. In order to weaken the radical movement, the Russians decided to apply conscription to young Poles, that is to say, all those suspected of belonging to secret political societies. The result was the Polish rebellion of 1863. Once again the rebels were most unlikely to succeed. Most of the landowners supported the rebellion because they did not want to be thought unpatriotic. The peasants were divided and the Poles under Prussian and Austrian rule gave no help. The Poles had the sympathy of France and Great Britain, but the hopes of western intervention recklessly excited by the Polish exiles (since the revolution of 1830) came to nothing.

The rebels never gained control of the large cities and were never strong enough or sufficiently united to attempt to fight a major battle. Although the suppression of the rebellion was severe, the Tsar kept to his plan of introducing reforms. The land settlement of 1864 gave freehold tenure to some 700,000 Polish families; compensation was paid by the Government –

not by the peasants – and recovered by a general tax on landowners. Another 130,000 holdings were created out of state lands for landless peasants. The Russians expected these measures to separate the landowners from the peasantry; the actual effect (as a less unimaginative bureaucracy would have realized) was that the peasants now had a stake in their country and were much readier than before to unite with other classes in resisting russification.

The failure to conciliate Polish opinion was one reason after 1880 for the increased russification of the country. The Government came to the conclusion that the Poles could be regarded only as enemies and took measures against the two strongest forces making for national unity, language and religion. The Polish language was not allowed for general instruction in secondary schools after 1885 or in the primary schools of Warsaw or, after 1890, in the university of Warsaw. The Roman Catholic Church could not be suppressed, but the Greek Uniates (who were of the Roman obedience, but practised Orthodox rites) were cajoled or bullied into conformity with the Russian Church.

Russification was extended to other nationalities of the Empire, partly owing to bureaucratic insistence on uniformity, partly for military reasons – the security of the frontier districts – and partly owing to an increased consciousness of Russian nationalism. A Russian writer described the old theory that the Tsar was the father of all his peoples as 'la polygamie érigée en système politique'; loyalty was required not to the Tsar but to the Russian people. This policy of russification through the compulsory use of Russian in the schools and in the business of local government was applied to the Baltic Germans, Lithuanians, Finns and Armenians who had been loyal hitherto to the regime. Once again the result was a reaction of protest and a growth of separatist feeling in these communities which, unlike the Poles, had no recent tradition of existence as independent states. The Grand Duchy of Finland had been ceded to Russia by Sweden in 1809[1] on terms giving the Finns even superior rights to those which they had held under Sweden. About the

[1] Russia had already acquired parts of Finland in 1713 and 1743.

o

last decade of the nineteenth century the Russian Government began to encroach upon these rights by its usual methods; Russian schools were established, a knowledge of Russian was demanded of all applicants for official posts and so on. When in 1895 the Finnish Diet refused an extra contribution of recruits for the army, the Tsar affirmed his right as Grand Duke to legislate on all questions affecting Russia and the Grand Duchy; the Finns had to give way.

The Ukraine had provided a different problem for the Russian Government. Ukraine means, simply, borderland and the Slavs who had come southward to the Dnieper and Bug rivers after the Mongol invasions (in contrast with those who established the Muscovite and later the Russian state to the north) had developed through constant fighting a community life and traditions of their own. They were not brought into the centralized system of the Russian Empire until the time of Catherine the Great. Until the nineteenth century they were content to call themselves Russians but, as in other parts of central and south-eastern Europe, a nationalist movement was begun by a small, articulate minority who made a Ukrainian language out of peasant dialects and a literature out of peasant folklore. Nicholas I and Alexander II tried to suppress this nationalism. The publication of works in the Ukrainian language was forbidden and the leaders of Ukrainian studies expelled from the universities. Russian historians 'wrote down' the Ukrainian version of history and every effort was made to suppress the 'national' Uniate Church. The Ukrainians, however, were more hostile to the Poles than to the Russians, and particularist rather than nationalist. They were protesting mainly against Russian mal-administration and over-centralization and most of them would have been content with genuine local autonomy.

Russification had nothing to do with the so-called Slavophil or later Pan-Slav movements. Neither of these movements ever became part of official Russian policy, although at times the government made use of them. The Slavophils were at the height of their influence before the Crimean War. They had no definite political programme; their emphasis was on the uniqueness of Russian culture and the need to conserve it from disruptive influences coming from the west. The Pan-Slavs were more politically-minded, less interested in a vaguely mystical Russian orthodoxy and more concerned with the defence of Slav interests generally against Magyars, Germans and Turks. Pan-Slavism was perhaps of greater importance outside than inside Russia. It had more influence in Russia itself after the humiliation of the Crimean War and the success of the nationalist movements in Germany and Italy. Politically this later stage of Pan-Slavism implied the disruption of Austria–Hungary and of the Turkish Empire in Europe to the advantage, in each case, of the Slavs. The stubborn hostility of the Poles, however, wrecked any chance of a great Pan-Slav union under Russian hegemony; the failure of Russia to get the terms she had planned after the Russo–Turkish War of 1877–8, the subsequent antagonism between Serbs and Bulgarians and the incompatibility between the Russian autocracy and the 'westernizing' nationalism of all the Balkan states deprived Pan-Slavism of political importance.[1]

From 1814 to 1914 the rival interests of Russia and Austria in the Balkans became an increasingly important factor in the foreign policy of each of the two Powers and was ultimately fateful for the peace of Europe. After the Vienna settlement, which was nearly wrecked by Russian and Prussian obstinacy over Poland and Saxony, the two Powers were drawn together, in spite of other differences, in a common fear of the spread of liberal ideas and a renewal of revolutionary violence in Europe. In 1849, Nicholas I assisted Austria to suppress rebellion in Hungary. Austria, however, was suspicious of Russian designs at the expense of the moribund Turkish Empire. Great Britain and France were not directly interested in south-east Europe, but were concerned to prevent Russia from controlling Constantinople and the Straits. In the treaty of Unkiar Skelessi (1833), secured from Turkey as the price of protecting the

[1] Gorchakov, the foreign minister of Alexander II, once said that he found it difficult to believe in the sympathy of the Slav peoples for an autocratic Russia. (Quoted in Sumner, *op. cit.*, p. 245.)

Sultan against the attacks of his rebel vassal, Mehemet Ali, Pasha of Egypt, Nicholas I appeared to have gone a long way towards getting this control. Russia, however, at this stage was more anxious to keep the British fleet out of the Black Sea than to get passage for her own ships of war (of which she had few) through the Straits into the Mediterranean and feared that, if she put pressure on Turkey to allow such passage, Great Britain and France might reply by seizing some Aegean islands as bases from which to blockade the Dardanelles. In 1840 an agreement signed by the Powers recognized the 'ancient rule' whereby the Straits were closed to warships other than those of Turkey in time of peace. Russia, however, increased her Black Sea fleet and strongly fortified the naval base of Sebastapol. After the Crimean War[1] Russia was compelled to agree to the neutralization of the Black Sea and therefore unable to keep a fleet in it or to refortify Sebastapol. She also had to cede southern Bessarabia and thus lost control of the northernmost mouth of the Danube.

The Russians were unlikely to accept these restrictions for long. They took the occasion of the Franco-Prussian War to denounce the neutralization of the Black Sea. Great Britain insisted on a European conference to give formal legitimacy to the Russian action, but could not maintain the Crimean decisions. The next step in the Russian weakening of Turkey began with revolution in 1876 among the Slavs of Bosnia and Herzegovina. The Serbs in the kingdom of Serbia came to their help (Russian officers joined the Serbian Army as volunteers) but the Turks defeated them and also put down a revolt of the Bulgarian peasantry. European intervention was therefore necessary, not only to save Serbia and to protect the Bulgars from the savagery of the Turkish irregular forces (Bashi-Bazouks from Circassia) but also because the other Powers could not allow Russia to act alone. Austria and Russia then agreed secretly that, if Russia went to war with Turkey, she would take back southern Bessarabia, allow Austria and Serbia to divide Bosnia and Herzegovina between them, and Serbia and Montenegro to share the Sanjak of Novi Bazar (a wild area

[1] See above, p. 187.

of great strategic importance as a corridor leading towards Salonika).[1] The ambassadors of the Powers now met and decided on reforms which the Sultan would be required to carry out in his European possessions.

The Sultan, counting as usual upon the conflict of interests between the Great Powers, refused their proposals, or rather overbid them by announcing that he would himself promulgate a constitution for all his European subjects. These promises were unlikely to satisfy Russia and, after the Sultan had rejected further proposals from Great Britain and Russia, Russia declared war on Turkey. The war was less successful at first than the Russians had hoped, but the Turks were defeated by January 1878. Before the fighting began Russia had signed another convention with Austria in which the Austrian claim to, or rather demand for, Bosnia was accepted and both signatories agreed that no new Slav state should be created as a result of the war. After her victory Russia announced the creation of such a state in Bulgaria, with access to the Aegean, while she refused to agree to the annexation of Bosnia by Austria.

Great Britain and Austria were unwilling to allow the proposed state of Bulgaria access to the Aegean. After much secret, or semi-secret bargaining, the Powers reached a settlement at the Congress of Berlin (1878).[2] Russia gave up the 'big Bulgaria', while Austria was permitted to occupy and administer, though not to hold in full sovereignty, Bosnia and Herzegovina. The Russian surrender was necessary because Bismarck, faced with the alternative of supporting Austria or Russia, felt bound to choose Austria. In 1879 Bismarck

---

[1] See also below, p. 246.

[2] The Congress of Berlin was a classical example of nineteenth-century diplomacy. The decisions were determined by secret agreements between the several participants before the Congress met; the meetings did little more than register these decisions. Great Britain had secret agreements with Austria, Russia and Turkey. The secrecy was not very well kept; the Anglo-Turkish agreement was sold to the 'Globe' newspaper by a copying clerk in the Foreign Office, but the Russian Government appears to have had a fairly accurate knowledge of its general tenor before the actual terms were published in the *Globe*.

followed up this decision by making an alliance with Austria which became the basis of German policy. Bismarck tried to maintain that he was acting as an 'honest broker', indifferent to Balkan questions as such, but his decision was ultimately to be fatal to the German Reich. For some time Bismarck delayed these consequences by his adroit diplomacy; he aimed at allowing Russian influence in the eastern half and Austrian influence in the western half of the Balkan peninsula. A division of this kind turned out to be impracticable, if only because the Balkan states themselves had territorial ambitions; Serbia was concerned in particular with the southern Slavs in the Habsburg dominions, now increased by the occupation of Bosnia-Herzegovina which Austria obviously intended to be permanent. Bulgaria was interested in Macedonia and Thrace which still remained part of the Ottoman Empire. Roumania did not give up hopes of getting back Transylvania and Bukovina from Hungary and southern Bessarabia from Russia.[1]

Bismarck's attempt to reconcile the rival ambitions – and fears – of Austria and Russia led him to make the 'reinsurance' treaty of 1887[2] with Russia in order to reassure the Russian Government at a time when a war party in Russia might have got the upper hand and persuaded the Tsar to attack Austria. Bismarck had been able to prevent Russia from taking the obvious though, to the Russians, not attractive step of making an alliance with France. After Bismarck's dismissal the Russian Government could be less sure that German policy would be directed with such skill towards avoiding war.

The Franco-Russian alliance did not come at once. In 1891 France and Russia agreed to consult together on common action in the event of a threat to peace. In 1892 the French and Russian general staffs approved a draft convention for mutual military aid. The draft convention was not finally agreed until the end of 1893. Both parties were extremely cautious about

---

[1] The Powers had acquiesced (in spite of a British protest) in the return of southern Bessarabia to Russia in 1878. Roumania, who had been the ally of Russia in the war against Turkey, was given nominal compensation in Dobrudja to the south of the mouth of the Danube.

[2] See above, p. 123.

committing themselves. The Russians did not want to be involved in a war for the French recovery of Alsace-Lorraine; the French disliked the Russian autocracy and did not want to be drawn into a war for Russian interests in the Balkans. For the first three years of the alliance Russia and France were more concerned with opposing Great Britain outside Europe than with a common European policy.[1] The terms of the alliance were extended after 1899 to cover not only the preservation of peace but the maintenance of the balance of power in Europe. The 'pointing' of the alliance against Germany was due primarily to the mistakes of German policy.

Another reason why the full effects of the Franco-Russian alliance were delayed was the preoccupation of the Russian Government in the 1890s and the first year of the twentieth century with the Far East – a preoccupation which the Germans encouraged since it relieved Austria-Hungary of Russian pressure in the Balkans. The Russian decision in 1891 to build a Trans-Siberian railway was taken in the interest of the economic development of Siberia. Witte,[2] who was Minister of Finance from 1892 to 1902, had in mind the development of trade with China, but the railway also had important strategic implications. Korea, theoretically a vassal state of China, in fact independent under conflicting Chinese and Japanese influence, was of interest to Russia, since near the straits dividing it from Japan, Russia could get access to an ice-free port south of Vladivostok. After the defeat of China by Japan in 1895, Russia, with French and German support, refused to allow Japan to acquire Port Arthur and the Liaotung peninsula, and soon competed with Japan in meddling in the internal affairs of Korea. In 1896 China agreed to the construction of a Chinese Eastern Railway under Russian control across Manchuria to link up with the Trans-Siberian and thus shorten the Russian route to the Pacific.

In 1897 Germany used the murder of a German missionary

[1] See above, p. 129.
[2] Count Sergius Witte was the son of a German (or Dutch) Lutheran who had married into a Russian noble family. He was brought up in the Caucasus. He began his official career in the railway administration.

in China as a pretext to occupy the Chinese port of Kiaochow; the other Powers then demanded similar concessions; Russia obtained most of the Liaotung peninsula (including Port Arthur) and a concession for a South Manchurian railway. Korea was now even more important for Russia since the Japanese controlled the Straits of Shimonoseki between the Sea of Japan and the Yellow Sea, that is to say, between Port Arthur and Vladivostok. After the Boxer rebellion[1] Russia occupied the whole of Manchuria and did not fulfil her promise to leave it by stages. The British Government, afraid that Russia intended to increase her hold over the rapidly disintegrating Chinese Empire, came to an agreement in 1900 with Germany to maintain the integrity of China and the 'open door' to trade, but the German Chancellor (Bülow) stated in the Reichstag that Germany did not intend the agreement to apply to Manchuria. Japan, on the other hand, attempted a direct agreement with Russia. When these direct and indirect efforts to stop Russian encroachment on China failed, Great Britain and Japan signed (January 1902) an alliance recognizing Japanese interests in Korea and promising mutual assistance if either party to the alliance were attacked by two or more Powers. The Russians continued to delay their evacuation of Manchuria and to make new demands on China. They also began to occupy an area of north Korea under cover of a timber syndicate (which was itself a discreditable enterprise organized by a Russian adventurer with high connections).

[1] The Boxers were a secret society, partly religious, partly political; they opposed western missionaries and the demands of western Powers for concessions in China. They organized risings all over China and in 1900, after murdering a Japanese diplomat and the German Minister in Peking, besieged the foreign Legations in the city. The Chinese Government, which had taken no steps to suppress the rebellion or to protect foreigners, was compelled to pay an indemnity. Most of the Powers gave their share of the indemnity to educational and other institutions in China. The address of the Emperor William II to the German contingent of the International Force (which in fact arrived after the relief of the Legations) was remembered later because it contained the words: 'Even as a thousand years ago the Huns under Attila made such a name as still resounds in terror, so may the name of Germany resound through history a thousand years from now.'

In February 1904 Japan went to war with Russia. The Russian commander at Port Arthur surrendered it to the Japanese in January 1905, though it could have held out much longer. The Japanese won victories in Manchuria, with heavy casualties on each side. At sea they completely destroyed not only the Russian Pacific fleet but also the Baltic fleet which reached Far Eastern waters in 1905. Japanese resources were strained to the limit and the Russians were finding it extremely difficult to fight a major war at the end of the Trans-Siberian railway, with the threat of revolution at home. Both sides therefore were willing to accept the mediation of President Theodore Roosevelt and the war ended in August 1905. Russia lost the Liaotung peninsula and the control of the South Manchurian Railway. The Japanese had stopped the Russian advance in the areas where this advance was most threatening to the interests of Japan, but both parties continued to oppose an 'open door' policy for China and in fact came to an agreement whereby Russian influence would be dominant in northern Manchuria and Outer Mongolia, and Japanese influence in Korea, southern Manchuria and Inner Mongolia. After the Chinese revolution of 1911 and the fall of the Manchu dynasty, Russia supported a revolution in Outer Mongolia; the Chinese revolutionary government had to recognize Mongolian autonomy, but in fact Russia controlled the country.

Nevertheless the period of rapid and aggressive Russian expansion in the Far East had come to an end. In these circumstances Russian policy was likely to be more active in the Near and Middle East. Events in south-eastern Europe would anyhow have revived the Austro–Russian conflict of interest which had been dormant for about a decade. The increasing tension between the different nationalities of the Habsburg Empire, the doubts whether this Empire would survive the death of the aged Francis Joseph, the growing economic domination of Turkey by Germany, the ambitions of the Balkan states and the moribund condition of the Ottoman Empire were bound to have important implications for Russia. The assassination of the Serbian King Alexander II in 1903 had been followed by the restoration of the former Russophil Karageorgevich dynasty[1] and an increasing breach between Austria and Serbia. In Turkey-in-Asia the German-controlled Baghdad railway cut directly across Russian plans for 'warm-water' expansion and was one of the reasons why the Russian Government in 1907 was willing to give up or at least to share a dominant influence over Persia in return for an agreement with Great Britain. The military weakness of Russia for some time after the Russo-Japanese War made it hazardous for her to go to war with a European Great Power, but the Russian Government was determined not to submit for a second time to the humiliation of a quasi-ultimatum with which Germany demanded that she should accept the Austrian annexation of Bosnia–Herzegovina. By 1913 the relations between Russia and Austria, with Germany supporting Austria, were such that any serious crisis might lead to war.[2]

Before the assassination of the Archduke Francis Ferdinand in 1914 brought about this crisis, Russia had made a remarkable economic and, at least superficially, a political recovery from revolutionary turmoil threatening the Tsarist regime in 1905. The mistakes of policy which had involved Russia in war with Japan, the mismanagement and disasters of the war itself did not provide the occasion – absolute defeat – for which Lenin and his fellow exiles were looking, but there was sufficient indignation and unrest to make it impossible for the Tsar altogether to resist the demand for political change. Russia still had neither a bourgeoisie nor an industrial proletariat comparable with those of the western European states; there was, however, an educated class, nearly all of whose members were alienated from the bureaucracy and its crass methods. Many officials themselves were convinced that the old machinery of autocratic rule could not continue. The economic policy of Witte had done much to stimulate economic growth, especially in the metallurgical industries, and the programme of railway building (one of Witte's predecessors fifty years earlier had

[1] See also below, p. 250.
[2] For the Balkan wars and their aftermath, see chapter on Austria-Hungary, pp. 250–254.

opposed railways because they encouraged useless travel) was a necessary condition of economic advance. Russian industry was highly protected and, inevitably, subject to bureaucratic planning, but it could be argued that the capitalists manipulated the Government as much as the latter directed the capitalists. The economic advances brought an increase in the number of factory workers which was disturbing to the Government, but little was done to remove the bad conditions which laid the workers open to revolutionary propaganda. Plehve, an unimaginative reactionary who was Minister of the Interior from 1902 until his assassination in 1904, supported a fantastic attempt to bring the labour organizations under official direction. This 'police socialism' had its own clubs, meetings and trade unions, but it was a dead thing from the start and within a year of his appointment the official leader, a certain Father Gapon, went over to the socialists proper.

The revolution of 1905 began with a movement among the propertied class which predominated in the *zemstvos* against the irresponsibility and blunders only too manifest in the conduct of the war. In November 1904 a congress of *zemstvos* was held privately, but with official sanction; the congress decided that the only way to end the arbitrary rule which allowed these mistakes was to establish in Russia the public and private rights recognized in western European countries and to secure them by means of a national representative assembly. The Government refused these proposals, but promised a number of administrative reforms. The protests of the *zemstvos* had been against the administration and no effective change was likely until the principle of autocracy was abandoned and the bureaucracy brought under control.

With the fall of Port Arthur on 2 January 1905, the expansionist policy of the regime and its servants was seen to have collapsed. The working class in St Petersburg now took a hand in the protests. After a great strike in the capital a delegation of workers under the leadership of Father Gapon drew up a workers' petition for submission to the Tsar. The Tsar's ministers advised him not to receive the delegates or their petition. On the morning of Sunday, 8 January, Father Gapon led a procession of 18,000 workpeople towards the great square outside the Winter Palace. The procession came into collision with the troops; the troops were ordered to fire and continued to shoot wildly into the crowds. They even shot at children who had climbed trees to see the procession. The number of killed was at least 700; some estimates suggest 1,000.

During the next four months the agitation for reform became more menacing. In July 1905 another congress of *zemstvos*, composed mainly of the more conservative members of these bodies, again asked for a national assembly. The Tsar promised to call a 'representative assembly' of the people, but the police confiscated newspapers announcing this promise and prosecuted their editors. Meanwhile there was more news of defeats in the Far East; political strikes continued and disorders broke out all over Russia among the peasants as well as the town workers. Even the conservative press defied the censorship and attacked the administration. In mid-August the Government took a step towards surrender by announcing that an elected assembly (*Duma*) would be called; its work would be consultative and elections to it would be by indirect voting with four categories of voters.

These concessions were too few and too late. The congress of *zemstvos* was not satisfied and the political strikes went on. The Government then made a second surrender. On 30 October the Tsar issued a manifesto promising full civil liberties and a Duma elected on a wide franchise, but still with indirect election. Three days earlier the St Petersburg workers had set up a Soviet (Committee) of representatives chosen in the factories. The Soviet lasted for fifty days until the authorities felt strong enough to arrest its leaders; other industrial towns followed the example of the St Petersburg workers. In December about a thousand people were killed during riots in Moscow. Some of the disturbances were said to have been caused by *agents provocateurs* with the intention of enabling the administration, in the interest of public order, to go back on the Tsar's promises. A subvention of 20,000 roubles was reported to have been given from government funds for the writing of pamphlets against the new constitution. The attempts of the Soviets to force the Government into more concessions by political strikes caused a certain public reaction against incessant disturbances. Mutinies in the army and navy, however, gave the authorities greater alarm. In June the crew of the battleship *Potemkin* had mutinied at Odessa. 10,000 men were involved in the troubles and several ships were sunk in an outbreak at Sebastopol.

The administration therefore could not avoid fulfilling the promise of an elected Duma and indeed had to call one for financial reasons. They wanted a foreign loan and could get it only if public order were restored and the Duma were summoned. Many Russian intellectuals, including Maxim Gorki, protested against this proposal for a loan on the ground that, if the Government secured financial independence before a constitutional regime had been established, they would use it to suppress the revolution and retract all the political concessions. None the less, the loan was obtained; it came from France, with the approval of a radical, anti-militarist, anti-clerical French ministry which feared that the Franco-Russian alliance, already weakened by Russian defeats, would otherwise collapse and German predominance be established in Europe.

The French loan was received in April 1906. Witte in his *Memoirs* described it as 'the loan that saved Russia'. In this same month the first Duma met. The Tsar's promises of 30 October had included a new status for the Committee of Ministers by turning it into a Council with its president as a kind of Prime Minister. This approach to parliamentary government and a Cabinet system did not go very far. Witte, the first President of the Council, had a general responsibility for policy and a certain authority over his colleagues, but the Duma had no control over them. They were appointed by the Tsar; the Duma could not remove them. The President might report the wishes of the Duma to the Tsar; the Tsar need not pay attention to them.

Nicholas II got rid of Witte, whom he disliked and distrusted, before the meeting of the first Duma. Even so, if the Tsar and the reactionaries to whom he listened had tried to work with the Duma and had encouraged the emergence of parties with a programme less radical than that of the revolutionaries, the transition to genuine parliamentary government might have been made or at least begun. No such transition was even attempted. On 20 July the members of the Duma, like the representatives of the Tiers Etat at Versailles in 1789, found themselves locked out of their hall of meeting. The reforms for which they had asked, including measures to meet the peasants' demands for land, were rejected.

A second Duma was called in March 1907. The history of its predecessor was repeated. The deputies, excited, suspicious and unpractical, were more radical than those of the first assembly. The Government did not try to work with the moderates and to win over the majority to a sense of realities, that is to say, to the acceptance and immediate execution of those reforms which could be carried out without political risk or extreme administrative difficulty. The Tsar dissolved the second Duma in June 1907 and, before calling a third assembly, altered the franchise by decree in order to secure the election of a conservative, landowning majority. This third Duma, however, was not totally reactionary; it persuaded the administration to accept a number of limited reforms and Stolypin who had been appointed President of the Council at the time of the dissolution of the first Duma, was a constitutional conservative, disliking reactionary absolutism and at the same time regarding Russia as not yet fit for a parliamentary regime. Stolypin was especially interested in improving the condition and character of the peasantry by getting rid of the communal ownership of land and collective responsibility for taxation, consolidating the peasants' holdings and increasing the facilities for the purchase or rent of land. He also did much to provide for primary education. Between 1906 and 1914 the number of Russian primary schools increased fourfold (even so, the total was only about half the number required). It is, again, impossible to say whether, given the necessary time, this long-range policy of creating a 'solid peasantry' would have succeeded. Before 1917 the holdings of some 1,300,000 peasant householders – about one tenth of the possible number – had already been consolidated. They were not enough to satisfy peasant discontent.

The nine-tenths who still lived under the old system were getting poorer with the increase of population and the greater pressure for land; the nobility and gentry and their families – about a million persons – still held about 100 million acres of land (over a third of it was mortgaged to the Nobles' Land Bank), while nearly 100 million peasant families had only 400 million acres. Thus, unless the tempo of reform were greatly increased, agrarian discontent would lead the peasants to support revolution.

The rapid growth of the Russian economy after 1905–6 had not made the urban workers less discontented. Between 1900 and 1913 the production of coal in Russia had doubled and that of pig-iron and steel had increased by over 50 per cent. There were in 1913–14 some three million factory workers – nearly 800,000 of them employed in textile industries – about a million miners and some 800,000 railway workers. This urban population was still small in comparison with the ocean of peasants, just as the total industrial production of Russia was far below that of the industrial countries of western Europe. On the other hand, Russian industry was mainly concentrated in large units and these again were located in certain areas, with the greatest concentrations in the regions of St Petersburg and Moscow. Housing and conditions of work were very poor; trade unions remained unorganized, ineffective and suspected by the Government. Hence the working class in the industrial areas was more open to revolutionary propaganda carried out by the underground methods to which the workers themselves were driven. There were a number of political strikes between 1910 and 1914; the suppression of a strike (which had broken out mainly for economic reasons) at the Lena goldfields in Siberia cost about 500 lives.

Stolypin was assassinated in September 1911. His successor, Kokovtsev, was an able man, but unable to overcome the senseless opposition of the Tsar and his entourage to constitutional change and genuine reform of the hated bureaucracy. Kokovtsev was dismissed in January 1914 owing to his protests against the interference of the monk Rasputin in matters of state. Rasputin was a peasant monk of dissolute habits who had gained an extraordinary hold on the Tsar and Tsarina because he had twice predicted, against the diagnosis of the doctors, the recovery of the ailing young Tsarevitch.[1] Rasputin in fact belonged to no party; he was merely an ignorant, reactionary charlatan with no programme other than a crass support of autocracy. The fact that the Tsar and Tsarina allowed this sinister adventurer (they called him 'the man of God') to interfere in every department of state is in itself enough to show that revolution could hardly have been avoided. Rasputin was at last murdered by high-born conservatives in December 1916; there was no other way of getting rid of him, but the Tsar still refused to listen to the warnings not only of ministers but of his own Grand Ducal relations and the Allied ambassadors in St Petersburg that public discontent had reached a dangerous height.

The revolutionaries remained, as before, totally hostile to the regime. Once more it is impossible to say whether, under a less oppressive and inefficient regime, a sufficient number of them would have abandoned their absolute hostility to the Russian state and would have accepted (Lenin, from his point of view, described the Mensheviks as certain to do so) the bourgeois liberal reforms without attempting to move forward to the second stage of the revolution. The dispute between Bolsheviks and Mensheviks continued; the language used by each party of the other in the years before 1914 was as violent as most of the internal controversies of the left. Lenin spoke of Trotsky's 'incredible bombast'. 'It is impossible to argue with Trotsky on any point of substance, since he has no opinions.' Trotsky wrote in 1913 that the 'whole foundation of Leninism at the present time is built on lying and falsification and carries within itself the poisoned element of its own disintegration'.[2]

Nearly all Russian revolutionaries, whatever their particular affiliations, agreed that a socialist, and not a merely bourgeois revolution could not succeed in Russia unless it were supported by the aid and example of successful revolution elsewhere in

[1] The Tsarevitch suffered from haemophilia.
[2] See E. H. Carr, *The Bolshevik Revolution, 1917–23* (London, 1950) vol. i, p. 63.

Europe. They had also argued that their opportunity would come after the military defeat of their own country. Defeat in the Russo-Japanese War was not sufficiently drastic to prevent the recovery of the autocracy. The situation in 1917 was very different. The war had begun in 1914 with an outburst of patriotic feeling in Russia, as in the other belligerent countries, which was disconcerting for the extreme left since it swept aside all chance of mass proletarian action to stop the fighting. In western Europe, notwithstanding the immense suffering and distress and the growing concern of the peoples that their governments seemed unable to get peace either by victory or negotiation, there were signs of unrest but no immediate loss of control by authority. In Russia, as defeat followed defeat and the internal economy fell into increasing disorder, one fact was tragically clear. Russia had no leadership able to prevent the country from drifting into anarchy. The Tsar remained as remote as he had been in peace time from the desperate realities of his empire, unwilling to accept such sensible advice as he received and unable either to get rid of or to keep his advisers. In the last year of his reign there were four Prime Ministers, four Ministers of the Interior, three Foreign Ministers. Ministerial offices continued to be filled from the bureaucracy and in the months when decisive action, with strong popular backing, was essential, one mediocrity succeeded another and nothing was done to satisfy the mounting demand for change. It was ominous for the army that there had been six different Chiefs of Staff between 1905 and 1914. On 8 March 1917 the Tsar wrote to his wife: 'I shall take up dominoes again in my spare time.'

This day, 8 March, was the beginning of a week of disturbances in which the autocracy collapsed. Rioting broke out in St Petersburg over the shortage of bread; there was actually sufficient food in the city, but no proper system of distribution. On this and succeeding days the police fired on crowds demonstrating in the streets. The factory workers struck and joined the crowds. There was more firing; the soldiers now began to take the side of the rioters. On the morning of 12 March a regiment of the Guards mutinied and by the end of the day most of the St Petersburg garrison had come over to the people.

The rioters had neither leaders nor a programme, but on the evening of 11 March the St Petersburg factory workers had re-established the Soviet which the Government had suppressed in 1905. The Duma appointed a Provisional Committee to deal with the breakdown of authority. The President of the Duma sent a warning to the Tsar on 11 March that 'the last hour had come'. No answer was received. On 14 March the Duma agreed to the appointment of a Provisional Government; the St Petersburg Soviet agreed to give it a conditional support. Next day the Tsar, at the request of the Provisional Government and with the approval of the High Army Command, abdicated in favour of his brother, the Grand Duke Michael, but the Soviet and the soldiers of the St Petersburg garrison would have no more to do with the family of Romanoff.

A month later Lenin, and shortly after him Trotsky, arrived in St Petersburg, the latter from Canada, the former transported from Switzerland in a train provided by the Germans. The Provisional Government thus had to deal with the most dangerous of the revolutionaries at a time when the Russian people had created a situation which the Bolshevik minority could turn to their advantage. The Russian people interpreted the fall of the autocracy as the end of the war. The peasants began to sieze the lands to which they had so long thought that they had a right; the soldiers, except those in actual touch with the enemy, began to desert and to go home in order to claim their share of the land.

Neither the Liberal programme of radical reform and a responsible, balanced government, nor the war against Germany meant anything to these masses of men who had reached the final point of endurance and submission. The Ministers of the Provisional Government realized that Russia was still fighting a war with Allies and that, if Germany won this war, the Russian revolution would have no chance of survival. The masses did not concern themselves with the political future; the Bolsheviks hoped that the Russian abandonment of the war would be followed by similar mass action in the other belligerent countries.

In fact the Allies of Tsarist Russia won the war and, in so

doing (notwithstanding their confused and puny interference in Russia), saved the Bolsheviks from destruction. Lenin did not expect this victory of the western parliamentary democracies; the western victors did not expect that Lenin and his small band of professional revolutionaries would be able to lift Russia out of the anarchy into which she had fallen. It is still not possible, in the short perspective of fifty years, to pass a final, historical judgement on Lenin and his achievements, but his genius as a world figure stands out far more in the sphere of practical action than in the region of ideas.

Lenin's notions of the world in which he lived were narrow and inadequate; his analysis of contemporary events and his forecasts of world revolution everywhere in Europe were almost totally mistaken (they were proved wrong so soon that he had to make rapid adjustments to a new situation). Even the consequences of his own actions in Russia were far from what he had planned. On the other hand his positive achievement in restoring order and authority in the huge Russian state was more remarkable than the success of Peter the Great and those other rulers of Russia whose force of character and violent determination had altered the course of the nation's history.

5. Austria–Hungary

The four countries whose composition and recent history I have outlined developed into nation-states at different times and in different ways, but in each case this development could be called a consolidation based upon a sense of common nationality, of belonging to a single community, even if minorities within these communities had been absorbed and were held there by force. France was already a fully articulated nation-state at the beginning of the nineteenth century and the problem which Frenchmen had to solve was how to establish the institutions which would secure the exercise of sovereignty by the people and not by an absolute ruler. Germans and Italians had first to merge a number of independent sovereignties in order to form a united Germany and Italy and then to find an adequate place in the world for these new states. The Austrian Habsburgs, on the other hand, had to look for a way of keeping together under their rule a number of separate nationalities which were in danger of falling apart and so disrupting the State.

Austria, originally an 'eastern March' peopled by Charlemagne with German settlers, was overrun by the barbarians against whom it was intended as a barrier. The March was re-established by Otto the Great in the tenth century as the Duchy of Austria. After more centuries of violence the Duchy came into the possession of the house of Habsburg which also acquired and managed to keep (except for a short interval) the sovereignty of the Holy Roman Empire. War and politic marriages added to the possessions of these Habsburg rulers until in 1519 the Emperor Charles V inherited, in addition to the original nucleus of Habsburg lands, the Netherlands, Franche Comté, the kingdoms of Naples, Sicily and Sardinia, Spain and the whole of the Spanish Empire.[1]

[1] It is hardly necessary to point out that the facts in this and succeeding paragraphs will become clearer by looking at a historical atlas of Europe in the fifteenth, sixteenth and seventeenth centuries.

Charles V gave his Austrian lands to his younger brother, Ferdinand, who had married the daughter of the King of Bohemia and Hungary. On the death, without male issue, of this king in battle against the Turks in 1526, Ferdinand was accepted as heir by the two kingdoms and thus ruled over more non-German than German subjects. Bohemia and Hungary had their own separate histories. Bohemia was predominantly Slav, with a German admixture; the early national consciousness of its Czech inhabitants was shown in the popular support of the religious reformer, John Hus.[1] The Magyars of Hungary were neither Teutonic nor Slav; they spoke a language which had no affinity with any other European tongue except Finnish. The independent kingdom of Croatia (once a province of the Byzantine Empire) had been linked with Hungary since the early twelfth century. The Magyars had also extended their sovereignty over the Slovaks to the north-west and Transylvania to the south-east. The Slovaks had never had an independent status and nearly all of them were peasant serfs. Transylvania had a mixed population of Magyars, Roumanians and Germans (these latter had come into the country as settlers in the thirteenth century). The Magyars had obtained for themselves, about the time when King John of England was forced to grant the concessions embodied in Magna Carta, somewhat similar rights against their own sovereign. In the so-called Golden Bull of 1356 they secured a national assembly to which the third estate sent members from the counties and towns, though their votes counted for less than those of the nobility.

The willingness of Hungary and Bohemia to accept a Habsburg sovereign was mainly due to the menace of the Turks. After defeating the Magyars at Mohacs in 1526, the Turks had overrun a great part of Hungary. The Habsburg monarchs slowly won back much of this lost territory; the highest point

[1] John Hus (1373–1415) became Rector of the University of Prague in 1402. He accepted the teaching of the English John Wyclif and was excommunicated after protesting against the burning of Wyclif's writings by the archbishop of Prague. Hus and his heretical doctrines became increasingly popular in Bohemia. He was invited under a safe-conduct to the Council of Constance, but when he got there he was imprisoned and, after a refusal to recant his beliefs, burned at the stake.

of Turkish aggression was in 1683 when they beseiged Vienna and might have captured it but for the help of a Polish army which came to the assistance of Austria under the Polish king, John Sobieski. From this time Turkish power declined rapidly; after 1718 the Danube and the Save formed roughly the frontier between the Habsburg dominions and the Ottoman Empire. The Habsburgs had also to fight protestantism which, before the Counter-Reformation, seemed likely to drive out the Catholic Church, especially from Hussite Bohemia. There followed a catholic revival, of which the reforms of the Council of Trent were evidence, and in which the Jesuits were the most remarkable instruments. This national reconversion – no other term is adequate – was enforced by long and bloody fighting; the Bohemian protestants were utterly defeated at the battle of the White Mountain near Prague in 1621. Most of the Czech nobility who were not killed in the battle went into exile and lost their estates; the Czech nation was reduced to a peasantry and, in stamping out heresy, the Habsburgs also destroyed almost all that remained of Bohemian liberties and national existence.[1] The division between catholic and protestant Germany after the terrible Thirty Years War in the first half of the seventeenth century reduced the Holy Roman Empire to little more than a titular sovereignty; the Habsburgs became more interested in Italy and the lower Danube lands and, in any case, began to suffer from the aggressive territorial ambitions of the Hohenzollerns. Frederick II of Prussia compelled the Empress Maria Theresa to surrender Silesia (part of the old dominions of the Bohemian Crown) to Prussia, though Maria Theresa later took her share in the partition of Poland. Maria Theresa and, with less caution, her son, Joseph II, while nominally respecting the rights of Hungary and what little was left of the rights of Bohemia, attempted to modernize, that is to say to centralize, the administration of their multi-national and multi-lingual empire. Centralization was bound to lead, at least linguistically, to germanization. Neither Maria Theresa nor Joseph II was German in a nationalist sense; they merely took the practical line that a central administration for the monarchy

[1] They even destroyed Czech books.

must be German. Obviously, however, this germanization would be resented if circumstances brought about a revival of nationalist feeling in the non-German lands. Joseph II's reforms were meticulous and far-reaching; they included the institution of a secret police to spy on officials. The agricultural reforms did not abolish serfdom, but improved the legal status and lightened many of the burdens of the peasants.

Joseph attempted too much and paid too little attention to vested rights and interests. In 1788 he had to give way to Hungarian opposition and in 1789 to revoke his attacks on the liberties of the Netherlands. He delayed too long about this revocation with the result that in January 1790 – a month before the Emperor's death – the Estates of Flanders declared open rebellion. Joseph II's successor was his brother, Leopold, Grand Duke of Tuscany. Leopold was a wiser and more conciliatory man, but he died within two years of coming to Vienna and these two years had been disturbed by the increasing turmoil of events in revolutionary France. The Habsburgs could have nothing to do with the French revolutionary idea of the sovereignty of 'la nation'. They were also unable to hold out later against the armies of Napoleon. After the battle of Wagram in July 1809 and the treaty of Vienna in the following October, they gave up hope of further resistance. Metternich,[1] who became Foreign Minister, told the Emperor Francis a month after Wagram that Austria must confine herself to 'manœuvre, evasion and compliance. In this way alone can we hope possibly to maintain our existence until the day of general deliverance.' Two years earlier Metternich had commented upon Napoleon's career that 'it is curious that Napoleon, while tormenting and modifying incessantly the relations of all the European states, has not yet taken a single step which will tend to assure the permanence of his successes.'

The House of Habsburg fell back on its old policy of dynastic

[1] Count Metternich (b. 1773) was a Rhinelander and (like his father) entered imperial service. His marriage with a daughter of the Austrian Chancellor Kaunitz opened his way into high Viennese society. From 1803 to 1806 he was Ambassador in Berlin and from 1806 to 1809 Ambassador in Paris.

marriages. The Emperor gave his daughter, Marie Louise, as a wife to Napoleon and then awaited his chance to join the final coalition which brought about the defeat and collapse of the French Empire. In the European settlement of 1815 Austria did reasonably well. She lost her former outlying territories in the Low Countries, but gained Venetia and the Dalmation possessions of the Venetian republic, and recovered Lombardy. Members of the Habsburg family ruled Tuscany, Modena and Parma and Austrian influence predominated in the kingdom of the Two Sicilies. Austria also kept Polish Galicia and reasserted her position in Germany by getting the Presidency of the new Confederation. Her financial recovery, though slow and never complete, was enough to keep the Empire going.

The fundamental weakness of this heterogeneous Empire was its incompatibility with the liberal and nationalist ideas which had survived the military defeat of the French armies. The combination of liberalism and nationalism was not to be lasting in Europe; it continued long enough to embarrass a state which was both multi-national and opposed to all forms of popular sovereignty. A concession to liberal demands in any part of the Habsburg Empire might open the way to disruption and therefore had to be resisted. In order to prevent the contagion from spreading, Austrian policy had to be anti-liberal everywhere in Europe. Austria suppressed liberal movements in Italy; Austria and Prussia suppressed them in Germany.

The Emperor Francis I,[1] hard-working, conscientious, narrow-minded – he approached the political question like a carpenter making holes with a gimlet – maintained this policy of negation; it never occurred to him to do otherwise, and Metternich, a far abler man who had little influence on domestic policy, though he agreed with its negative character, also tried, without inner hope of success, to check the spread of liberalism in Europe. Francis died in 1835; his son and successor, Ferdinand, was almost a half-wit; under his nominal direction the leaders of the administration disagreed among themselves, but

[1] Francis II ceased to be Holy Roman Emperor with the abolition of the Empire in 1806. He then assumed the title of Emperor of Austria and, as the first of his kind, became 'Francis I'.

Austria-Hungary 225

continued their negative policy while the tide of revolution mounted.

'The 'system', if such a name can be given to it, was unlikely to survive a combined attack from different quarters; the revolutionary assault which would destroy the regime might come from any one of various discontented elements. The crisis began in 1845. Harvests were bad in this year and again in 1846. There were disastrous floods in Galicia and in North Italy, an outbreak of cattle plague in Hungary, potato blight in Silesia. Conditions were no better in 1847; food prices more than doubled and unemployment increased in industrial areas. Everywhere in the countryside the peasants were agitating for the abolition of their compulsory labour services (*robot*) or just refusing to perform them. Hunger typhus broke out in various parts of the Empire and Vienna was full of starving people.

The most surprising and, from the Austrian point of view, the most dangerous political development occurred in Italy, where the election in 1847 of a supposedly liberal pope – Pius IX – started a belief that he would head an anti-Austrian movement throughout the peninsula. Rioting began in Milan and spread to other parts of Italy at the end of 1847. Early in 1848 a rebellion broke out in Sicily and extended to Naples. King Ferdinand promised his subjects a constitution. Other Italian princes had to follow with similar concessions. Charles Albert of Piedmont, who was afraid of his own position if he did not himself lead the movement against Austria, began to move troops to the border of Lombardy. The Austrian military position was difficult; over a third of their infantry in Lombardy-Venetia were Italian.

The news of the revolution in Paris in February 1848 had immediate repercussions throughout the Habsburg Empire. The Czechs asked for a reformed Diet and an administration centralized in Prague for the lands of the Bohemian Crown. In Hungary, Kossuth[1] demanded and obtained an independent,

---

[1] Louis Kossuth (1802–94) came of an impoverished Hungarian noble family. His father was a lawyer and the son at first worked with him. He came into prominence over his illegal publication of reports of the proceedings of the Hungarian Diet and later edited a 'patriotic' newspaper

responsible Hungarian ministry with complete financial control. In Vienna popular disturbances compelled the resignation of Metternich, and the Emperor was forced to agree to a constitution with a single parliament (Reichsrat) and a responsible ministry for all the Austrian lands.

In Italy riots broke out in Milan; Radetsky, the Austrian army commander, had to leave the city and retire to the fortresses of the so-called Quadrilateral;[1] a large number of his Italian troops deserted. The military governor of Venice surrendered the city without attempting resistance and the citizens proclaimed a republic. Charles Albert issued a proclamation sympathizing with the Lombards and Venetians and on 23 March crossed the frontier into Lombardy. Other Italian princes either ran away or declared for the Italian cause against the Austrians; even the pope allowed papal troops to be concentrated at Bologna. Finally the meeting of the Vorparlament at Frankfurt[2] seemed to be taking the German question out of the hands of the sovereigns and their governments; the surrender of the king of Prussia to the Berlin rebels and his declaration that henceforward Prussia would be merged into Germany was ominous for the isolation of Austria. On 17 May the Emperor Ferdinand started out from his palace in Vienna, apparently on an afternoon drive. He went on driving through the night and the next day until on 19 May he had reached Innsbruck.

At this point an observer might have thought that the Habsburg Empire was certain to break up or at all events that it could never recover its former position. In fact, the conservative forces now began to regain control and the liberals and nationalist opposition to disintegrate. There were a good many reasons for this disintegration. The physical force behind the

[1] Mantua, Peschiera, Verona, Legnano. These fortresses secured the entry into Italy from the north.
[2] See chapter on Germany, p. 109.

---

with a very wide circulation. Kossuth was a brilliant writer and orator and his fiery enthusiasm for Hungary gave him a leading position in the years 1848–9; but he was less good as a man of action and the great fault of his policy was his total neglect of and even contempt for the aspirations of the Slavs.

revolution in Vienna had come largely from the proletariat who were driven to rebellion out of misery and hunger, and from students who had not thought out the consequences of their actions and were easily diverted into extravagant and impracticable political plans. On the motion of one of the students the Committee of Security, which was in fact controlling the city after Ferdinand had left it, brought forward a motion in favour of providing work or maintenance for the unemployed. This measure, like the establishment of the National Workshops in Paris, drew to the capital large numbers of workless men from outside it; they came from all parts of Austria, including Bohemia, and added greatly to the threat of further disorder. The middle class, who had been satisfied with the fall of Metternich and the grant of a constitution, were alarmed at the danger of social revolution and had no wish for the overthrow of the economic order. The disappearance of the Emperor and of a large number of the wealthier classes from the city had dislocated business and the provincial towns were regarding the growing anarchy in the capital with suspicion. The interest of the peasants everywhere was limited to securing the end of what remained of their servitudes. Furthermore the nationalists who were demanding self-government for themselves weakened their position by refusing similar demands from other minorities within their own areas. The Magyars, in particular, maintained everywhere their own linguistic and administrative control, at first in the naïve belief that the minorities in the lands of the Hungarian Crown would be satisfied with the assertion of Magyar rights against Austria. They alienated the Croats and other southern Slavs who then took the obvious line of supporting the Austrian Army in its attack on Hungary.

The attitude of the army was indeed the key to the situation. Prince Windisch-Graetz, a determined if not brilliant commander,[1] put an end in the second week of June to rioting in

[1] Field-Marshal Prince Windisch-Graetz (1787–1862) had fought in the Napoleonic wars and was almost a caricature of a conservative military grandee. He had been in command of the Austrian troops in Bohemia since 1840.

Prague by threatening to bombard the city if it did not surrender. He then declared the whole of Bohemia under a state of siege, arrested the leaders of the disturbances (which he alleged to have been fomented by foreign agitators) and forcibly imposed quiet. One nationalist revolution had thus been suppressed. An even greater success for the army came in Italy. If Radetsky[1] had been defeated by rapid Italian action, the Habsburg monarchy would almost certainly have collapsed elsewhere. Charles Albert, however, was afraid of intervention by the republican French and of republican movements in north Italy. The Piedmontese took Peschiera in May, but failed to capture Verona. In June Radetsky, who had already received some, though not enough, reinforcements, reoccupied Vicenza. In July he completely defeated the Piedmontese at Custozza and drove them out of Lombardy. Charles Albert signed an armistice on 8 August; the army of Radetsky, and particularly its Croatian regiments, were now available for the more difficult fighting against Hungary.

The Hungarians had refused the Croat demands in October and, after fruitless negotiations, Jellacic, the Ban (Viceroy) of Croatia, invaded Hungarian territory. The Hungarians defeated him without much difficulty and forced him to go back into Croatia. The situation in Vienna seemed to have become more out of hand, but the conservative military commanders could now begin their counter-action. The new Austrian Reichsrat which was to settle the details of a constitution opened in Vienna three days before the battle of Custozza and at once fell into disputes over the languages to be allowed in its discussions. In August and September there were riots in the city by the workers on the public works – mostly unskilled forms of labour – provided by the authorities. The riots, which were supported by the students, were put down with considerable loss of life; the Government closed the University and sent all the non-Viennese labourers to work on railway building some distance from the capital, while the non-Viennese students went

---

[1] Count Radetsky (1762–1858) had also fought (with greater distinction than Windisch-Graetz) in the Napoleonic wars, especially in Italy. He was extremely popular with his soldiers.

home. After more rioting early in October, the Emperor Ferdinand, who had come back to the capital from Innsbruck in June, was again taken from Vienna – this time to Olmütz. Windisch-Graetz was now given full powers to restore order in Vienna. He had a force of some 70,000 troops and repeated the ruthless tactics which had succeeded at Prague. The arrival of a detachment of Hungarians, for whose aid the left-wing Viennese radicals had asked, only caused Windisch-Graetz to be more severe in his treatment of the rebels.[1]

The Viennese bourgeoisie welcomed the restoration of order; the revolutionary movement was over. A new ministry was formed under the presidency of Prince Schwarzenberg, a brother-in-law of Windisch-Graetz. Schwarzenberg was the type of man, like Mirabeau, suited for 'the day after a revolution'.[2] Hitherto – again like Mirabeau – he had rather wasted his talents; he now showed great energy and, from his own point of view, great ability. His political convictions were somewhat uncertain; he believed in order and in the Habsburg monarchy as a guarantee of order, but he was not opposed to a limited constitutional regime. He chose able ministers and had a clear view of what he wanted. One of his first acts was to secure the abdication of the Emperor Ferdinand (partly in order to be able to repudiate the concessions promised by him to Hungary) in favour of his nephew, Francis Joseph. In a proclamation announcing his accession, Francis Joseph repeated the promise of constitutional government, but insisted upon the unity of all the peoples of the monarchy in a single body politic.

Before dealing with Hungary Schwarzenberg was able to free himself of any trouble in Italy and to be assured that the Frankfurt Parliament would not cause difficulties about the position of Austria in Germany. Charles Albert, in the belief that he might now get French help without the danger of

[1] Windisch-Graetz never bothered himself to find excuses for extreme severity, but he was able to claim that the revolutionaries had broken their word to him. They had agreed to surrender the city but, on the approach of the Hungarians, they repudiated their promise in the expectation that Hungarian help had arrived in force.

[2] Schwarzenberg (1800–52) had begun his career in the army, but on the advice of Metternich had changed to the diplomatic service.

republicanism, denounced the armistice which he had signed after Custozza. He was again easily defeated by Radetsky and had to abdicate. Venice held out a little longer, but in August the Austrians were back again in possession of their Italian provinces. As for Germany, the Frankfurt Parliament had answered the refusal of Austria to separate the German and non-German lands of the Empire by excluding her from the new Germany and offering the crown to Prussia. The King of Prussia, much as he wanted such a crown, was unable and unwilling to take it from the Frankfurt liberals and against the resistance of Austria. The Frankfurt Parliament thus collapsed.

The subjection of Hungary was a more difficult matter. The Magyars, under Kossuth's impulsion, refused to give up any of the concessions made by Ferdinand or even to recognize Francis Joseph until he had been crowned King of Hungary and taken an oath to respect the Hungarian constitution. In April 1849 the Hungarian Diet announced the deposition of the House of Habsburg from the throne of Hungary and the full independence of the country with Kossuth as President Regent. The extreme nationalists had now gone too far for moderate Hungarian opinion. Many deputies to the Diet disagreed with the deposition of the sovereign and – a more serious matter – many Hungarian officers felt debarred by their military oath from supporting a regime which had repudiated their lawful king. The Austrian Government appealed to the Tsar for help. Nicholas I wanted everywhere the suppression of rebellion against monarchy and was particularly concerned with the nearness of Hungary to his own dominions; furthermore a considerable number of Polish refugees had joined the rebel Hungarian Army. The Tsar had already allowed Russian troops to go to the help of the Austrians in Galicia. With this force, and over 175,000 Austrians against them, the Hungarians could not escape total defeat. They surrendered in August 1849; Kossuth and about 4,000 others escaped into Turkey; the ringleaders who were caught were treated with great severity.[1]

---

[1] General Haynau (nicknamed in England 'General Hyena'), who was in command in Hungary, already had a sinister reputation for severity in Italy. Haynau was remarkably obtuse in his failure to understand his own

Austria–Hungary 231

The Emperor Francis Joseph, upon whom ultimate responsibility now rested for the preservation of the Empire, was a young man of eighteen. He reigned for sixty-eight years, during which he showed a certain flat consistency of aim, though not of tactics. Towards the end of his life Francis Joseph held a position not unlike that of Queen Victoria in her later years. He had signed all the laws which had made the modern Austro-Hungarian state; his existence was a guarantee against a catastrophe – the break-up of this state – which appeared likely after his death, though few of his subjects really wanted its total dissolution. Francis Joseph was the only person in his dominions whose interests were general in the sense that they were concerned with the Empire as a whole; he was the keystone of an arch representing the thrust of the various nationalities. His position would have been difficult enough if he had been an exceptionally able man. He was not stupid; he had a remarkable knowledge of languages, a good memory and a natural shrewdness, as well as genuinely good manners,[1] but he was unimaginative (he was completely without interest in literature, art or music), insensitive and narrow-minded. He worked hard and regarded himself always as the impersonal servant of the house of Habsburg, whose continued existence was necessary to his subjects and must be put before everything else.[2] An Austrian historian has written of him that 'he neither

---

[1] One of his Ministers said of Francis Joseph that the only way to make him accept any proposal which he disliked was to be brusque almost to the point of rudeness with him. He was so unused to treatment of this kind that he became too much disconcerted to resist it.

[2] In his later years the Emperor became a close friend of a charming and good-hearted Viennese actress, Katherina Schratt. He used to have breakfast with her almost daily – at the early hour of 6 a.m.!

---

unpopularity. When he visited England a little later he was mobbed by the workmen of Barclay's brewery (one of the sights of early Victorian London). Lord Palmerston's answer to the Queen's wish for an apology for this indirect insult to a foreign sovereign was to speak of the 'want of propriety' on Haynau's part in coming to a country where he was regarded as a 'moral criminal'. When Russell, as Prime Minister, later asked Palmerston not to entertain Kossuth after he had come to London from Turkey, Palmerston replied that he could not allow the Prime Minister to dictate to him what guests he might receive at his private house.

loved nor hated; he approved or disapproved'. His own personal life was tragic. His wife left him to wander distractedly around Europe and was assassinated by an anarchist; his son killed himself in tragic circumstances. In every blow of fate, personal or political, Francis Joseph sacrificed his own feelings and expected others to do the same. For this arid routine of service he looked primarily for assistance from the high aristocracy – the nobility of birth (there were three nobilities in Vienna, the nobility of birth, that of service and the so-called 'banker's nobility'). These highly bred figures were in fact not of much use to him. They had been dropping out of most of the important ministerial posts and few of them had any taste for the routine work of the central administration. They were not to be found in large numbers even in the army.

Francis Joseph and his advisers were convinced that the only safe policy for the Empire was one of complete centralization in the higher ranges of government, but without a central assembly or real parliamentary institutions to whom the ministers would be responsible. On Schwarzenberg's advice the Emperor moved away in stages from the early promises of 1848 and then from a constitution promulgated after dismissing the Reichsrat to a new constitution in 1851. This new constitution, if such a title can be given to it, cancelled all the fundamental rights previously promulgated except the abolition of peasant servitudes and the equality of citizens before the law. After Schwarzenberg's sudden death in April 1852 Francis Joseph decided not to appoint another Minister President but to exercise control in person. Since he also regarded foreign affairs as especially within his personal direction, and since after the resignation of the Minister of War in 1853 no successor was appointed, the Emperor had in fact restored the old bureaucratic absolutism.

This period of absolute rule lasted until the military defeats of 1859 and the loss of Lombardy.[1] Administratively these years were not entirely barren. Most of the peasants in the Empire were transformed into small freeholders. There was a rapid advance in railway building, with the usual economic advan-

[1] See above, pp. 156–158.

tages, though the State finances never got out of difficulty and lack of money was one reason for the disgraceful condition of the army in 1859. The regime obviously did nothing to satisfy the nationalist aspirations which had been beaten down but not destroyed in 1848–9. There was, however, little open disaffection except in Lombardy-Venetia and in Hungary. Hungarian discontent was the most dangerous feature. The loss of the Italian provinces, though economically serious, would not be vital to the Empire; but it could hardly survive the defection of Hungary. A less clumsy diplomacy on the Austrian side might have avoided the war of 1859 against France and Piedmont; a less incompetent conduct of the war would almost certainly have forced Napoleon III, and therefore Piedmont, to withdraw from it on terms more favourable to Austria than those actually agreed. Francis Joseph was too much afraid of revolution at home to call on his subjects to fight the war to a finish and in any case the Austrian financial position was now almost desperate. Diplomatically Francis Joseph, who still hoped for an Italian federation which Austria might dominate, was almost as much tricked by Cavour as Napoleon was tricked after the war.

After this military failure Francis Joseph was compelled to make political concessions to his subjects. He agreed to an enlarged Reichsrat with representatives chosen from the Landtage[1] of the different lands of Austria to consider financial reform. The new Reichsrat in turn demanded other reforms; the Emperor, with his usual reluctance, issued a Diploma in October 1860 giving the Reichsrat a good deal of control of local affairs and making its consent necessary for taxation. A few months later Francis Joseph went a little further; the Reichsrat now had to consent to legislation, though the Government could act on its own authority when the Reichsrat was not sitting and the Emperor still rejected the principle of ministerial responsibility. A more significant concession was a change in the composition of the Reichsrat which greatly increased the

[1] The Landtage were almost exclusively assemblies of the greater and lesser nobility and in no sense representative of the population as a whole.

importance of the German bourgeoisie. Ultimately the Reichsrat extorted from the Emperor a recognition that the ministers should be responsible to itself as well as to the monarch.

These changes totally failed to satisfy the Hungarians, who would accept nothing less than the abolition of the centralist regime and the full restoration of the rights of the Hungarian Crown and constitution. The Slavs, or most of them, also objected to the continued centralization.

Once again the dénouement came after military defeat. The Austro-Prussian War of 1866 was a deliberate act of Prussian policy;[1] Prussia had long regarded war as inevitable in order to get rid of the old Confederation which, on Schwarzenberg's insistence, had been restored in 1851 (though without the inclusion, as Schwarzenberg had wished, of the non-German Habsburg lands). Bismarck had prepared for the war by a clever manipulation of the Slesvig-Holstein question and by the diplomatic isolation of Austria in Europe; Moltke had prepared for it by the reorganization of the Prussian Army. The Austrian Foreign Minister, Count Mensdorff-Pouilly, was an amiable cavalry officer; the Austrian Army had again been starved owing to lack of money and also because the Austrian-German liberals distrusted it for its support of high conservative policy. Francis Joseph early in 1866 had wanted to rearm the infantry with the new breech-loading rifle already adopted by the Prussians, but no money was available. The Emperor himself was responsible for the worst military blunder in his appointment of General Benedek to command in the all-important Bohemian theatre of war, where he would have to meet Moltke, and of the Archduke Albert to command in the secondary Italian theatre. Benedek was a good fighting officer, familiar with the campaigning area in Italy where he had done well in the 1859 war; the Archduke was much more skilled and better trained to deal with the Prussians. Benedek knew his own limitations and accepted the Bohemian command against his will. The deciding factor with the Emperor seems to have been his fear of the effect upon the dynasty of a defeat of an army led by a member of the imperial house. Benedek was defeated in

[1] See above, pp. 117–118.

Bohemia (partly through the culpable neglect of his subordinates)[1] within three weeks.

The military defeat of 1866 and the establishment of a North German Confederation – from which Austria was excluded – under Prussian hegemony meant that the attempt to maintain centralism at Vienna was now impossible. The Austrian Germans were still the largest single national group in the Empire, but they were outnumbered to the extent of three to one by the other nationalities and two to one by the Slavs.[2] A federation of the Monarchy would therefore have put the Germans in a minority. The obvious solution and the line of least resistance was an equal partnership between the Germans of Austria and the Magyars of Hungary, though such a solution would dissatisfy the Slavs. The German–Magyar partnership was worked out in the *Ausgleich*, or compromise, of 1867 in which each side made concessions.[3]

Under the terms of the *Ausgleich* Austria–Hungary[4] was not a single state but a unit formed of two states linked by the person of the ruler, with certain common ministries and a common army. There were separate parliaments, but no common Austro-Hungarian parliament. The Magyars would never have agreed to a common parliament since they would have been outvoted in it. A curious system of 'delegations' was set up to provide some form of communication between the two parliaments. Sixty members from the Austrian and sixty from the Hungarian parliament met alternatively in Vienna and Budapest. They held separate meetings and communicated with each other in writing. If after three such communications they could not agree, they held a plenary session with an equal number of delegates

---

[1] Francis Joseph never allowed Benedek to publish his own justification.

[2] See also below, p. 237.

[3] The violent denunciation of the *Ausgleich* by the exiled Kossuth actually helped the Magyars to get the settlement through, since it made the Austrians readier to make concessions.

[4] The name 'Austria–Hungary', without the addition of 'Reich', was accepted after some discussion. In fact there was neither an official 'Austria' nor an official 'Hungary'. The official designation of Austria was 'the kingdom and lands represented in the Reichsrat' and of Hungary, 'the lands of St Stephen's crown'.

from each side. These delegates then settled the matter in dispute by a majority vote without discussion. If there were no majority, the decision was left to the common sovereign, the Emperor-King.

Since there was no common parliament, there could be no general ministerial responsibility to an elected body. There were common Ministers for Foreign Affairs, Finance and War. They were appointed and could be dismissed by the Emperor; they reported to the Delegations, not to the Austrian or Hungarian parliaments. The Foreign Minister was thus isolated from direct parliamentary control; he met the other common Ministers and the Austrian and Hungarian Ministers-President in an informal Crown Council – the only approximation to a common Cabinet – but other Austrian and Hungarian Ministers attended only on invitation. In the summer of 1914 neither the Austrian nor the Hungarian parliaments were called to meet between March and the outbreak of war.[1] At the decisive sessions of ministers between 7 and 19 July, when the ultimatum to Serbia was settled, the only persons present were the Emperor, the Foreign Minister, the Finance Minister, the two Ministers-President, the Chief of the joint General Staff and a naval representative.

Francis Joseph regarded the *Ausgleich* as a final settlement of the relations between Austria and Hungary, while the Hungarian nationalists thought of it only as a stage in the assertion of complete Hungarian sovereignty. None the less, and in spite of continual bickering and bargaining, especially on financial questions, the settlement of 1867 remained in force until 1918 and was the determining factor, directly or indirectly, in the history of the Habsburg Empire as a whole, as well as in the uneasy and confused relationship between the two legally dominant partners and the other nationalities claiming special recognition.

This jarring and jostling of the nationalities prevented the

---

[1] The Austrian Reichsrat was prorogued in March 1914 owing to the persistent obstruction of business by the Czechs. This obstruction was in retaliation for similar tactics by the Germans in the Bohemian Landtag. During the war the Reichsrat building was used as a hospital.

development of a sound parliamentary life in either half of the dual state, while the lack of political leadership except in the negative form of protests and lobbying for separate interests gave too great an influence to the bureaucracy, especially in Austria. Ministries tended to be formed of officials because there was no one else to take office. The bureaucracy had the faults of all over-powerful administrative services; resentment of criticism combined with dislike of responsibility, over-respect for routine and hierarchical gradation, collective arrogance and, above all, too great an emphasis on police supervision. Austria-Hungary was a police state in the sense that police supervision was not limited to the prevention and detection of crime. The police were less oppressive and more humane than in Russia and better-mannered than in Prussia. Nevertheless, police supervision existed and stifled a great deal of the free public criticism essential to a healthy political life. The danger in this respect was intensified by the fact that most of the high judicial posts in the Empire were given to legal officials. Promotion to these posts went to men whose compliance was known and who were unlikely to take an impartial line in cases affecting the activities and interests of the bureaucracy.

Owing to the dominance of the bureaucracy the conflict between the nationalities became very largely a struggle, not for political power to be won by a free vote, but for the control of the civil service. The demand for national schools, that is to say, for schools in which instruction was given in the vernacular language of the area concerned, was fundamentally a demand for machines to produce officials who could speak the local languages and belonged to the local national groups.

The situation was more acute in Austria than in Hungary because the Magyars were more able than the Germans to dominate their part of the monarchy. There were seventeen 'kingdoms and lands represented in the Reichsrat'. In the census of 1910 – the percentages had not changed much during the previous forty years – about a third of the population of some $28\frac{1}{2}$ millions was German, nearly a quarter Czech or Slovak, about 17 per cent Polish, nearly 13 per cent Ruthenian,[1] under

---

[1] Most of them in Eastern Galicia.

5 per cent Slovene, 2¾ per cent Serbian and Croatian[1] and under 3 per cent Italian or Ladin.[2] The nationalities were distributed roughly as follows: Upper and Lower Austria, the north Tyrol and Vorarlberg and the Salzkammergut were almost entirely German. There was a German majority in Styria and Carinthia; Germans were more numerous than any nationality in Austrian Silesia and formed a 25 per cent minority in Bohemia and Moravia. The Germans were better-off than any other of the Austrian nationalities; the average German paid twice as much in taxes as the average Czech and seven times as much as the average Austrian southern Slav.

The Slavs taken together were a majority in Austria, but they were neither geographically contiguous nor united in language, culture and political aims. The Poles and the Czechs were 'submerged' nationalities in the sense that they had been deprived of their independence by force, but there was little collaboration between them. The Poles were more interested in the Polish question than in the future of Austria; the Austrian Poles were only a narrow majority in their own area and were willing to sell their support to the centralizing policy of the monarchy in return for the maintenance of their local predominance. The Czechs and Slovaks had no interests outside the monarchy and for a time looked only for equal status with the Germans and Magyars. The Slovenes wanted at least the use of their own language in government and education and at most an Illyrian kingdom which would include the Croats. The Serbs, or most of them, wanted to leave the monarchy and to unite with the kingdom of Serbia. The Italians of Trieste and Fiume hoped for union with Italy and those of the Tyrol at least for local independence. The Italians on the Dalmatian coast wanted protection from the Slavs of the hinterland and supported the German centralists.

---

[1] The Serbs and Croats had a common language, but the fact that the former had been Christianized long ago from Byzantium and the latter from Rome gave them different religious allegiances, alphabets and historic traditions.

[2] Ladin, the fourth language of modern Switzerland, was spoken by peasants in the area of Austria bordering on the Grisons and the Engadine.

These circumstances explain why the Germans were able to keep their predominance and yet failed to carry through a constructive policy based upon it. After 1866 the Germans, or at least the German liberal bourgeois, wanted to 'westernize' Austria on a German basis. They therefore worked for centralization which meant, as in Maria Theresa's time, germanization. They claimed that culturally the German element was stronger than any other. A German deputy once went into the Landtag of Carinthia carrying, as he said, the whole of Slovene literature under his arm. The Czechs had a much stronger case against German domination. After the middle years of the century a Czech national revival made rapid progress. The national movement was spread through Czech schools, Czech co-operative societies, savings banks and other economic organizations. Sport was not neglected; the gymnastic organization known as the Sokol, founded in 1863, was far more than a society to promote physical fitness. The Czechs were no longer a nation of peasants; they possessed an active middle class which was finding its way into big business, a large number of industrial workers and a disproportionate share in the minor and middle ranks of the Austrian administration. In 1881 they opened a Czech National Theatre and in the following year a Czech University in Prague. Prague itself, from being almost entirely German-speaking, was becoming almost entirely a Czech city. The Czechs could not deny that a Czech who learned German widened his interests much more than a German who learned Czech, but this kind of argument carried no weight with nationalist enthusiasts, though obviously they did learn German.

Furthermore, the Germans themselves were divided. The dominant liberal party had to meet the opposition of the Catholic Church and the landed nobility to the centralizing policy which was essential to the realization of the liberal programme, but which would have lessened the importance of the provincial Diets, the only representative institutions in which the conservatives could retain their influence. The liberals also had to meet the small but noisy party of Pan-Germans who were willing to see the break-up of Austria and the absorption of her German citizens in the Reich rather than a solution of the Austrian problem which would take control out of German hands. Above all, the liberals were increasingly attacked from the Left as a capitalist party.

Austria was backward in social legislation, though her industrial population had been increasing very considerably since the 1850s. Until the collapse of the abolutist regime the workers had no means of making their grievances known, still less of using political pressure to remedy them. Before 1867 there was no general right of association. In 1870 the workers were given such rights which, almost by definition, included the right to strike, but they suffered from administrative repression when they tried to exercise this right. The Government still refused legal limitation on the hours of work for adult men. Other measures of social legislation were prepared but not carried into effect for another decade; a series of laws was then introduced – largely copied from German models. The laws were too often evaded and many workpeople turned in desperation to anarchism. An anti-anarchist law, with severe penalties, was passed in 1886.

From about this time there was a change for the better, owing, to a considerable extent, to the efforts of a few individuals. One of these reformers, Freiherr von Vogelsang, a member of a protestant Prussian family which had settled in Vienna and turned catholic, initiated a Christian Social Movement which did much to awaken the public conscience. Another reformer was Dr Viktor Adler, a well-to-do Viennese physician, who brought together a Social Democratic Party on Marxist lines out of the small existing socialist groups which, in Austria as elsewhere, had been wasting themselves in doctrinal quarrels. A third figure, Dr Karl Lueger, was a less disinterested politician. Lueger, the son of a Viennese concierge, obtained a name for himself by his attacks on vested interest and corruption. In 1875 he was elected to the Vienna Municipal Council and ten years later to the Reichsrat. After 1888 he joined with Vogelsang in forming a Christian Social Party. In 1895 the Christian Social Party won a majority on the Vienna Municipal Council and Lueger became Burgomaster of the city. Lueger was a remarkable administrator and did much for the municipal services of Vienna. His influence over the 'little men' – the small shopkeepers and artisans – was immense, but he was never a leader of the industrial workers and his activities had a discreditable side in their demagogic anti-semitism.[1]

The problem of the Jews in Austria and Hungary was a genuine one, though it could only be aggravated by anti-semitism. Before 1850 the Jewish population of Vienna was not more than a few thousands. Modern anti-semitism, in contrast with the traditional prejudices of medieval Christendom, became a serious factor only after the large-scale Jewish immigration into Austria, and particularly into Vienna, following the grant of full civil liberties in 1867. In 1870 the number of Jews in Vienna had risen to 40,000; it increased to 70,000 in 1880 and to more than twice as many in 1910. Most of the immigrants came from Galicia and most of them were poor, but those who climbed out of poverty soon established themselves in industry, banking and certain professions, especially in medicine. Their success caused a certain ill-feeling among the classes who suffered from the sharpness of Jewish wits and the traditional Jewish habit of going to the extremes of competition in a competitive society. The competition of small Jewish traders and artisans, the part played by Jews in the development of machine industry and the consequent displacement of handworkers gave an opportunity for demagogues to stir up anti-semitic feeling. The severe Austrian financial crisis of 1873 was commonly attributed to Jewish speculation. For obvious reasons the Jews tended to join the German liberal party; they also played a leading part in the development of Austrian socialism.[2]

The German liberals could go to a certain distance. They had

[1] Hitler gives Lueger extravagant praise in *Mein Kampf*. It would be unfair to Lueger to describe his career as an anticipation of that of Hitler, but their anti-semitism had the same roots.

[2] One difficulty in the way of a dispassionate treatment of the problem caused by this large Jewish infiltration was that the serious press of Vienna was almost entirely in Jewish hands and refused to admit that there was a real problem and not merely ill-founded and mischievous anti-semitic prejudice.

secured the fundamental laws securing parliamentary government of a limited kind, a limited ministerial responsibility, a much greater degree of civil liberty than Austrians had previously enjoyed, control of the budget and, against the resistance of the catholic hierarchy, civil marriage and secular direction of education. They made no headway, however, against the opposition of the non-German nationalities.

In all this mélange of nationalist squabbling and social discontent there was no German party strong enough or indeed willing to bring about a political solution on federal lines, and Francis Joseph had not the largeness of imagination to attempt a policy which involved a risk of disruption and certainly a weakening of the authority and exercise of the residual powers of the house of Habsburg. The political life of Austria inside and outside the Reichsrat thus jolted on in a continual wrangle between nationalist groups and a fight for existence by the Government. *Kuhhandel* (cattle-dealing) was the term used to describe the barter of local concessions in return for the support of an administration whose *raison d'être* was to get the budget passed. Since there was no possibility of government by leaders of a party with a parliamentary majority, the Emperor had to appoint officials as ministers; these ministers in turn used the powers under the constitution which enabled them to give provisional validity by ordinance to exceptional measures. Between 1907 and 1914 these exceptional powers are said to have been used seventy-six times.

There was indeed an alternation between different policies during the years from 1867 to 1914. Thus in 1879 Francis Joseph thought that, in view of possible danger of a war with Russia, some effort must be made to placate the Slavs, and especially the Czechs, but attempts at a compromise which would satisfy Germans and Czechs – one of the difficulties was over the areas with a mixed German and Czech population – broke down over the language question.[1] In 1897 Count Badeni,

---

[1] The absurdity which the quarrels over the language question could reach is shown by a dispute in the Reichsrat whether Czech reservists should answer 'present' in Czech or German at the first roll call after their call-up. For obvious reasons German had to be the language of command

a former Governor of Galicia, and one of the many officials to become Prime Minister, tried to settle the language question with the Czechs in ordinances that all officials in Bohemia and Moravia would have to be able to speak Czech and German and that business between members of the public and the administration should be conducted in the language of the citizen concerned.[1] The ordinances brought violent opposition from the Germans who disliked them as such and also feared that similar concessions would have to be made to the Slovenes and others. Badeni himself was wounded in a duel with one of the German extremists. The Germans of the Reich supported the opposition in Austria; the historian, Mommsen, wrote a letter of protest to the Viennese *Neue Freie Presse*. Badeni had to resign and, after two other governments had failed to get agreement, the ordinances were withdrawn. Another 'official' Prime Minister tried to settle the dispute by a return to an earlier proposal which would have divided Bohemia and Moravia into three language areas, German, Czech and mixed. The Czechs refused to give up the administrative unity of Bohemia and Moravia; the Germans refused to admit that there were any administratively mixed areas. After more disturbances Francis Joseph in 1905 decided to introduce universal suffrage in Austria and Hungary.[2] The idea behind this 'leap in the dark', as it was called on the analogy of the English Reform Act of 1867, was that a parliament elected on a franchise including the poorer classes would be more concerned with measures of social reform than with the nationalist disputes of the bourgeois which were making the conduct of public business impossible.

[1] These ordinances were in fact only an extension of previous rulings which applied mainly to the judicial services.

[2] The promise of the Tsar to give his peoples a constitution and to summon a Duma was almost certainly not without influence upon Francis Joseph's decision.

(amounting to about 200 words) in the Austrian, though not in the Hungarian, Army, but when a reservist turned up for mobilization he would be wearing civilian clothes. A quicker-minded bureaucracy would have settled the matter by an order that reservists in civilian clothes should answer by holding up their hands or taking two steps forward.

The franchise law passed in January 1907 gave practically universal male suffrage in Austria, though the constituencies were still weighted to the advantage of the culturally more advanced nationalities. The result was a great increase in the representation of the Christian Democrats and the Social Democrats – the clerical and anti-clerical parties of social reform – but there was still no dominant party either of government or of opposition. In the first Austrian parliament elected under the new franchise there were over thirty parties, small groups or, in one or two cases, single individuals purporting to represent a group. In 1911 – the last election before 1914 – nearly 3,000 candidates, representing fifty different parties or groups, contested the 500 and more seats. A body including Germans, Czechs, Poles, Slovenes, Ruthenians, Roumanians, Croats and Italians was unlikely to provide Austria with an effective form of parliamentary democracy. In the short time between the introduction of universal suffrage and the outbreak of war in 1914 Austria was back again in the routine of government by officials using the 'exceptional powers' and unable to do anything but adjourn the Reichstag in the face of total obstruction.

The internal position in Hungary was less complicated but no more satisfactory. In 1910 (and here as in Austria there had not been any great change in the distribution of nationalities during the last half century) the 'lands of St Stephen's crown', that is to say, the kingdom of Hungary with Transylvania, the kingdom of Croatia Slavonia, the town and district of Fiume, had a total population of just under 21 million. The Magyars were a larger percentage – 48 per cent, or just under 10 million (including 500,000 magyarized Jews) – of the Hungarian part of the monarchy than the percentage of Germans in Austria, but even in Hungary proper the figure was only 54 per cent.[1] The other nationalities consisted of 2,000,000 Germans (including German Jews), nearly 2,000,000 Slovaks, about 1,750,000 Croats and 1,000,000 Serbs, nearly 3,000,000 Roumanians (most of them in Transylvania) and just under 500,000 Ruthenes.

[1] This official Hungarian figure may be an exaggeration. It is certainly not an understatement.

The domination of the Magyars over their minority nationalities was greater than that of the Germans in Austria not only because there were proportionally more of them. They were more centrally placed and in the more fertile parts of the monarchy; they were also more ruthless in enforcing their rule. The richer classes in the country were mainly on their side and the whole machinery of the state – courts, administration, army and schools – were at their disposition. They could therefore do much to deprive the subject peoples – one can hardly avoid the term 'subject' to describe these 'second-class citizens' – of the instruments of national culture. Magyarization was enforced in every possible way and down to minor details. Public notices were written and posted up in Magyar in the non-Magyar areas; place names were changed. A non-Magyar defendant in the courts had to pay for an interpreter if he wanted one.

These efforts at magyarization had considerable success in the towns and neighbourhood of Magyar density, but they failed elsewhere and by 1914 the resentment and unrest among the non-Magyars had increased. In 1905 a Congress of Nationalities in Prague demanded that Hungary should become a multinational state. The demand brought great indignation from the Magyars who obviously rejected it. On the other hand, there was little the Magyars could do to counter the attraction for the non-Magyars of their co-nationals in neighbouring states. The Transylvanians wanted union with Roumania; the Serbs, and to some extent the Croats, wanted union with Serbia; the Czech movement in Bohemia and Moravia attracted many of the Slovaks of Hungary.

The Magyars could not feel easy about their position. Their backwardness in social legislation was a danger to themselves. They tended to leave business and, to a large extent, the liberal professions to the Jews.[1] Hence there was no middle class

---

[1] The Jews in Hungary, as in Austria, were late arrivals. In the last years of the eighteenth century they were not more than one per cent of the population. By 1850 they had risen to 343,000 and by 1900 to 850,000 or 8·49 per cent of the population. Nearly a quarter of the population of Budapest was Jewish.

comparable with the German bourgeoisie, while there was considerable foundation for the anti-Magyar complaint that Hungary was controlled by a partnership between great Magyar landlords and Jewish bankers. The uneasiness of the Magyars was shown in the pressure which they put upon Austria to affirm their position and in their blocking of any changes in the constitution of the dual state which would have weakened Magyar predominance in Hungary. In particular they were bound to oppose every plan of a federalist kind and therefore any genuine solution of the Czech problem in Austria. Similarly they opposed concessions to the southern Slavs.

The failure to reach a settlement with the southern Slavs ultimately brought Austria–Hungary to destruction. This possibility was not realized when the Powers in 1878 agreed to the Austrian occupation of Bosnia–Herzegovina (not annexation, though Turkish sovereignty was not expected in future to be more than a legal fiction which would ultimately disappear). Serbia at this time was hardly more than a client state of Austria and had objected as strongly as Austria to the Russian proposals for a 'big Bulgaria'. Bismarck hoped for Austro-Russian agreement on the basis of Austrian predominance in the western, and Russian predominance in the eastern Balkans. In addition, however, to the real wishes of Austria and likewise of Russia to secure predominance over the whole peninsula, there were two great difficulties. What was meant by the Balkans? Did the term include Dalmatia, Croatia, Slovenia, Constantinople and, by a strategic extension, the Aegean islands? What was to happen if the Balkan peoples themselves had conflicting ambitions and if these ambitions extended to claims over Austrian and Russia as well as Turkish territories?

In fact the Balkan peoples did have such ambitions. They were predominantly peasant societies with a small black-coat class brought up in the traditions of revolution and easily succumbing to the temptations of power. The Roumanians had a somewhat bogus claim to Latin, that is to say, western origins, and a small, exotic and very rich aristocracy which was on the whole useless from the point of view of national leadership. Greece had a considerable mercantile and seafaring population with affiliations in most of the great Mediterranean ports and a distant, romantic claim to the legacy of the Byzantine Empire. Serbia and Bulgaria also had memories of short-lived medieval greatness.

The foreign dynasties, whose establishment was recognized and indeed to a large extent imposed by the Great Powers on the Balkan states after their liberation from the Turks, were also of little use; the position was even worse in Serbia where two indigenous dynasties, Obrenovich and Karageorgevich, each going back to the era of liberation, expelled and re-expelled one another. From the early days of their existence these 'emerging' nation-states depended upon and angled for the support of the Great Powers; the failure of the latter to act collectively in encouraging social and economic development in the Balkans added to the trouble. In the early years of Greek independence the political parties in the country were known generally as 'English', 'Russian' and 'French', but the rivalry of the Great Powers did no good to their clients. Owing to this rivalry the Turks had been left in 1878 with a considerable remainder of their old empire in Europe. This territory included Thrace, with the fortress of Adrianople, and Macedonia, with a mixed population of Greeks, Turks, Serbs, Bulgars (not to mention a body of migratory pastoral Vlachs from Roumania). The seacoast from Salonika to Gallipoli[1] was mostly Greek in population, with Bulgars in the hinterland. Hence the conflicting claims in the event of an ultimate break-up of Turkish power in Europe and the concentration of each of the Balkan states on getting Great Power support for its claims.

In accordance with his plan of bringing Austria and Russia together on the basis of a division of interests, Bismarck formed a so-called League of the Three Emperors in 1879. The League was renewed in 1884, but strained to breaking-point by the union of Bulgaria with the separate principality of eastern Rumelia established under the treaty of Berlin. The Russians had at first wanted this union but they had made themselves

---

[1] Salonika, and to a lesser extent other places, had large colonies of Spanish Jews who had settled there after the expulsion of the Jews from Spain.

unpopular in Bulgaria by their high-handedness and now realized that an enlarged Bulgarian kingdom would try to escape their control. Serbia asked, after the habit of the age, that she should receive 'compensation' for the Bulgarian increase of territory. Bulgaria refused to give anything. Serbia then went to war, was defeated and saved only by Austrian intervention. Russia, on the other hand, at the end of 1886 threatened to assert her influence in Bulgaria by force. Austria made it clear that she would go to war if Russia invaded Bulgaria. Germany would have supported Austria, France might have attacked Germany in order to recover Alsace-Lorraine and Great Britain might have come into the war to keep Russia out of Constantinople. In other words, the European war which broke out in 1914 over dominance in the Balkans might have come a quarter of a century earlier.

War did not break out; neither Russia nor Austria felt in a favourable position for fighting. Bismarck closed the German money market to Russian loans and therefore made it impossible for Russia to obtain a loan in Germany.[1] At the same time Bismarck showed that Germany would not support Austrian aggression against Russia. He signed with Russia the so-called 'reinsurance treaty', under which Germany was pledged to neutrality in an Austro-Russian war unless Russia were the aggressor, and Russia was pledged to neutrality in a Franco-German war unless Germany were the aggressor. Germany also promised diplomatic support to Russia on the questions of Bulgaria and the Straits.[2] Finally, in 1887, Bismarck informed Russia of the terms of the Austro-German treaty of 1879 which made it plain that Germany was pledged to support Austria in the event of a Russian attack on her.

The reinsurance treaty was not renewed after Bismarck's dismissal, but Russian interest was now concentrated on the Far East. In 1897 Austria and Russia signed an agreement that the two Powers would work together for the preservation of

[1] See also above, p. 124.

[2] Since Bismarck was encouraging Great Britain and Italy to oppose Russia on these questions, the treaty could be justified only by its success in preventing war. For the treaty see also above, p. 123.

the *status quo* in the Balkans. If territorial changes became inevitable (in other words, if the Ottoman Empire collapsed) the Two Powers would prevent any one of the Balkan states from becoming strong enough to dictate to the others.

There was no further crisis in Austro-Russian relations until the Austrian annexation of Bosnia-Herzegovina in 1908. Russia had been compelled after her unsuccessful war with Japan to give up at least for the time her expansionist plans in the Far East and was again actively interested in the Balkans. The Young Turk revolution had overthrown the incompetent Ottoman autocracy[1] and a reformed Turkish Government might well claim the return of Bosnia-Herzegovina to Turkish administration. Meanwhile Austrian relations with Serbia had deteriorated. Officially these relations had been satisfactory up to 1903, but the demand for a greater Serbia at Austrian expense was gathering strength. In the first years of their occupation of Bosnia-Herzegovina the Austrians had to meet a serious Moslem rebellion (the population consisted roughly of 800,000 Serbs, 400,000 Croats and 600,000 Moslems). After 150,000 troops had been brought in to suppress the rebellion, there were no more disturbances on a large scale. The Austrian administration of the provinces was on the whole good and far better than anything the Bosnians had known, though they did not welcome law and order with much eagerness. The Austrians introduced western improvements, better communications, higher standards of agriculture, primary and a certain number of technical schools, but the Bosnians had to pay for them and the Government did almost nothing to satisfy the peasants by getting rid of the oppressive rights of the landlords.[2] Bosnians

---

[1] The Young Turk party had come into existence in opposition to the infamous misgovernment of the Sultan Abdul Hamid II. In 1901 the Sultan was able to suppress the movement for a time, but it re-emerged in 1908. Abdul Hamid was deposed in 1909.

[2] Most of the Moslem peasants owned their land; most of the Christian peasants paid dues to landlords. Nearly all the landlords were Bosnian Slavs whose ancestors had been given the choice of becoming Moslems or losing their lands. The Christians who belonged to the Catholic Church were classed as Croats, and those of the Orthodox Church as Serbs. The Austrians maintained full religious toleration. The Sultan was prayed for

were given only subordinate places in the administration and both Croats and Serbs, especially the latter, became increasingly disaffected.

The demand for a greater Serbia at Austrian expense was thus getting stronger. In 1903 the Serbian king and queen were murdered and the heir of the rival Karageorgevich dynasty came to the throne. The new King Peter was known to be Russophil and to support the Serbian expansionist party. In 1904 the Serbian Government signed a treaty and planned a customs union with Bulgaria. Austria protested that the customs union infringed her own 'most favoured nation' rights in relation to Serbia. In January 1906 Austria retaliated against the Serbian action by refusing to transport Serbian agricultural exports, mostly pigs, over her railways. This 'pig war' lasted until 1908; Austria gained nothing by it, since it turned peasant opinion in Serbia against her.

In 1906 Count Aehrenthal became Austro-Hungarian Foreign Minister. Aehrenthal was an ambitious man who wanted Austria to take a more important place in Europe. His first *coup* was to get Turkish consent to a railway through the Sanjak of Novi Bazar which would link up with the Turkish railways and thus give Austria direct access to Salonika. The Russian reply to this move was to support a project for a line from the Danube through Serbia to the Adriatic. About the time of Aehrenthal's appointment, Izvolsky became Foreign Minister of Russia. Izvolsky was as determined as Aehrenthal to assert his country's interests in the Balkans. Neither man was particularly scrupulous;[1] both were arrogant and willing to take dangerous risks. The Young Turk revolution seemed to give them an opportunity for a bargain.

Aehrenthal wanted to secure the annexation of Bosnia-Herzegovina. He realized that he could not do so without

[1] The British Ambassador to Vienna once said directly to Aehrenthal: 'That is the truth, but your Excellency does not love the truth.'
See footnote (3), p. 141.

---

in the mosques and Moslem recruits to the army were required to perform their religious duties more strictly than in many parts of the Ottoman Empire in Europe still under Turkish control.

Russian consent. He believed that he might get this consent by allowing 'compensation' to Russia elsewhere, in other words, agreeing to an alteration in the regime of the Straits which would allow the passage of the Russian Black Sea fleet into the Aegean. In September 1908 Aehrenthal and Izvolsky met at Buchlau, the Moravian country estate of the Austrian Ambassador to Russia. Here they came to an agreement on a deal to the mutual advantage of Austrian and Russian interests. They realized that the consent of the other signatories of the Treaty of Berlin was necessary, but they did not put their agreement into writing and did not fix a date for announcing it nor for asking the consent of the other Powers concerned. This neglect of traditional procedure is more explicable in the case of Aehrenthal than of Izvolsky because the signatories of the treaty, though they (other than Germany) might disapprove of the Austrian annexation of Bosnia–Herzegovina, were more likely to reject an alteration of the regime of the Straits in favour of Russia.

Aehrenthal announced the annexation of Bosnia–Herzegovina in October 1908 before Izvolsky had made sure of the consent of the Powers to his proposal about the Straits. He then found that neither Great Britain nor France would accept the proposal.[1] Serbian opinion was greatly excited by the Bosnian annexation and, in the hope of getting Russian support, demanded compensation. Russia, however, at this time was hardly able to fight Austria and altogether unable to do so if Austria were supported by Germany. Germany gave notice of her support in the form of a sharp demand – almost an ultimatum – in March 1909 to Russia. Russia had to accept the annexation and Serbia to give up her demand for compensation.

After the crisis was over the Emperor William II, with his

---

[1] Since the acquisition of Alexandria as a naval base, the British Government no longer regarded the exclusion from the Mediterranean of Russian warships coming from the Black Sea as a necessary safeguard to British lines of communication. Grey, however, was unwilling to relax the international rule about the Straits in favour of Russia alone. He also did not want to weaken the new Turkish revolutionary government and was disturbed by Russian high-handedness in the sphere of influence in Persia allocated to them under the Anglo–Russian agreement.

usual bombast and tactlessness, announced that Germany had stood by her ally and 'confronted the world in shining armour'. Germany had thus indirectly strengthened the Anglo–Russian *entente* as she had earlier strengthened the Anglo–French *entente* by her clumsy interference in the Moroccan question. It was also clear that Russia, as soon as she had recovered militarily from the disasters of the Far Eastern war, would not accept another humiliation from Austria and Germany. Aehrenthal died in February 1912. He was succeeded as Foreign Minister by Count Berchtold, a great landowner who had been for five years Austrian ambassador in St Petersburg. Berchtold was less inclined than Aehrenthal to adventurous policies but, as his actions in 1914 showed, was much too ready in a crisis to take risks which a man of higher intelligence and better judgement would have seen to be foolish. Sazonov, who succeeded Izvolsky as Russian Foreign Minister in 1912, was also more conciliatory and, unlike Izvolsky, did not let his policy be deflected by personal vindictiveness.

Nevertheless, the consequences of Aehrenthal's *coup* could not be abated. Serbia was now irreconcilably hostile and Austria no less determined to make her harmless. Russia was equally determined to improve her position in the Balkans and to resist further German demands. Germany might try to restrain Austria from provocative action, but if Austria considered it necessary for her own existence to risk war with Russia, the Germans, having alienated the other Great Powers (Italy, the third party in the Triple Alliance, was hardly more than a nominal ally), would have to support her. Germany had indeed put herself in the position which Bismarck had worked always to avoid; in a world of five Great Powers, Germany was one of two, not one of three.

Russian diplomacy from the summer of 1909 began to work for a league of the Balkan states which would bring about the expulsion of Turkey from Europe and incidentally prevent further Austrian and Austro–German expansion in the Balkans. In the spring of 1912 Serbia and Bulgaria and Serbia and Greece signed military agreements ostensibly directed against Turkey but potentially applicable against Austrian interference. The

Balkan allies (joined by Montenegro) attacked Turkey in October 1912 and, to the surprise of the Great Powers, quickly defeated her. Then came the problem of dividing the spoils. Not for the first time the Balkan states rejected the advice of their protectors. One question was the future of Albania. Serbia wanted to annex the northern part of the country and thus to gain a port on the Adriatic. Austria refused to allow Serbia access to the Adriatic; the Serbian port might well become a Russian naval base. Russia supported the Serbian claim.

After much discussion the belligerents, at a conference in London, agreed to a British and German proposal to make Albania into a separate state.[1] In January 1913, while the conference was still discussing the boundaries of the new Albanian state,[2] Turkey denounced the armistice which had been signed early in December and re-opened the war.[3] The Turks were again heavily defeated and lost the fortress of Adrianople. The Balkan states now accepted the mediation of the Great Powers. Turkey gave up all her European territory except an area adjoining Constantinople and the Straits.

At this point the victors fell out among themselves. Serbia, having reluctantly accepted her exclusion from Albania, demanded a revision of the frontiers agreed between herself and Bulgaria and refused to give western Macedonia to the Greeks. The Tsar tried to mediate in the dispute, but Bulgaria suddenly attacked Serbia and Greece. With the help of the Roumanians, who also wanted compensation from Bulgaria for her gains, the Serbs and Greeks easily defeated the Bulgarians, while Turkey took the chance to recover Adrianople. Austria would have

[1] The Kaiser is reported to have said: 'I shall not march against Paris and Moscow for the sake of Albania and Durazzo.'

[2] Montenegro was claiming the port of Scutari. Austria, however, was no more willing to satisfy the ambitions of Montenegro than those of Serbia.

[3] The denunciation of the armistice followed a dramatic scene in Constantinople. Enver Bey, the leader of the Young Turks, with other Turkish officers, invaded the Council Chamber at Constantinople, denounced the surrender of Adrianople, deposed the Grand Vizier, shot the Turkish Commander-in-Chief and appointed himself Minister of War.

gone to the help of Bulgaria to prevent further Serbian expansion, but Germany would not support her. Even so, Austria sent an ultimatum to Serbia when she refused to withdraw her troops from Albania. This time the Powers acquiesced in the Austrian demand and the Serbs had to give way.

Berchtold and the Austrian military command were now sure that the only way of making Austria safe from Serbian ambitions was to attack the Serbs and reduce their state to a nullity. Within nine months the opportunity came for carrying out this plan. The Archduke Francis Ferdinand and his wife, on a visit to Sarajevo, the Bosnian capital, were murdered by a Bosnian Serb. The assassin and his accomplices – also Bosnian Serbs – were Austrian subjects but connected with secret Serbian societies; their weapons had come from a Serbian military arsenal. The Powers strongly condemned the assassination – Serbia had a bad name since the murders of 1903 – and although the extent (if any) of direct complicity of the Serbian Government in the assassinations was not known, and indeed never has been proved,[1] the Austrian Government could have gone a long way to secure the suppression of secret and open action against her by the Serbs. Francis Joseph and his advisers, however, repeated the mistake which they had made in 1859 with regard to Piedmont. They decided, if Germany agreed, to go to war with the intention of disrupting the Serbian state. Germany gave Austria her full support without even knowing what the Austrian plans were.

After it had become clear that a war against Serbia could not be localized, as Germany and Austria had rashly assumed (though indeed the extent of this assumption is still doubtful), Austria refused to be content with the occupation of Belgrade and drastic measures against Serbian intrigue and propaganda. The German high command, though again there had been

---

[1] It would appear that the Serbian Government knew of the assassins' intentions and tried to stop them from getting into Bosnia, but failed to do so owing to the connivance of local frontier officials with the terrorist organization. The Serbian Government then warned the Austrian Government in general terms of the danger to the Archduke if he went to Sarajevo, but gave no details about the plot.

curiously little correlation of plans between the Austrian and German General Staffs, thought that a German–Austrian combination could defeat France and Russia in a short war during which British intervention, if it took place, would make no difference.

Epilogue

In an introduction to these chapters I described European civilization as a unity in diversity, a unity made up of a number of nation-states, sharing what might be called a common culture, but each of them with a unique history, special characteristics and often divergent interests. I mentioned the danger of conflict arising out of these divergent interests and the attempts made to get rid of such a danger. I said that the attempts had not been altogether futile, though they had never had lasting success. The idea of an overriding European interest, a common *respublica*, was never entirely lost and expressed itself in different forms; the conception of Christendom, a European balance of power, a Concert of Europe, a League of Nations to which non-European nations could belong and which was indeed sponsored largely by an American President, although the United States never joined it. Even after the calamitous breakdown of this latter attempt to prevent internecine war, a new organization, the United Nations, ultimately to be world-inclusive in membership, was set up to safeguard the peace, and in this most recent instrument for the settlement of disputes three out of the five leading members were European.

After considering certain features common to a greater or lesser extent to all the greater European nation-states, I went on to outline the diversities between these Great Powers as shown in their respective histories – differences of location, tradition and experience, for example, between Edinburgh and Moscow, the countryside of southern England and that of southern France, between the states with semi-absolute rulers and those which had become in fact as well as in name parliamentary democracies.[1]

[1] Similar differences are found in America. Thus, on crossing the Rio Grande between the Texan city of El Paso and the Mexican city of Juarez,

I cannot avoid in conclusion asking whether the sum of these differences has been more important than the less obvious expression of their unity, and whether the nation-state, for so long the vehicle of European greatness, has not become an anachronism (in spite of the fact that all over the world societies hitherto backward have rushed to claim separate national polities for themselves). Have national rivalries been the cause of the decline of European civilization, and does the future of the civilized world (if it is to have a future) henceforward lie outside this small continent, whose citizens have twice in my own lifetime fought one another to desperation and who are outnumbered by other peoples able to use the skills created by European technology, but with little respect for, or even understanding of, the subtler qualities which have distinguished European civilization? The immense achievements for all humanity of our European civilization in the past are no more of a guarantee of a European future than were the achievements of Athens a guarantee for the future of the Greek city state or those of Florence and Venice for the political future of Italy.

I am only a historian and, although historians have had, and even today some of them still venture to have, pretensions to forecast the future, I think that such claims are idle. All I can do is to put before you certain considerations of which account should be taken in any attempt to understand and obtain guidance from the past. In the first place let me remind you of what I have said about the fact of 'progress', the development of a high civilization carrying with it always the possibility of 'regress'. If we are in a time of regress now, we should remember that this phenomenon has occurred before in European history, that it lasted for several centuries and was followed by the recovery of most of Europe and a long spell of advance with only local recessions. Moreover, the contemporary recession does not apply only to the states of Europe. Observers elsewhere, especially in North America, had equal misgivings

---

I had the strong impression that I had gone down a subway in Stockholm and come up again to find myself in Naples.

about the future of their own continent and, although this fact may seem only to add bleakness to a world situation, civilization in Europe is not alone wilting while elsewhere there is hopeful springtime.

In the second place we ought to remember, in judging an age, and especially in comparing past with present, that the recent past, which was itself only lately a 'present', inherited, judged and tried to improve upon a more distant past. The nineteenth century was not just the beginning of a decline which has become more obvious to us in the twentieth century; it was also an advance on the century which preceded it. Some lessons were learned, some improvements consciously made. We also know (though we have tended to forget) from our own successes and failures that, in J. S. Mill's words which I quoted earlier, there is 'only a certain order of possible progress'. This is obviously true of technical advance. Modern urban drainage schemes could be put into effect only after the invention of cheap drain pipes and the necessary traps, gullies and methods of sewage disposal.[1] What is true of an ordered advance in material things (there is no 'army of progress' progressing in all directions at once) is true of social advance. Social progress in the nineteenth century depended on the collection of statistical information, the dissemination of the knowledge thus gained, the conclusions drawn from it by public opinion, and the legislative and administrative activities of governments in enforcing change. The 'order of possible progress' applied to matters like the development of an honest and efficient administration; an end to bumbledom and inefficiency was likely only if there were an educated public large enough to demand honesty and efficiency.

Thus we should see the nineteenth century as much against the background of the eighteenth century as in relation to its own 'unfinished business' and its legacies to our present time. Both the eighteenth and nineteenth centuries (if we prolong the latter to 1914) ended, to the discomfiture of much enlightened opinion, in international war of a new type. The decline

[1] Doulton's glazed earthenware pipes were not put on the market until 1846.

of the early optimism about the French revolution ('bliss was it in that dawn to be alive', etc.) into the confusion, bellicosity and corruption of the later revolutionary governments, followed by the anti-climax of Napoleonic military autocracy, was as unforeseen by most people as the rise of bolshevism and fascism in and after the First World War. Nevertheless the optimism of the nineteenth century was broader-based than that of the first period of the French revolution. There were in the nineteenth century new features in society; changes for the better, not yet universally accepted, but widespread, in the attitude of the strong towards the weak, of men towards women, in the treatment of prisoners, the protection of children and indeed of animals. These changes can be described as a general growth of a sense of social responsibility, that is to say, the responsibility of individuals for the prevention of evils which could be removed by collective action.[1] This increase in public sensitiveness and pity for the helpless, as I have said, was not uniform throughout society; those who were affected by it in one direction were inconsistent in failing to support it in other directions which seem to us even more obvious. In Great Britain, Peel, who from 1823 onwards carried through Parliament large reforms in the savage penal code of the eighteenth and earlier centuries, had opposed Martin's bill in 1822. Wilberforce, whose zeal for the general abolition of the slave trade and, later, of slavery, cannot be attributed to a desire to put an end to the competition of slave-grown sugar in British markets, never went much beyond private charity in the alleviation of extreme poverty and inhumane working conditions within a mile of his house in London. None the less the change in public opinion was real. There is a fundamental difference between the unthinking acquiescence of Defoe and the attitude of Charles Dickens towards child labour. When the socialist and successful

[1] Richard Martin ('Humanity Martin') secured in 1822 the passing of a bill through Parliament to prevent 'the cruel and improper treatment of cattle' – the first legal measure in the United Kingdom for the protection of animals. The Royal Society for the Prevention of Cruelty to Animals was founded two years later. One can imagine the astonishment of a decent man like Samuel Pepys if Martin's measure had been introduced into the House of Commons in the last half of the seventeenth century.

manufacturer, Robert Owen, told a parliamentary commission that he thought it unnecessary for children under ten to work in cotton mills, he was asked whether there would not be 'a danger of their acquiring vicious habits for want of a regular occupation'. Parliament, however, agreed with Owen and in an act of 1819 laid down an age limit of nine years.[1]

One may also notice that, in spite of the militarism of certain countries and the increasing burden of armaments, especially in the second half of the nineteenth century, the general attitude towards war was slowly changing. The idea of 'glory' was less dominant; there is a significant difference between the flamboyant public expression of victory on the inscription on the base of the Marlborough column in Blenheim Park and the restraint of the Guards' Crimean war memorial in Waterloo Place. The criticism of the Germans for their part in bringing about the outbreak of war in 1914 (whether or not they were singled out too much as having sole responsibility) had an element not found in the condemnation of the wars of the eighteenth century. Aggressive war had always been deplored by the victims; it was not regarded as a punishable crime until the early twentieth century.

The content of political liberty was also widened in the nineteenth century. As I have said, absolutism, though it held its own over large areas in Europe, was everywhere on the defensive and at the end of the century seemed likely to disappear. The so-called Whig interpretation of British history has exaggerated the merits and concealed the narrowness of the landed and commercial magnates of England between the revolution of 1688 and the passing of the first Reform Act in 1832, but the value of the Whig defence of the rule of law and of

[1] The act of 1819 applied only to cotton mills and still allowed the employment of children aged between nine and sixteen for twelve hours a day, exclusive of meal-times. Even so the House of Lords threw out the bill when it was first introduced. Fourteen years later, when the age limit was raised from nine to thirteen and the hours of work reduced to nine a day, Cobbett ridiculed the opponents of the new act by saying that they seemed to base the industrial welfare of England on '30,000 little girls. If these little girls worked two hours a day less, our manufacturing supremacy would depart from us.'

political liberty cannot be set aside because their ideas of the content of liberty had later to be enlarged.

Throughout this slow transformation of opinion and rapid technical advance, the governments of the nation-states gained in power as their agents extended their control over more and more fields of domestic activity. The increase in the population of Europe, the organization needed to provide the conditions of a civilized social life strengthened the central authority. Every major reform entailed complicated legislation and more officials for carrying the legislation into effect. This increase in state power had its dangers; its ultimate consequences might be destructive of the liberty it was intended to safeguard. There was some truth, especially in regard to Russia (where indeed officials as a class nearly always abused their powers), in Alexander Herzen's bitter comment that the modern state was 'Jenghiz Khan with the electric telegraph', but the comment cannot be applied to the social reforms introduced into every country – not wholly excluding Russia – before 1914. Meanwhile the subjects of the nation-states maintained their loyalty and tended to identify western civilization primarily with their own particular nationality. Other institutions which might have challenged the power of the State declined in strength. The Christian Churches in most countries lost to the State, or at any rate to secular authorities, their monopoly of school and university education. The safeguard of elected parliaments was more theoretical than real in many so-called democratic states; public opinion associated representative institutions too often with log-rolling and jobbery, and the professional politician was satirized and derided in the press and in the literature of imagination.[1]

In spite of (perhaps, one might say, owing to) their domestic power, the European governments made little real effort to transcend the concept of closed national sovereignty and to find adequate methods of settling rival claims and interests without war. Europe indeed did not consist only of the Great

[1] It would be hard to find a nineteenth-century play of which the hero was a successful politician.

Powers. The Scandinavian states, Belgium (in spite of a growing antagonism between its French and Flemish speaking citizens), the Netherlands and Switzerland were stable societies without interests and ambitions likely to lead to war.[1] Spain and Portugal maintained their political isolation and underwent military *coups* and revolutions of a local intensity which hardly affected the rest of Europe. Even in 1900 the effete and incompetent rule of the Turkish Sultans had not been entirely removed from south-east Europe, while the Christian nations which had secured their independence had failed to be much more than disturbing elements in the European state system.[2]

Here again one can notice the lack of common action by the Great Powers in the general interest of Europe. The economic development of the Balkan states was left mainly to the haphazard provision of capital – where profit was to be had from it – by cosmopolitan financiers or at best by governments wanting to further their own special interests in the areas concerned. The politicians of these small states occupied themselves by getting what they could out of the Great Powers and by marking out in advance as much territorial gain as possible for themselves when the Turkish Empire should finally collapse. These territorial ambitions were mutually incompatible and in some cases at variance with the interests of the rest of Europe. In such a situation there were the elements of disaster.

Nevertheless, although there was no effective attempt to bring about European unity or to limit the actions of independent sovereign states, it is not altogether accurate to speak of a 'European anarchy' before 1914. I have shown that even Bismarck, in spite of his contempt for what seemed to him the politically unreal conception of a European solidarity, attempted by his system of alliances to maintain the peace of the European continent after 1871. This peace, at least between the Great Powers, was kept for half a century, if only by shifting compromises and 'papering over cracks'. During these years the

---

[1] The dissolution of the union between Norway and Sweden and the revival of a separate Norwegian state in 1905 were carried out by peaceful agreement.

[2] See above, p. 246.

European Powers, whatever one may say of their aims and methods, managed to partition vast areas in Africa among themselves without recourse to war. After the Crimean War there was no war between the Great Powers over the succession to the Ottoman Empire. War in the Far East between Russia and Japan had immense indirect political consequences as the first war for several centuries in which an Asiatic Power defeated a European Power, but in the years after 1905 Russia and Japan reached an 'adjustment of interests' over the border areas of China. In many matters not affecting what they regarded as their vital interests the Great Powers improved the machinery and widened the scope of international co-operation.

There was, however, a sinister increase in the accumulation of armaments. Nothing in international law and no international agreements prevented an 'armaments race'. I have mentioned the failure in the twenty years before 1914 of efforts to secure by agreement a general limitation of armaments. The inventiveness of their own experts and those of their armament industries drove the European governments to heavier expenditure; the taxpayers protested, but paid; the parties of the left urged that the money could be better spent on social reform. Nevertheless the curious fact – or so it seems in retrospect – is the lack of any really strong public pressure, at least in continental Europe, to stop a competition, wasteful in itself, which might end in war of a more frightful kind than anything hitherto known.

Why was this possibility of catastrophe not envisaged more clearly and why was there not a more urgent political campaign and movement of public opinion to avert it? The political parties of the extreme left were indeed committed to the full Marxist prognosis and therefore to regard a general war as a likely event signalling the collapse of capitalism and ushering in social revolution and the peaceful regime of a classless society. Such a prognosis was incompatible with efforts to avert this almost inevitable war and thus save capitalism and at least delay indefinitely the revolution. The revolutionary parties were not pacifist in the sense of being opposed to violence as such. Russian revolutionaries looked to the military defeat of their country as an occasion for their action. Theoretically, however, the socialist parties might short-circuit the revolutionary process and, by using the power of numbers – the general strike – at the right moment to prevent the outbreak of the capitalist war, might take a direct step to overthrow their capitalist governments. The socialist parties of Europe, in spite of their divisions, were the only parties with any kind of organization transcending the closed national sovereignties. They held congresses at which they passed resolutions in favour of a refusal by the workers to take part in a capitalist war from which they would gain nothing. The governments, however, had no reason to treat these resolutions very seriously. There was something unreal about the assumption that the outbreak of a European war must be due to capitalist machination – the greed of armament manufacturers, the desire for colonial markets and the like. Even if these factors (which certainly existed) had been the only likely causes of war and there had been no danger from the political desire to extend national power (and, more important, no fear of losing it to a rival), the chances of working class action strong enough to compel or seriously to embarrass governments were slight. The conscript armies of the continental Great Powers were made up largely of peasants who distrusted the socialists of the cities. The conscripts from town and country alike had undergone the discipline of military service and knew what penalties they would suffer if they disobeyed the call to mobilization. The only chance of successful general strike would have come, and gone, before war had broken out. Once hostile action had started and there were visible signs of a coming enemy invasion, the traditional appeal to national patriotism would be enough; each of the belligerent governments would claim to its citizens that their country was the victim of attack. In Germany in 1914 the socialist, Bebel, said that, whatever Germans might think of their own government, it was better than anything the Russians would impose on them.

A further difficulty for the socialists was that, with few exceptions (I have mentioned Jaurès as one of them), the socialist leaders everywhere were more continuously interested in the domestic problems of their own countries than in questions of foreign policy involving the war and peace of Europe. They knew indeed very little about the detail of the foreign policy of their own states. Throughout the nineteenth century the conduct of foreign affairs remained in the hands of the traditional upper class. Even in Great Britain parliament was given little information about foreign policy. Socialist criticism could therefore have little weight because it was too often based upon ignorance of the facts. On 5 August 1914 Ramsay MacDonald asserted that the foreign policy of Grey had been 'a menace to the peace of Europe for the last eight years'.[1]

There were thus no effective counter-measures in the European states to meet the danger that the diplomatic moves and methods, which had prevented for nearly a century the outbreak of a general European war, might suddenly fail to do so. Moreover, the prospect of war was not seen, except by a minority, as a total threat to European civilization. The common expectation was that a war, although it would cause terrible loss of life and much material destruction and dislocation, would be short and that a return to 'normality' would follow. The General Staffs of the European armies thought in terms of a short war. The German General Staff planned a rapid defeat of France and then a rapid overthrow of Russia. Military operations would consist of a few violent 'encounter battles'. The French also planned a swift offensive against the Germans. All the belligerents in 1914 ran short of ammunition before the end of the year. The British military authorities had provided their Expeditionary Force with sufficient ammunition and reserves for four great battles, each lasting for three days. No army was adequately equipped for anything like siege warfare on a vast scale and no one envisaged the horrors (and, one might add, the intellectual bankruptcy) of a war of attrition.[2] The politicians and civil services did not prepare in advance for

[1] Early in 1915 the *New Statesman* described a pamphlet (sponsored by the Independent Labour Party) as showing that there was 'neither honesty nor intelligence in the pacifist cause'.

[2] The Germans, having the largest munitions industry, were better able than the other belligerents to meet the situation.

the total adaptation of civilian resources to military purposes. In Great Britain the Committee of Imperial Defence had produced a useful book of instructions for departmental use in case of war; the book did not mention possible measures to deal with a banking or financial crisis. Some economists and many politicians indeed believed that no country could afford a long war.[1] *The Times* military correspondent on 8 August 1914 wrote that German experts had suggested 'ways and means' for carrying on a war as long as six months: 'No one has been able to see beyond that period.' Grey, who feared a general collapse of credit in the event of war, does not appear to have considered that Great Britain might become involved in a vast military effort on the European mainland.[2]

If there was little understanding of the character and immensity of the calamity into which Europe might fall,[3] and if public opinion in every European country thought of a war as a disaster, but not more so than previous great wars, and as unlikely to get out of hand in the sense that it would be impossible to stop it, there was also a body of opinion which regarded war itself as a grimly inevitable and even salutary phenomenon in the activities of nations. War brought suffering to the innocent, but it also called out qualities which tended to disappear in a long peace and without which societies declined into self-indulgence and greed for profit. Such a view was not confined to professional militarists and was more likely to affect

---

[1] One book which had a very wide circulation, *The Great Illusion* by the journalist Norman Angell, took the line that war had become so costly that there could no longer be any victors.

[2] Grey said in his speech to the House of Commons giving the case for British intervention (3 August 1914): 'If we are engaged in war, we shall suffer but little more than we shall suffer even if we stand out.'

[3] Lord Kitchener, who in 1914 forecast a long war, took few measures other than enlisting soldiers to prepare for it and, when trench warfare set in along the whole of the western front, said that he did not know what to do about it. *The Times* stated on 8 August that 'it is evident that few people have given the matter (i.e. the length of the war) much serious thought.' At the beginning of the war the British public, having no conscript army and trusting in the ability of the navy to save them from invasion, devised the slogan 'Business as usual' to provide against the widespread unemployment which would be caused by a fall in demand.

a generation which had not itself endured the miseries of a great war. There were signs of this mood that war raised the moral level of a people by asking for self-sacrifice in Great Britain at the time of the Crimean War after the long peace of forty years between the Great Powers. The soliloquies of the hero, if he may be so called, in Tennyson's *Maud* are a remarkable example.[1] In 1859, four years after the publication of *Maud*, Darwin's *Origin of Species* provided new arguments for those who held war to be a natural and normal feature of society. Political writers have always tended to fortify their arguments by analogies from the physical world. The hypotheses of natural selection and the survival of the fittest in a perpetual struggle seemed to justify the test of war as evidence of national vigour and successful might as conferring of itself a stark moral right. These tenuous analogies encouraged much vague and unhistorical talk about 'young nations' and about the alleged follies of liberal pacificism. After another 'long peace' between the Franco-Prussian War and the outbreak of war between the Great Powers in 1914 there was another move in continental Europe in favour of what was commonly called (on another ill-defined scientific analogy) 'dynamism'.

It is unsafe to try to correlate too closely fashions in political thinking with those in literature and the arts, but there was a certain affinity and interaction between the political advocacy of violence as exemplified in the writings of Sorel,[2] the disillusion of extremists of the left and right over the unsatisfying results of political democracy and the so-called Futurist movement in literature and the arts in the years immediately before 1914. The Futurist movement was begun, or at all events publicized, by the Italian poet, E. F. T. Marinetti, who wrote a book on *Futurism* and organized an exhibition of Italian futurist paintings in Paris in 1911. As an artistic and literary protest against jejune academic standards, Futurism had something – though not much – to be said for it; the English *New Statesman*

[1] It is fair to add that the bellicose sentiments of the hero in *Maud* were not necessarily those of Tennyson himself. A sharper acceptance of the popular mood can be read in Charles Kingsley's novel, *Two Years Ago*.
[2] See above, p. 102.

described it as a 'display of penny fireworks'.[1] On its political side it expressed in an exaggerated form the discontent of Italians at the low level on which democratic institutions worked in their own country. The movement provided a pseudo-intellectual setting for the early revolutionary career of an unstable character like Mussolini. Modern writers, however, have tended to set too much importance upon this cult of violence before 1914 and to forget that these noisy exhibitions were set in a stable society in which, over most of Europe, public opinion had no cause to feel seriously alarmed by them and could therefore tolerate displays of intolerance by a minority.

Nineteenth-century forecasts of the future of western civilization were as wide of the mark as those projected in earlier periods of history. Popular opinion took little notice of them and largely discounted talk of war, immediate or remote.[2] The Great Exhibition of 1851 in London may be taken as the high point in the acclamation of technical advance. Opinion in general, which had already become habituated to 'railway speed', now accepted such advances as a matter almost of routine and expected them to continue indefinitely and to bring a better living for all and a levelling up of standards in the 'backward' areas of the world. It is not a paradox to say that revolutionaries of every school shared in this optimism, and indeed the violence with which extremists of the left denounced the existing order was often proportionate to their confidence in the beneficial results which would follow its violent over-

---

[1] The *New Statesman* (July 1914) commented: 'Signor Marinetti's glorification of war, violence and cruelty is like Kipling at fourteen writing in a school magazine, if you could imagine Kipling emancipated from religion and belief in British law and order.'

[2] This is less true of continental than of British opinion. Two British music-hall songs of the decade before 1914 show the total unconcern (and ignorance) of the British people. One of these songs had the light-hearted line 'There'll be trouble in the Balkans in the spring'. The other, a somewhat ludicrous panegyric of King Edward VII, had as its refrain 'There'll be no war, so long as we've a king like good King Edward, there'll be no war. 'E 'ates that sort of thing.'

Epilogue 269

throw. A temperamental cocksureness and arrogance (for which the psychologists of today would give an easy explanation) affected the judgement of many of these advocates of change by violence but, apart from the interia of society, their own differences and mutual excommunications did much to discredit the parties of revolution. It is significant that in the latter half of the nineteenth century, after the 'new learning' – no lesser term is adequate to describe the more systematic study of society[1] – the most widely read analyst of the trend of the times was not Marx but Herbert Spencer.[2] Herbert Spencer is largely forgotten today, but his book on education, published in 1861, was translated into languages as widely separate as Arabic and Mohawk, and his encyclopedic writings after 1870 had an immense influence not only in Great Britain and America but in India and Japan.[3]

The ablest investigators into the new science of political economy in the nineteenth century were less inclined than most of their predecessors of the later eighteenth century to feel optimistic about the future. They were indeed less concerned with general forecasts than with establishing their own subject on a sound basis. J. S. Mill, who had one of the best

[1] In 1851 *Fraser's Magazine* (one of the high quality literary journals published in London between 1830 and 1882) wrote of 'the new science of sociology, as it is barbarously called'.

[2] Herbert Spencer (1820–1902) was almost entirely self-taught. He left school at the age of sixteen and began his career as a railway engineer; he did not establish himself as a writer until after he became sub-editor of *The Economist* in 1848. From this time he expounded his views – he was, increasingly, a strong individualist – in a series of overlapping volumes covering philosophy and politics in a 'system' on a supposedly scientific basis. The trouble about all such scientifically based systems is that the scientific basis rapidly becomes out of date. Benjamin Kidd (1858–1916), another self-taught philosopher of society, has fallen into a deeper oblivion than Spencer. Kidd's *Social Evolution* (1894) was also translated into many languages and was followed by another large work on *The Principles of Western Civilization*. Kidd wrote the article on sociology in the 1911 edition of the *Encyclopaedia Britannica*, but his theories were never taken as seriously as those of Spencer.

[3] It is of interest that the lectureship founded at Oxford University to commemorate the name and work of Herbert Spencer was endowed by an Indian nationalist.

minds of the nineteenth century, wrote also on political subjects and combined a philosophical – and practical – radicalism with a fear that the mass pressures of democracy might well be a threat to political liberty. At the turn of the century, however – in 1798 – Thomas Malthus[1] published an *Essay on Population* which had a very wide public influence. Malthus took a gloomy view of the future of civilization and even regarded humanitarian efforts for the relief of misery as likely to defeat their own purpose. He argued from the available (and, in fact, insufficient) data that population increased in a geometrical ratio, while the means to support it increased only arithmetically. Hence nothing but 'the checks of misery and vice' kept the increase in numbers from going beyond the means of subsistence. Measures of social relief merely tended to aggravate the subsistence crisis by interfering with the harsh but ineluctable process of nature. No other political economist was as starkly 'dismal' as Malthus, but others warned of particular dangers for the future. W. S. Jevons (1835–82), for example, forecast economic disaster at least for Great Britain from the exhaustion of her coal supplies.

Most of the economists and sociologists of the nineteenth century give the impression of dealing only with the externals and arrangements of society (as so many of the historians were content to deal only with its politics) and to ignore the deeper question whether the lines on which society appeared to be developing would or would not lead to greater human happiness. For an answer to these questions about *la condition humaine* – man and his destiny – one would normally go to the religion, art and letters of an age. The nineteenth century was a time of widespread though decreasing religious conformity and of the disintegration of traditional religious doctrine. The extent of the

[1] The Rev. T. H. Malthus (1766–1834), after holding a Cambridge fellowship, became professor of history at Haileybury College (founded by the East India Company for the training of their cadets). Malthus, who was an amiable, cheerful man, did not invent his theory, but was the first to give it a systematic presentation. He modified his views later to the extent of admitting that the rate of growth of population might be reduced by what he called 'prudential checks' or, in our own terminology, deliberate family limitation.

decline in personal religion among the educated classes in Europe as the years passed was masked by the fact that, except in matters like the laicization of education, the general attitude towards religious doctrines and institutions was not one of persecution but of indifference. The official response of the established churches in Europe and, particularly, of the Roman Catholic Church to this indifference counted for little. The papal curia appeared to be concerned less with the defence of religion as such than with the maintenance of its own status and temporal possessions. The language in which the high ecclesiastical authorities denounced the increasing secularization of society was too often one of incomprehensive invective, and alienated from the Church or silenced the most acute religious critics and scholars. Even in England, where religion was much less restricted by a narrow fundamentalism, the clerical protest against 'indifference' repelled as many religiously minded people as it drew to its support. The occasion of Keble's sermon on 'National Apostacy' (he accused parliament of a 'direct disavowal of the sovereignty of God'), which was the beginning of the Oxford Movement, was a proposal for the suppression of ten out of twenty-two Irish bishoprics,[1] and Keble's defence of the Church of England included a stubborn refusal to admit Dissenters and Roman Catholics to Oxford and Cambridge. In France the most remarkable warnings against the consequences of religious indifference came from the Abbé Lamennais. F. R. de Lamennais (1781–1854), a Breton priest, began his career with the views common to most French counter-revolutionary writers that the only hope for civilization was the restoration of the authority of religion. He moved from a general criticism of society to a criticism of the Church itself; he thought on lines similar to those of the Oxford Movement

---

[1] The annual income of these twenty-two bishoprics amounted to £150,000 a year. They ministered to about a seventh of the population; the other six-sevenths would have nothing to do with them. The leaders of the Oxford Movement did not in fact confine themselves to the defence of Church property and sectarian exclusiveness, but the Movement never extricated itself from its local setting; its support and driving force came mainly from the clergy who tended to tie themselves to ecclesiastical trivia – much of it liturgical – which had little meaning for the laity.

that the Church in France had become merely 'une chose qu'on administre'; his solution was not to oppose but to support the general principles of liberalism. Lamennais' writings had a large European circulation, and about 1830 his increasing political radicalism (including support for the Polish rebellion) alarmed the authoritarian governments of Austria, Prussia and Russia. Lamennais, somewhat naïvely, appealed to the papacy for support; the Pope, Gregory XVI, was an old man who had been a monk before the outbreak of the French revolution. The Pope condemned his opinions; Lamennais left the Church and went over to the side of revolution.

Lamennais was a confused and intemperate thinker with great powers of writing and remarkable flashes of insight. He described the future of the indifferentist society which he foresaw. The progress of industry and invention, the development of new means of credit would bring about an immense material activity, but it would have no solid foundation. 'Up to the moment before this palace of folly and illusion vanishes into the gulf of universal ruin, human beings will boast about the progress of civilization and the prospects of society. Nevertheless reason will decay before men's eyes. The simplest truths will appear strange and remarkable and will scarcely be tolerated.'[1]

In compiling an anthology of nineteenth-century warnings against the emptiness and irrelevance of most of the gadgets and improvements and material preoccupations of the age, one has to look mainly to secular writers. In Great Britain one might set Carlyle's reiterated condemnations against Macaulay's superficial assumption (except for occasional doubts coming from his knowledge of fallen empires) that the future of the

[1] From a non-religious or, at all events, from a non-Christian point of view, the French positivist, Auguste Comte (1798–1857), was as much alarmed as was Lamennais at the danger to the stability of society from the disintegration of established beliefs and the absence of a dominant 'system' of social and moral ideas. Comte thought that a new 'system', such as he himself devised, was 'the only way of putting an end to the disorder which, if it should continue, will have no less a consequence than the total dissolution of the social order'. The total dissolution of the social order was, of course, just what the anarchists and other extreme revolutionaries wanted.

world would be a spread of English Whiggery. Carlyle, however, for all his influence upon the youth of his time, almost always, like Nietzsche, overstated his case. Few writers have spent more words in expressing their preference for action over talk.

The great poets of the nineteenth century, like those of earlier ages (Dante's damnations of local Italian politicians are only incidental to the theme of the *Divine Comedy* and the genius of Milton's *Lycidas* does not lie in his attacks upon contemporary clergymen), are rarely concerned in their poetry with a systematic analysis of the trend of society and still more rarely with prognostications about the future, but their indirect judgements are more convincing than those of the writers of treatises. Wordsworth's sonnet

> 'The world is too much with us; late and soon,
> Getting and spending we lay waste our powers'

was written about twenty years before the first steam locomotive pulled a passenger train along a railway line. Blake's strangely prophetic 'Improvement makes us straight roads, but the crooked roads, without improvement, are roads of genius' appeared in 1790 in *The Marriage of Heaven and Hell*.

Nearly three generations later William Morris in England attacked the vulgarity and ugliness of contemporary living, not only because these defects were repellent in themselves, but because they were debasing the quality of life and thereby endangering the future of civilization. Morris believed that this danger had arisen from the substitution – in the interest of greater private profit for the few – of the craftmanship which had formerly given workmen satisfaction in their work. Morris was a Marxist before he had read a line of Marx (whom he never found an attractive writer), but he was not a spiritual Luddite. He thought that machinery, like government, was a necessary evil and indeed not an evil but a benefit as far as it actually saved men from burdensome work. If this latter test were applied, and machinery used to save labour of labourers and not merely the pockets of capitalists, men would soon find that (as with government) they had been exaggerating the need of machines and could do with fewer of them. As things were, the deadening influence of nineteenth-century conditions, the 'blindness of society to beauty' would 'draw down a kind of revenge some day'. 'If civilization is to go no farther than this, it had better not have gone so far. It is simply an organized injustice, a mere instrument for oppression, so much the worse than that which has gone before it as its pretensions are higher, its slavery subtler, its mastery harder to overthrow because supported by such a dense mass of commonplace well-being and comfort.' Morris thought that future historians would neglect the nineteenth century because there was nothing in it worth recording, just as in the ideal future commonwealth described in his *News from Nowhere* the parliament buildings at Westminster had become a storehouse for gardeners because they were not wanted for any higher purpose.[1]

I have quoted English examples. Let me conclude with two judgements made by sensitive and imaginative Frenchmen about the probable future of European civilization. Unlike Great Britain, whose political revolutions had come in the seventeenth century, France and the United States were post-revolutionary countries in a more recent sense. Their political and social evolution, in spite of obvious and immense differences, might be expected to be on lines which other European states would ultimately follow. The development of American democracy was therefore (until the writings of Bryce) studied more carefully and with greater detachment in France than in Great Britain. Renan in 1883 (he was then sixty) summed up in the preface to his *Souvenirs d'enfance et de jeunesse* what he thought of the European future:

'The world is moving towards a kind of americanism, which

---

[1] Morris, however strongly he attacked the ugliness and mean spirit of his age, did not hope overmuch from revolutionary change. A sentence in *The Dream of John Ball* is as good a summary of the course of history as one could find, but it is nearer to the views of the Greeks than to any form of the modern doctrine of progress. 'Men fight and lose the battle, and the thing they fought for comes about in spite of their defeat, and when it comes turns out to be not what they meant, and other men have to fight for what they meant under another name.'

offends our highly cultivated ideas, but which, once the crises of the present age have passed, may well turn out to be no worse than was the *ancien régime* for the only thing that matters, the liberation of the human spirit. A society in which personal distinction counts for little, in which talent and intellect (*ésprit*) have no official recognition, and high office does not carry distinction, in which politics are left to those without status and to people of the third class, and the good things of life go chiefly to intriguers, to the vulgar, to charlatans who cultivate the art of advertisement, or rogues who live always just outside the range of the penal code, such a society, I repeat, cannot please us.... Everything becomes less outrageous, but everything is vulgar. Nevertheless, one may hope at least that this vulgarity will not busy itself with persecuting free intelligence.... Maybe a condition of general vulgarity will be an essential requisite for the happiness of the chosen few...'

Renan's view may be taken perhaps as the nostalgia of an old man for the Brittany of his childhood, 'la vieille Europe qui s'en va', as he called it elsewhere. Alexis de Tocqueville was a less sentimental observer, more scientific in his observation of the facts. Like Renan, he also did not forecast cataclysmic revolution or the destruction of civilization by a war fought with increasingly terrible weapons. None the less, at the end of the third volume of his *Democracy in America* he wrote a warning of what might happen to the civilized world through the gradual undermining of liberty by a benevolent but impersonal, omni-competent state.

'... I ask myself in what form will despotism reappear in the world. I see an immense agglomeration of people, all equal and alike, each of them restlessly active in getting for himself petty and vulgar pleasures which fill his whole being. Each of them, left to himself, is a stranger to the fate of the others. A vast, protecting power overshadows them. This power alone is responsible for securing their satisfactions and for watching over their fates. The power is absolute, concerned with every detail, smooth in operation, takes account of the future, and is not harsh.... The power wants all citizens to be happy, provided that happiness is their sole aim. It works willingly for their well-being, but insists upon being the source of this well-being and the sole judge of what it should consist. It gives them security, foresees and supplies their needs, facilitates their pleasures, conducts the principal business of their lives, manages their industries, divides their properties and regulates their inheritances and, in short, saves them from the trouble of thinking and the difficulties of living.

This tutelary power is continually at work to render less useful and more infrequent the use of free will; the sphere of liberty of decision is thus restricted more and more until every citizen loses, as it were, the control of himself. Equality has conditioned men for all these transformations and prepared them to accept such things and even to welcome them as beneficial.

After having brought the individual, stage by stage, into its mighty hands and moulded him to its wishes, the sovereign extends its tentacles over the community as a whole, and covers the surface of society with a network of little rules, complicated, detailed and uniform, but from beneath which the more original minds and the more vigorous personalities can find no way of extricating themselves and rising above the crowd. The sovereign does not break the wills of the subjects; it enervates them, bends them to its purpose, directs them, rarely forcing them to act, but continually preventing them from action; it does not destroy, but merely prevents things from coming to life; it never tyrannizes, but it hampers, damps down, constricts, suffocates, and at the last reduces every nation to the level of a flock of timid and industrious animals of whom the Government is the shepherd....

This kind of regulated servitude, well regulated, placid and gentle, could be combined – more easily than one would think possible – with the forms of liberty and could even establish itself under the shadow of the sovereignty of the people.'

Such was a forecast in the middle years of the nineteenth century of the society likely to emerge from the much vaunted progress of the time; the end of European civilization, not in some lightning stroke of calamity, but as a ship, bereft of masts and rudder, might drift into the Sargasso Sea.

Books for Further Reading

A list of suggestions for further reading is provided for each chapter. This first list includes general histories, works on certain aspects of European civilization, and books on international affairs which have not been included in other lists.

INTRODUCTION

General Histories

The *New Cambridge Modern History of Europe*, each volume of which is a collective enterprise by specialists, is widely recognized as the standard work. This period is covered in:

Vol. IX *War and Peace in an Age of Upheaval, 1793–1830*, ed. C. W. Crawley.

Vol. X *The Zenith of European Power, 1830–1870*, ed. J. P. T. Bury.

Vol. XI *Material Progress and World-Wide Problems, 1870–1898*, ed. F. H. Hinsley.

Vol. XII *The Shifting Balance of World Forces, 1848–1945*, ed. C. L. Mowat.

Each volume of the 'Rise of Modern Europe' series, edited by William Langer, is written by a single author, and may be preferred for that reason. The following are relevant:

W. LANGER, *Political and Social Upheaval, 1832–1852*, New York, 1969.

C. J. HAYES, *A Generation of Materialism, 1871–1900*, New York, 1941.

O. J. HALE, *The Great Illusion, 1900–1914*, New York, 1971.

The *Cambridge Economic History of Europe* adopts the same method as the N.C.M.H. Vol. VI, *The Industrial Revolution and*

After, 1965, covers the nineteenth century. Two parts are already published, a third expected.

'European Civilization'

Books are included in this list for want of a better place. It does not pretend to be comprehensive and omits the creative arts.

C. SINGER *et. al.*, *History of Technology*, Vols. 4 and 5, 1958.

C. M. CIPOLLA, *Literacy and Development in the West*, 1969.

General Accounts of European Thought

FREDERICK COPLESTON, *A History of Philosophy*, Vol. VII, 1963, unfortunately covers only the German philosophers.

JOHN PLAMENATZ, *Man and Society*, Vol. II, is an excellent introduction and commentary to Hegel, Marx and the French Socialists, and it gives another view of 'Progress'.

BERTRAND RUSSELL, *History of Western Philosophy*, 1961, has a short but good section on the nineteenth century.

EMILE BRÉHIER, *The Nineteenth Century: Period of Systems, 1800–1850*, tr. W. Baskin, 1968, complements Copleston to some extent.

A. G. N. FLEW, *An Introduction to Western Philosophy*, 1971, may be found useful as a systematic treatment of ideas, rather than individual thinkers. It excludes political theory.

Individual Thinkers

G. W. F. HEGEL, *The Philosophy of History*, tr. J. Sibree, 1899, new edn. 1956, is the least unreadable of his major works, and is a useful background to Marx.

K. MARX, *Das Kapital*. Many editions.

K. MARX and F. ENGELS, *The Communist Manifesto*, also in many editions.

SIR ISAIAH BERLIN, *Karl Marx*, new edn., 1960.

GUISEPPE MAZZINI, *The Duties of Man*, with other essays, ed. Thomas Jones, n.d.

F. W. NIETZSCHE, *Thus Spake Zarathustra*.

ERNEST RENAN, *The Life of Jesus*, ed. Howell Smith, 1935.

HERBERT SPENCER, *Education*, 1861 and 1929. *The Man versus the State*, 1884, new edn., ed. D. Macrae, 1969.

ALEXIS DE TOCQUEVILLE, *Democracy in America*, 2 Vols. tr. G. Lawrence

International Relations

L. ALBRECHT-CARRIÉ, *Diplomatic History of Europe, 1815–1945*, 1958.
A. J. P. TAYLOR, *The Struggle for Mastery in Europe, 1848–1918*, 1954.
F. H. HINSLEY, *Power and the Pursuit of Peace*, 1963.
C. HOLBRAAD, *The Concert of Europe*, 1968.

Special Topics

H. NICOLSON, *The Congress of Vienna*, 1946.
H. W. V. TEMPERLY, *England and the Near East: the Crimea*, 1936.
G. B. HENDERSON, *Crimean War Diplomacy*, 1947.
W. E. MOSSE, *The Rise and Fall of the Crimean System, 1855–71*, 1963.
W. E. MOSSE, *The European Powers and the German Question, 1848–71*, 1958.
A. J. P. TAYLOR, *The Italian Problem in European Diplomacy, 1847–49*, 1934.
C. W. CLARK, *Franz Joseph and Bismarck*, 1934.
L. D. STEEFEL, *The Schleswig Holstein Questions*, 1932.
L. D. STEEFEL, *Bismarck, the Hohenzollern Candidacy and the Origins of the Franco-German War of 1870*, 1962.
MICHAEL HOWARD, *The Franco-Prussian War*, 1962.
W. L. LANGER, *European Alliances and Alignments, 1871–1890*, 1950.
B. H. SUMNER, *Russia and the Balkans, 1870–1880*, 1937.
W. L. LANGER, *The Diplomacy of Imperialim, 1890–1902*, 1950.
E. L. WOODWARD, *Great Britain and the German Navy*, 1935.
L. ALBERTINI, *Origins of the War of 1914*, tr. I. Massey, 1952.
B. E. SCHMITT, *The Coming of the War*, 1930.

Colonies

J. HOBSON, *Imperialism*, 1900, is a contemporary view.

R. KOEBNER, *Imperialism*, 1964, studies the development of the concept.

A. J. P. TAYLOR, *Germany's First Bid for Colonies*, 1938, deals with Bismarck's colonial policy.

J. A. GALLAGHER and J. ROBINSON, *Africa and the Victorians*, 1961, though it deals primarily with the British experience, is by far the best work of history about colonialism in the nineteenth century.

FRANCE

General Books

BODLEY, J. E. C., *France*, 2 Vols., rev. edn. 1902.
BROGAN, SIR DENIS, *The Development of Modern France*, Rev. edn. 1967.
BURY, J. P. T., *France 1814–1940*, rev. edn. 1969.
COBBAN, A., *A History of Modern France*, 3 Vols., 1965.

Special Topics

CLAPHAM, SIR J. H., *The Economic Development of France and Germany, 1815–1914*, 4th edn. 1936.
PHILIPS, C. S., *The Church in France, 1789–1907*, 2 Vols., 1929 and 1936.
WOODWARD, SIR E. L., *French Revolutions*, 1934.
Three Studies in European Conservatism, 1929. Newington, 1966.
SIMPSON, F. A., *The Rise of Louis Napoleon*, 3rd edn. 1949.
MARX, KARL, *The Class Struggles in France, 1848–1850*, ed. Dutt, 1934.
ZELDIN, T., *The Political System of Napoleon III*, 1958.
DUNHAM, A.L., *The Anglo-French Treaty of Commerce of 1860 and the progress of the Industrial Revolution in France*, 1930.
LORWIN, V. R., *The French Labour Movement*, 1954.
EDWARDS, STEWART, *The Paris Commune, 1871*, 1971.
CHAPMAN, G., *The Third Republic of France*, 1962. *The Dreyfus Affair*, 1955.
THOMSON, D., *Democracy in France*, 5th edn. 1969.

GERMANY

General Books

RAMM, AGATHA, *Germany 1789–1919*, 1967. The best in English, with a full bibliography.
CARR, W., *A History of Germany, 1815–1945*, 1969. Useful bibliography.
MANN, GOLO, *History of Germany*, tr. Jackson, 1968. Interesting, if idiosyncratic.

Special Topics

HAMEROW, T. S., *Restoration, Revolution, Reaction. Economics and Politics in Restoration Germany 1815–71*, Princeton, 1958.
WOODWARD, SIR E. L., *Three Studies in European Conservatism*, 1929. New impr. 1966.
CARR, W. H., *Schleswig-Holstein, 1815–1848*, Princeton, 1966.
HENDERSON, W. O., *The Zollverein*, 2nd edn. 1959.
EYCK, F., *The Frankfurt Parliament*, 1968.
NAMIER, SIR L. B., *1848. The Revolution of the Intellectuals*, British Academy Raleigh Lecture, 1944.
VALENTIN, V., *1848, Chapters of German History*, 1940.
BÖHME, HELMUT, ed., *The Foundation of the German Empire*, tr. Ramm, 1971. Documents on unification with excellent bibliography by the translator.
SIMON, W. M., *Germany in the Age of Bismarck*, 1968. Documents.
PFLANZE, O., *Bismarck and the Development of Germany 1815–1870*, Princeton, 1963.
TAYLOR, A. J. P., *Bismarck, the Man and the Statesman*, 1955.
EYCK, E., *Bismarck and the German Empire*, 1950.
ANDERSON, E. N., *The Social and Political Conflict in Prussia, 1858–1864*, Lincoln, U.S.A., 1954.
STEEFEL, L. D., *Bismarck, the Hohenzollern Candidacy, and the Origins of the Franco-German War of 1870*, Cambridge, Mass., 1962.
BALFOUR, M., *The Kaiser and his Times*, 1963.

RÖHL, J. G., *Germany without Bismarck*, 1967.
SCHORSKE, CARL, *German Social Democracy, 1905–1917*, Cambridge, Mass., 1955.
CRAIG, GORDON, *The Politics of the Prussian Army, 1640–1945*, 1955.
KOHN, HANS, *The Mind of Germany*, 1961.

ITALY

General Books

MACK SMITH, DENNIS, *Italy, a modern history*, 1959. Full bibliography.
SETON-WATSON, CHRISTOPHER, *Italy from Liberalism to Fascism 1870–1925*, 1967. Good, up-to-date bibliography.
CROCE, B., *History of Italy 1871–1915*, 1929.
BERKELEY, G. F. H., *Italy in the Making, 1815–1848*, 3 Vols., 1932–40.
SPRIGGE, C. J. S., *The Development of Modern Italy*, 1943.
ALBRECHT-CARRIÉ, R., *Italy from Napoleon to Mussolini*, 1950.
MACK SMITH, DENNIS, *The Making of Modern Italy, 1796–1870*, 1968. Documents with commentary.

Special Topics

HALES, E. E. Y., *Revolution and Papacy, 1769–1846*, 1960.
JEMOLO, A. C., *Church and State in Italy, 1850–1960*, 1960.
WEBSTER, Q., *Christian Democracy in Italy, 1860–1960*, 1961.
WOODWARD, SIR E.L., *Three Studies in European Conservatism*, 1929. New impr. 1966.
GREENFIELD, K. R., *Economics and Liberalism in the Risorgimento: A Study of Nationalism in Lombardy*, Baltimore, 1934.
GREW, RAYMOND, *A Sterner Plan for Italian Unity: The Italian Society in the Risorgimento*, Princeton, 1963.
MACK SMITH, DENNIS, *Cavour and Garibaldi, 1860*.
RAMM, AGATHA, *The Risorgimento*, Historical Association Pamphlet.
HILTON-YOUNG, W., *The Italian Left*, 1949.

NEUFELD, M. F., *Italy: A School for Awakening Countries*, Ithaca, U.S.A., 1961.
CLOUGH, S. B., *Economic History of Modern Italy*, 1964.

RUSSIA

Two nineteenth-century books retain their value as first-hand accounts of life in Russia:
LEROY-BEAULIEU, A., *The Empire of the Tsars and the Russians*, 3 Vols., French edn. 1881–9, tr. N.Y. 1893–96, repr. 1970.
MACKENZIE-WALLACE, SIR D., *Russia*, rev. edn. 1912.

General Books
PARES, SIR BERNARD, *A History of Russia*, 1926. rev. edn. 1955. Good bibliography.
SUMNER, B. H., *A Survey of Russian History*, rev. edn. 1947. Good bibliography.
SETON-WATSON, H., *The Russian Empire*, 1967. The best modern book with an up-to-date bibliography.
The Decline of Imperial Russia, 1952.

Special Topics
The Cambridge Economic History of Europe, Vol VI, contains the best account of the Russian economy as a whole.
EMMONS, T., *The Russian Landed Gentry and the Peasant Emancipation of 1861*, 1968.
MAZOUR, A. C., *The First Russian Revolution, 1825*, 1937.
LAMPERT, E., *Studies in Rebellion*, 1957. Essays on Belinsky, Herzen, and Bakunin.
HARE, R. G., *Pioneers of Russian Social Thought*, 1951.
VENTURI, F., *Roots of Revolution*, 1960.
KROPOTKIN, PRINCE PETER, *Memoirs of a Revolutionist*, 2 Vols., 1899.
CARR, E. H., *Michael Bakunin*, 1937. *The Bolshevik Revolution*, Vol 1, new edn., 1966.
SCHWARZ, *The Russian Revolution of 1905*, 1967.
LENIN, V. I., *What is to be done?* tr. V. Utrchin, 2nd edn., 1962.

STAVROU, T. G., ed. *Russian under the Last Tsar*, Minneapolis, 1969.
BARING, MAURICE, *An Outline of Russian Literature*, 1914.

AUSTRIA-HUNGARY

General Books

MACARTNEY, C. A., *The Hapsburg Empire, 1790–1918*, 1968, is the best and most recent book in English, with an excellent bibliography.
WICKHAM STEED, H., *The Hapsburg Monarchy*, 4th edn., 1919, is the best contemporary account of the empire in its last years.

Special Topics

LANGSAM, W. C., *The Napoleonic Wars and German Nationalism in Austria*, N.Y., 1930.
NAMIER, SIR L. B., *1848. The Revolution of the Intellectuals*, British Academy Raleigh Lecture, 1944.
MAURICE, C. E., *The Revolutionary Movement in Italy, Austria, and Hungary in 1848*, 1887.
RATH, R. J., *The Viennese Revolution of 1848*, Austin, Texas, 1952.
REDLICH, J., *The Emperor Francis Joseph*, 1930.
EISENMANN, L., *Le Compromis austro-hongrois de 1867*, 1904.
KANN, R. A., *The Multi-National Empire*, 2 Vols., N.Y., 1950.
WISKEMANN, E., *Czechs and Germans*, 2nd edn., 1967.
SETON-WATSON, R. W., *A History of the Czechs and Slovaks*, 1943. *The Southern Slav Question*, 1911.
WEST, REBECCA, *Black Lamb and Grey Falcon*, 1941. A brilliant work illustrating the conflict between Serbs and Austrians.
JASZI, O., *The Dissolution of the Hapsburg Monarchy*, 1929. A Hungarian Liberal's interpretation.

Index

Abdul Hamid II, Sultan, 140, 249 n. 1
Aberdeen, Lord, and Crimean War, 190 and n. 1; fall of his ministry, 190 n. 2
Abyssinia, Italian interests, 172, 173, 174
Acland, Sir Henry, *Memoir of the Cholera at Oxford... 1854*, 3
Action Française, 102 n. 1
Adler, Dr Viktor, 240
Adowa, Italian disaster, 174–5, 177
Adrianople, 247, 253 and n. 3
Aehrenthal, Count, and annexation of Bosnia-Herzegovina 141 and n. 1, 176, 250–1; railway project, 250; meeting with Izvolsky, 251; death, 252; results of his *coup*, 252
Africa, British acquisitions, 34; European partition, 37; Anglo-Saxon settlements, 37–8; German colonial trade, 40, 127
Agadir incident, 134 and n.
Aggression, exaggerated by Hobbes, 45; its natural objects, 45; antidotes, 45–6; alleged salutary effects of war, 266–7
Agriculture, as a basis of society, 9; government protection, 27–8; mechanization, 29–30; bad harvests and calamities, 33; American competition, 33; Austrian, 223, 225; French, 64–5, 74, 103; Italian, 162, 163; Russian, 191–2, 214–15
Alaska, Russian sale to U.S., 34 n., 182 n. 3
Albania, becomes a separate state, 253
Albert, archduke, in Italy, 234
Alexander I, tsar, 186; and Poland, 184 n., 199; Council of Ministers, 187; succession, 189
Alexander II, tsar, and secret police, 187 n. 2; moderate liberalism, 187–8, 191, 194, 196; fear of revolutionary ideas, 188; compared with his father, 190–1; abolition of serfdom, 193–4; assassination, 194, 195; and Poland, 200; and Ukraine nationalism, 202
Alexander III, tsar, 195
Alexander II, king of Serbia, assassination, 209
Alexandria, 141, 251
Alfred the Great, Danish treaty, 43 n. 1
Algeciras Conference (1906), on Morocco, 176
Algeria, deportation to, 76–7, 77 n.
Alps, tunnels and Passes, 29 n. 1; Italian boundary, 148
Alsace, demand for annexation, 17; transfer of territory by conquest, 43; Jewish population, 96
Alsace-Lorraine, annexation by France, 61; by Germany, 64, 122
America, European immigrants, 15; and European agriculture, 33; vast physical differences, 256 n.; study of her political evolution, 274–6
Angell, Norman, *The Great Illusion*, 266 n. 1
Anglican Prayer Book, 6, 23 n. 2
Anglo-Japanese alliance, 130, 133, 208
Anglo-Russian agreement, 136 139–40
Anti-semitism, in France, 96–7, 97 n.; in Austria, 241 and n. 1
Aosta, cretinism, 162
Aristotle, on the State, 5
Arnold, Matthew, education enthusiast, 3

Armaments, Anglo–German naval race, 135–8; Italian expenditure, 171; lack of international legislation, 263

Army Act (1879), 48

Arts, the, and concept of human progress, 6–7; interaction with advocacy of violence, 267–8

Asia, European boundaries, 13–14; Russian expansion, 182, 183

Asia Minor, earlier 'waste lands', 5 n.; Christian–Moslem hostility, 22; German railways, 127; European interests, 206

Assumptionist order, anti-semitism, 96; and *La Croix*, 96; dissolution, 97

Augustenburg, duke of (father and son), claims to Slesvig–Holstein, 116, 117, 145 and n., 146, 147

Austria, and 1848 revolution, 26, 109, 110, 112; and European community, 49; and Congress of Vienna, 52; autocratic intervention, 54; Napoleon III and, 81, 233; and German Confederation 104, 107–8, 112, 113, 224; other relations with Germany, 115, 117–18, 123; and Slesvig–Holstein question, 116, 117; Balkan rivalry with Russia, 122, 203; reinsurance treaty with Russia, 176; armaments race with Italy, 177; anti-liberalism 203, 224; early history, 220; centralization and germanization, 222–3, 239–40; mounting tide of revolution, 225; anti-Italian developments, 225–6, 230; disintegration of nationalism, 226 ff.; military failure, 233; character of Landtage, 233 and n.; and the *Ausgleich*, 235 and n. 4; bureaucratic dominance, 237, 244; liberal-Catholic Church opposition, 239; social reforms, 240–2, 244; effect of universal suffrage, 244; occupation of Bosnia–Herzegovina, 246, 249; relations with Serbia, 249, 250, 252–4

Austria–Hungary, vii; political restraints, 25; tariff impositions, 33; capital investment abroad, 40; relations with Russia, 57, 123, 140; position in triple alliance, 58; nationalist movements, 58, 236; Bismarck and, 123; Dual Alliance with Germany, 130; multi-national state problems, 140, 142, 237, 242; and Sarajevo assassination, 143; Italian-speaking population, 177; creation in 1867 (*Ausgleich*), 235, 236; German–Magyar compromise, 235; acceptance of designation, 235 n. 4; constitution, 235–6, 242, 244; and ultimatum to Serbia, 236; bureaucratic dominance, 237; a police state, 237; population distribution by nationalities, 238; Jewish problem, 241; *Kuhhandel* period, 242; language problems, 242 and n., 243; and universal suffrage, 243–4; failure to reconcile southern Slavs, 246

Austrian Government, and German Confederation, 108; restoration under Francis Joseph, 112; and Slesvig-Holstein, 117–18; creation of Reichsrat, 226, 228; prorogued in March 1914, 236; nationalities represented, 237; fight for existence, 242

Austrian Netherlands, revolt of 1789, 43; *see also* Belgium

Austro–Italian War (1848), 112, 226–8

Austro–Prussian War (1866), 83 161; an act of Prussian policy, 234

Backward countries, British policy, 38; rush to acquire sovereignty, 257

Badeni, Count, and Czech–German language question, 242–3, 243 n. 1

Bakunin, Mikhail, anarchist, Italian followers, 168; overshadowed by Marxism, 197; biog., 197 n. 1

Balance of power, and prevention of calamities, vii, 46; changing concepts, 47–9, 55, 56; failure as peacekeeper, 49; effect of defeat of Napoleon, 50–1; Gentz's basis of constitution, 51–2; invoked by Treaty of Vienna, 52; used to justify

Balance of power, *cont.*
  autocratic intervention, 54; destroyed by Prussian militarism, 56; superseded by military aggrandisement, 56–7, 58; pre-1914 equilibrium, 57–8; Franco–German alliance, 207
Balbo, Cesare, 154
Balkans, Austro–Russian rivalry, 122, 123, 140, 184, 203, 246, 248–9; 1912–13 wars, 142, 178, 210 n. 2; Racconigi treaty, 176 and n.; westernizing nationalism, 203; extent and peoples, 246–7; imposed foreign dynasties, 247; Russian diplomacy, 252; haphazard economic development, 262; territorial ambitions, 262
Baltic states, linguistic enclaves, 17; and balance of power, 146; Russian advancement, 183; education, 185 n. 1; compulsory use of Russian, 201
Baratieri, General, and Adowa, 174 and n.
Barrère, Camille, 175
Basques, 61
Batum, 183
Bazaine, Marshal François, 88 and n. 2
Bebel, Ferdinand August, 127, 264
Belgium, two-language state, 17, 262; and French Revolution, 43; guaranteed independence, 84, 126; industrial progress, 108; invasion under Schlieffen plan, 125–6, 126 n.
Benedek, General, in Bohemia, 234–5, 235 n. 1
Benedetti, Vincent Count, 84; and Spanish crown dilemma, 86; Ems telegram, 87 and n. 1
Benedictines of Solesnes, 97
Berchtold, Count, succeeds Aehrenthal, 252, 254
Bergson, Henri, his influence, 102
Berlin, 105; Royal University, 106; population, 108; 1848 revolution, 110, 226; expulsion of Social Democrats, 121
Bessarabia, 204, 206
Bessemer, Sir Henry, steel process, 29

Bethmann-Hollweg, Theobald von, 128 n. 1, 143
Bismarck, Otto, Prince, application of means to ends, 27; Prussian objective, 27, 83–4, 113–19 *passim*; and protection, 32; Slesvig-Holstein policy, 55 and n. 2, 83, 116–18, 147, 234; and isolation of France, 57, 129; and Napoleon III, 81–4, 119–20; and need for war, 85; and Spanish crown, 85–7, 119–20; 1871 peace terms to France, 89 n.; and liberalism, 113–19 *passim*; and army reform, 115, 116; elimination of Austria, 117, 234; and Russia, 119, 122–3; and France, 119, 120; dominating position as Chancellor, 121–6; dismissal, 121; and Catholic Church, 121; international aims, 122–3, 247; and an Austrian alliance, 122, 123, 205–6; 'reinsurance treaty' with Russia, 123, 175, 206, 248 and n. 2; relations with the Emperor, 124–5; inability to collaborate, 125; and colonial expansion, 126–7; public appearance, 128 n.; and Triple Alliance, 172–3; Balkan diplomacy, 206, 246; and Russian loans, 248; and European peace, 262
Bizerta, 172
Blake, William, 273
Blanc, Louis, and unemployment (*L'Organization du travail*), 73–4; co-operative plan, 74, 75–6
Bohemia, 221; Czech nationals, 111, 221 and n., 225, 243; and Habsburgs, 221; suppression of revolt, 227–8; German nationals, 236 n., 238
Bologna, papal troops, 226
Bolsheviks, origin of term, 199; dispute with Mensheviks, 216; minority group, 218; and abandonment of the War, 218–19; unforeseen rise, 259
Bonald, Louis, Vicomte de, 68
Bordeaux, meetings of National Assembly, 88, 89, 90
Bosnia-Herzegovina, Austrian annexation, 141–2, 176, 177, 210, 249, 250–1; Slav revolution, 204; Russia and, 210, 250–1; Austrian occupa-

Bosnia-Herzegovina, *cont.*
tion, 246, 249; Moslem rebellion, 249; peasant population, 249 and n. 2; religious toleration, 249 n. 2
Bosnians, assassination of archduke, 254; and Austrian occupation, 249 and n. 2, 250
Boulanger, General, 92
Bourbons, misrule, 25; return to Naples, 26, 149 n. 1; return after Waterloo, 67, 68, 82 n. 2; claimant to throne (1871), 91-2; Church hopes of, 93, 94
Bretons, 61
British Empire, unplanned growth before 1815, 34, 38; trade foundation, 34; association of free peoples, 36
British Government, 51; and colonial self-government, 38; and autocratic intervention, 54; relations with Germany, 130; and *Entente Cordiale* (1904), 130-2; and Egypt, 131 n.; and naval superiority, 136; and expenditure on armaments, 136; and closure of Straits, 141 and n. 2, 251; and Slesvig-Holstein, 146; and Sicily, 162 n. 2
Browning, Robert, 30 n., 161
Buchar, L., and colonial development/national power connection, 39
Buchlau, Aehrenthal-Izvolsky meeting, 141, 251
Budapest, alternate seat of government, 235
Bukovina, 206
Bulgaria, Russian predominance, 123, 246, 247-8; peasant revolt, 204; and access to Aegean, 205; interests in Asia Minor, 206; union with Rumelia, 247; relations with Serbia, 248, 250, 253
Bülow, Prince von, 125; Chinese policy, 208
Byzantium, 247; sack of in 1204, 22; source of Russian Christianity, 180; and Serbo-Croats, 238 n. 1

Cabot, John, 7-8
Calais, English occupation, 18 n. 2

Calvinists, territorial establishment, 48
Canada, 40, 63-4
Canning, George, and Vienna Treaty, 54
Capitalism, last barrier before utopia (Marx), 9; Cobden and, 35 n.; Hobson and 'under-consumption', 39-40; French attacks, 70, 74; weak Russian adherents, 198, 211; socialist association with war guilt, 264
Carducci, Giosuè, 171
Carinthia, 238
Carlyle, Thomas, 272-3
Carnarvon, Lord, and word 'imperialism', 35
Carolingian Empire, 21
Castlereagh, Robert Stewart, viscount, 52, 55; and use of 'national' forces, 43-4; and diplomacy by consultation, 53, 57
Catherine the Great, 180; and 'private serfs', 186; and the Ukraine, 202
Catholic Action, in Italy, 167
Catholics, and Treaty of Westphalia, 48 and n. 2; absurdities of counter-revolution, 68, 93; and Rome as the capital, 82, 85; widening breach with modern society, 93; and education in France, 93-4; and Italian liberalism, 155; and new kingdom of Italy, 167-8; abstention from political participation, 168
Cavour, Count Camillo Benso di, 149; place of origin, 44; and Napoleon III, 81, 82, 156-7, 157 n. 1, 158; on Windsor, 154 n.; compared with Bismarck, 155, 156; and Garibaldi, 155, 159-60; and the Church, 156, 160; responsibility for unification, 156; *Il Risorgimento*, 155
Cayenne, deportees, 79
'Central Society for commercial geography and German interests abroad', 39
Chamberlain, Joseph, 130
Chambord, Henri comte de, and French throne, 91 and n.
Charlemagne, 21, 22, 220
Charles III, king of Spain, 149 n. 1

Charles V, Emperor, 220-1
Charles X, king of France. 68-9, 78 and n. 2
Charles Albert, king of Sardinia, 152; invasion of Lombardy, 153, 225, 226; armistice with Radetsky, 228, 229-30; abdication, 230
Charles Martel, defeats Moslem invaders, 21-2
Chateaubriand, François vicomte de, 68
Chaucer, Geoffrey, use of term 'nation', 18 n. 1
China, 5; homogeneous, well-protected empire, 10-11; British 'open door' policy, 36, 208, 209; Russian advancement, 130, 182, and n., 207; Boxer rebellion, 208 and n.; fall of Manchu dynasty, 209; Russo-Japanese adjustment of interests, 263
Christendom, concept of temporal state, 2; unity in Middle Ages, 22, 256; dyarchy of Pope and Emperor, 22, 47; Fénelon on, 48; anti-semitism, 241
Christian Democrats, Austrian, 244
Christian of Glücksburg, Prince, 146
Christian Social movement, Austrian, 240
Church, Christian, and transference of tradition, 21; a universality of persons, 22; and heresies, 23; and Counter-Revolution, 93; loses contest against secular state, 166, 261, 271; neglect of popular misery, 166; diverted by rise of socialism, 167; reaction to indifference, 271
    French, and Napoleon III, 78, 93; and conservatives, 92, 94; and education, 93-4; opposition to republic, 94; and Dreyfus case, 95, 97; denounces Concordat, 98; position of clergy, 99 n. 1
    Russian (Orthodox), character of schismatics (Old Believers), 180-1, 181 n.; state domination, 181; Holy Synod, 181; absorption of Greek Uniates, 201
Civilizations (high), exampled in Europe, vii, 1, 256; accompanied by dangers as well as achievements, vii, 4, 10, 256; high material standards, 3; ancient/modern comparison, 3-4; marked by greater rationalization, 4; 'waste land' view, 5 and n., marked by an organized state, 5-6; post-War degradation, 8-9; unequal pace of achievement, 10-11; alleged work of an élite minority, 11; prohibit censorship of the mind, 11-12; pressure on human beings, 12; produce extremes, 13; European development, 13 ff; pace of material and social advance, 258; changing attitude to war, 260

Clark, Sir George, and territorial transfers, 43 n. 1
Cobbett, William, and child labour, 260 n.
Cobden, Richard, and preferential colonial trade, 35 n.; and *laissez faire* capitalism, 35 n.; Treaty, 31-2
Colonial settlement, colonies, 7; viewed as a burden, 34 and n., 35 and n.; loss of America, 34-5; European comparisons, 39, 63; economic value, 40; German brutality, 128; Italian ambitions, 171-2
Colonial Society, German, 39
Colombus, Christopher, 7, 8 n.
Combes, Émile, anti-clericalism, 98
Common Customs Union (*Zollverein*), 108, 118, 151-2
Commune, the, defeat in 1871, 66, 90-1; creation by National Guard, 89; nature of the revolution, 89-90; horrors of civil war, 90-1, 94
Communist Manifesto, 26 and n.
Comte, Auguste, and 'automatic progress', 9; his new system, 272 n.
Concert of Europe, 53-4, 171, 256
Condorcet, Marquis de, *Esquisse d'un tableau historique* ..., 2 and n., 3
Confédération Générale du Travail (C.G.T.), 101, 102-3
Confederazione Generale del Lavoro (C.G.L.), 170
Congress of Berlin, Bismarck and, 123, 171, 205; Italian delegation, 171, based on secret agreements, 205 n. 1

'Congress Poland', 184 n.
Congress of the Second International (1905), 101 and n.
Congress of Vienna (1815), 51 n., 104; and territorial transfers, 42; behaviour of Great Powers, 52; and return of Italian sovereigns, 151; and Poland, 184 n.
Congress of Westphalia, 48 and n. 2
Conrad, Joseph, on patriotism, 45 n.
Constantine, Grand Duke, viceroy of Poland, 189
Constantinople, 17, 246; Patriarchate, 181; fear of Russian control, 203; Enver Bay and Young Turks, 253 n. 3
Council of Trent, 222
Counter-Reformation, Catholic, 8, 222
Crédit Foncier, foundation, 31, 96
Crimea, the, foundation, 180
Crimean War, 29, 119, 267; Great Britain and, 54, 190 n. 2, 263; immediate causes, 189–90; and Pan-Slavism, 203; and Black Sea, 204
Crispi, Francesco, 173–4; and Adowa, 174–5
Croatia, 221; and Hungary, 221, 228; Christianization, 238 n. 1
Croatia-Slavonia, kingdom of, 244, 246
Croats, percentage of Austria-Hungarian population, 238, 244; relations with Serbs, 238 n. 1, 245; in Bosnia, 250
Cromer, Evelyn Baring, Earl, 131 n.
Custozza, battle of, 228
Czechs, deprived of sovereignty, 42, 238; nationalist movement, 111, 225, 238, 239; in Bohemia, 221, 222; destruction by Habsburgs, 222; and Reichsrat, 236 n.; % of Austro-Hungarian population, 237; and language question, 242 and n. 1, 243

Dalmatia, 238, 246
Dante Alighieri, vision of Eternal law, 6; idea of dual authority, 47, 48 n. 1; damnation of politicians, 273
Danzig, 14, 104, 184 n.
Dardanelles, 183, 204; *see also* Straits
Darwin, Charles, and justification of war (*Origin of Species*), 267

De Lesseps, F., 97
Delcassé, Théophile, and *Entente Cordiale*, 132; and Triple Alliance, 175
Denmark, rights in Slesvig-Holstein, 55, 83, 111, 116, 145–7; Austro-Prussian victory, 117, 146–7; provision of joint parliament, 145; abrogation of Salic Law, 145 n.
Directory, the, 61
Diseases, Athenian and Roman plagues, 3–4; fourteenth century pestilences, 4; Black Death, 9; malaria, 161–2; cretinism, 162
Drefus, Capt., 95 and n.; repercussions of his case, 96
Drumont, Édouard, *La France juive*, 96
Dual Alliance (German/Austria-Hungary), 130
Duisberg-Ruhrort, water-borne trade, 14
Dupont de l'Eure, Jacques, 75

Eastern Question, 122–3, 184
Economic nationalism, rise of, 28, 32; individual justifications, 33; transfer of competition to states, 33, 41; projection into 'uncivilized world', 34, 40–1
Education, French, 30, 93, 94, 98; German, 105 and n., 108; Italian, 163, 166; Polish, 201; Russian, 185 and n. 1, 196, 214
Edward VII, king, 58 n., 140 n. 1, 268 n. 2
Egypt, financial defaults and reforms, 31 n. 2, 127, 131 n.
Empire, use of term, 35
Enfantin, Barthélemy Prosper, Saint-Simonian, 71
Engels, Friedrich, 90 n.; and Communist Manifesto, 26 n.
England, and world naval control, 7; surrender of princely power, 18–19; vernacular culture, 23 and n. 1; mutual antagonism with France, 49, 60; membership of European community, 49; 'insularity', 60; origin of 'socialism', 70 and n. 1; universities, 105 n.; and employment of children, 260 and n.; clerical protest against indifference, 271

Entente Cordiale, settlement, 130–1; German reaction, 132–3, 137, 176; strengthened after Agadir, 134–5, 252; Italy and, 176
Enver Bay, 253 n. 3
Eritrea, Italian colony, 174
Europe, Europeans, centre of high civilization, vii, 1, 13–14; dark ages, 8; twentieth century regression, 8–9, 11; geographical characteristics, 13–15; growth and transfer of populations, 14–15; share of world's wealth, 14; racial/political disunity, 16–17; impact of French Revolution, 19, 259; early ignorance of foreign lands and goods, 21 and n.; year of revolutions (1848), 26, 199; triumph of force over idealism, 26–7; ignorance of forthcoming transformation, 27; periods of economic malaise, 33, 75; lack of accurate statistical information, 49; membership of its community, 49; changed face after Napoleon, 50; periods of unemployment, 110; result of failure of German liberalism, 113–14; what is her future? 257 ff.; contemporary recession, 257; nineteenth-century advancement, 258–9; growing sense of social responsibility, 259–60; lack of common unifying efforts, 262; failure to foresee or circumvent disaster, 263–4; periods of peace, 267; political advocacy of violence, 267–9; decrease in religious influence and conformity, 270–1

Far East, 130, 140, 207–9, 248–9; extension from Eastern Question, 184
Fascism, 102; origins of its *clichés*, 177; unforeseen rise, 259
Fénelon, François de Salignac, Archbishop, and economic equity between neighbouring nations, 47–8, 48 n. 1, 57
Ferdinand I, Emperor of Austria, 109, 221, 224–5; promises a constitution, 225; and the Reichsrat, 226; abdication, 226, 227, 229

Ferdinand I, king of Two Sicilies, 153, 154; in Sicily, 162 n. 2
Ferdinand I, king of Spain, and Two Sicilies, 149 n. 1
Feudalism, an exercise of power, 6; incompetent magnates, 23; its opponents, 35 n.; abolition in Austria, 110
Fichte, Johann Gottlieb, *Der geschlossene Handelstaat*, 32 and n. 1
Finland, 184; Russia and, 201 and n., 202
First World War, unforeseen schism of Europe, 8–9; 265; an immeasurable calamity, 8, 266; recruiting poster, 37 n. 1; precipitated in act of assassination, 58, 142–3, 245; British naval superiority, 138, 144; implementation of Schlieffen plan, 143, 144; British intervention, 143; Russia and, 217, 218–19; criticisms of Germany, 260; alleged capitalist machination, 264; anticipated early ending, 265; general unpreparedness, 265–6
Fiume, 238, 244
Florence, 149, 160
Fourier, François Marie, his 'phalansteries' (*Théorie des Quatre Mouvements*), 72
France, vii, 48; compared with Britain, 7, 62, 74; linguistic boundaries, 17; retention of princely power, 19; fear of anarchy, 26; overthrow of Second Republic, 26, 62; technological improvements, 29; and 'limited liability' principle, 31; tariff impositions, 32; African acquisitions, 35; territorial threats to Britain, 36; and European community, 49; and Congress of Vienna, 52; 'national' history, 59–60, 60–2; influence of her civilization, 59–60; Third Republic, 62, 69, 91–2; geographical features, 62; population, 62, 63; laws of succession, 63; and Germany, 64; industry compared with agriculture, 64; political characteristics, 67; philosophy of Counter-Revolution, 68; division among republicans, 70; discontent with socio/economic con-

294 Europe 1815-1914

France, *cont.*
ditions, 73; disruption of Monarchy, 73; provisional governments, 75; defeat of 1848 insurrection, 76-7; Second Empire, 79-80; 1870 plebiscite, 80; and the Spanish crown, 85-7; Government of National Defence, 88; separation of Church and State, 98-9; absence of union organization, 99-101; revolt against reason, 102; loans to Russia, 124, 213; influence in Morocco, 131; and British in Egypt, 131 n.; high army estimates, 138; N. African ambitions, 172; and Triple Alliance, 173, 175; tariff war with Italy, 173, 175; intervention in Abyssinia, 173-4; as a nation-state, 220; and religious indifference, 271-2

Franchise, in republican France, 69-70; Bismarck and, 119, 124; in Italy, 64, 167-8

Francis II, Emperor, 223, 224, 224 n.; later Francis I Emperor of Austria, 224 and n.

Francis II, king of Naples, 158, 159 and n.

Francis Ferdinand, archduke, assassination, 58, 142-3, 178, 210, 254

Francis Joseph, emperor of Austria. 85, 112, 142, 209; sccession, 229; political concessions, 229, 233; character and achievements, 231 and n. 1, 232; personal life, 231 n. 2, 232; absolute rule period, 232-3; and the army, 234; and the *Ausgleich*, 236, 242; and possible war with Russia, 242; introduces universal suffrage, 243 and n. 2

Franco-Prussian War, vii, 30, 161, 204; outbreak, 80, 87, 120; and German unification, 80; pre-war machinations, 87; siege of Paris, 87-8; peace terms, 88-9, 89 n.

Franco-Russian alliance, 123; Germany and, 128; a threat to Britain, 129-30, 207; final agreement, 206-7; fear of its collapse, 213

Frankfurt Assembly (*Vorparliament*), 109, 110-11; middle class character, 110-11; consciousness of world mission, 111; projected German navy, 111 n.; offers crown to Frederick William IV, 112, 230; and Slesvig-Holstein, 146; and Austrian question, 226, 229; collapse, 230

Frederick the Great, 19, 49, 105

Frederick II, king of Prussia, 222

Frederick III, emperor of Germany, death from cancer, 124

Frederick VII, king of Denmark, 145-6

Frederick William I, king of Prussia, 106

Frederick William IV, king of Prussia, 226; and constitutional reforms, 109, 112; ambitions, 110; dissolves the Assembly, 111; refuses crown of united Germany, 112; and 'little' Germany, 113; insanity, 115 n.

Free trade, 31-2

Freemasonry, French, 92, 95

French, the, contrast, 'la nation' and 'le roi', 19; investment abroad, 40; treatment after defeat of 1815, 53; consciousness of intellectual preeminence, 60; underrate the Germans, 60 and n.; ignore English experience, 60; political experiments, 61-2; stability during political changes, 62; slow population growth, 63, 64; agricultural workers, 64-5; and political management, 67; character of middle classes, 69, 70, 101, 103; tradition of revolutionary violence, 100; stable society in 1914, 103; fishing rights off Newfoundland, 130 n. 2

French Academy, 79-80

French (Republican) Government, mutual distrust of Church, 94; anticlerical measures, 94, 97-8, 98 n., 99; and freemasonry, 95; and Dreyfus case, 97; denounces the Concordat, 98; and strikes, 103

French National Assembly, 88-9; and Third Republic, 91-2

French Revolution, 43; Condorcet and, 2 and n.; gives impetus to national sovereignty, 19, 24, 43-4; progenitor of 'liberals', 24; causes continental surprise, 60; destroys

French Revolution, *cont.*
old political system, 61; an urban achievement, 66; anti-Church policy, 92; influence on Germany, 106, on Italy, 150; early hopes from, 259
Freud, Sigmund, 13; his influence, 102
Futurism, correlation with advocacy of violence, 267–8

Galicia, 224, 225, 230, 237 and n.; Jewish immigrants, 241
Gallipoli, 247 and n.
Gambetta, Léon Michel, 87, 88; biog., 88 n. 1
Gapon, Fr, and 'police socialism', 211; workers' petition to the Tsar, 211–12
Garibaldi, Giuseppe, 149; birth at Nice, 44, 158; and Two Sicilies, 82; and liberation of Rome, 82, 159, 161; Cavour and, 155, 159; arrest in Piedmont, 158; exile in Caprera, 158–9; Sicilian landing, 159; hands over to Victor Emmanuel, 160; defeated by French 161
Genoa, 44; republic, 42, 50, 149, 151
Gentz, Friedrich von, 'Fragments on the Balance of Power', 51 and n., 52
German Confederation (with Prussia and Austria), establishment, 104, 107; and Austria, 104, 107–8, 224, 230; the Diet, 107–8, 109, 117; slow economic growth, 108; and 1848 revolutions, 108–9, 113; meeting of *Vorparliament*, 109, 110, 111; Slesvig-Holstein and, 145–7
German Government (Reichstag), and colonization, 38; elections, 128 and n. 2; relations with Great Britain, 130; and Egyptian affairs, 131 n. 132; and Agadir crisis, 134; and Russia, 142, 207; and British intervention in 1914, 143–4
German Reich, military based predominance, 56, 127–8, 144; population frontiers, 62, 63, 104; linguistic variations, 104; a federation of princes, 120, 148; Prussian domination, 120–1; Bismarck and, 122 ff. 144, 205–6; dependence on Chancellor/Emperor co-operation, 125, 144; advance in wealth, 126, 127; errors of high policy, 129 ff.; complaints of encirclement, 129, 135, 139
German states, religious equilibrium, 48; and European community, 49; settlement by Treaty of Vienna, 53; under Holy Roman Empire, 59; and a war with France, 84, 85, 87, 119; absentee sovereigns. 107; Prussian annexation, 118
Germans, blind obedience to Hitler, 8; belief in British plot, 58; numbers compared with French, 64; problems of unification, 104–5, 107, 148; middle class liberals, 109–10; treatment of Poles, 111; acceptance of authority from above, 114; *nouveaux riche* arrogance, 127; limitless belief in own superiority, 127–8; inefficiency in higher echelons, 144; midEuropean settlers, 221; and Austrian language question, 243; in Austria and Austria-Hungary, 235, 238–40, 242–3
Germany, vii; change in urban/rural population, 15; linguistic boundaries, 17, 104; and retention of princely power, 19; defeat of liberalism, 26, 109–13, 224; and unification, 26, 80, 83, 148; adoption of 'limited liability' principle, 31; pursuit of power by economic measures, 32; industrial over-building, 33; African empire, 35, 127; colonial expansion, 38, 126–7, 134; private investment abroad, 40; position in Triple Alliance, 58; differing political/geographical frontiers, 104–5; as a nation-state, 105–6, 108–9, 220; nature of her culture, 105–6, 127; self-image of world leadership, 111, 127; 'great' and 'little' solutions, 112, 113, 115; competition for her leadership, 115 ff.; diplomatic alliances, 122–3; plan for 'two-front' war, 126 n.; welfare benefits, 129; misjudgement of Britain, 129, 130;

Germany, *cont.*
and a secret treaty with Russia, 133; naval competition with Britain, 135 and n. 2, 136–8; relations with Turkey, 138–9; suppression of democratic press, 144; and Slesvig-Holstein, 145–7; intervention in China, 207–8; seventeenth-century catholic/protestant division, 222; merges with Prussia, 226; and Anglo-Russian *entente*, 252; General Staff hopes for war, 265 and n. 2

Gibraltar, British retention, 42
Gioberti, Vincenzo, *Del primato morale e civile degli Italiani*, 152
Giolitti, Giovanni, 169 and n., 170
Gladstone, William Ewart, 54, 128 n. 1; opposes naval programme, 130 n. 1
Gorki, Maxim, 213
Gortchakov, Prince, 34 n., 57, 203 n.
Great Britain, and oceanic trade and expansion, 7; geographical detachment from Europe, 14 and n.; technological inventions, 28, 29; adoption of 'limited liability' principle, 31; development of horticulture, 33; leading colonial power in 1815, 34; African acquisitions, 35; annexes N. Zealand, 35–6; attitude towards colonies, 36, 37; mood of 'jingoism' and self-satisfaction, 36; small army vis-à-vis European forces, 36; private investment abroad, 40; union of England and Scotland, 42–3; behaviour at Congress of Vienna, 52; opposition to autocratic intervention, 54; and Napoleon III, 55; belief in forthcoming German aggression, 58 n.; compared with France, 62, 74; and union organization, 100; and a standing army, 114; and Eastern Question, 123; German competition, 136–8; and Russian plans for Turkey, 189–90, 203; Whig defence of rule of law, 260–1; unpreparedness for war, 265–6, 266 n. 3; ignorance of her people of forthcoming war, 268 and n. 2
Great Powers, composition, vii, 256; emergence as independent sovereign states, 47, 256; Russian and Prussian entry, 49; misuse of power of intervention, 50, 54; and partition of Poland, 50 and n.; and overthrow of Napoleon, 50; lack of consultation with local population, 52; two European groups, 58; myths concerning opposition aggression, 58; position of Italy, 161, 171, 172; intervention in Turkey, 204–6; Chinese concessions, 208; and Bosnia-Hertzegovina, 246; and the Balkans, 247; diversities and similarities, 256; lack of common action, 262; periods of peace, 262–3; conscript armies, 264

Greece, earlier 'waste lands', 5 n.; Orthodox Church, 201, 202; population, 246
Greeks (Ancient), belief in cycles of change, 2; distinguish themselves from barbarians, 2; and terrible nature of man, 9–10; ignorance of history, 10
Gregory XVI, Pope, 272
Grey, Sir Edward, 265 n. 1; and the Straits, 141 n. 2, 241 n.; and Agadir, 134; and British intervention in 1914, 266 and n. 2
Guesde, Jules, 96
Guizot, François, rigid conservatism, 69

Habsburgs, 26, 43, 110; titular monarchs, 49, 105, 222; multi-national dominions, 107, 149 n. 2, 209, 220, 224; Germany and, 142; and national unity, 220; Hungary and, 221–2, 230; and protestantism, 222; and Hohenzollerns, 222; and revolutionary France, 223; and Napoleon, 223; dynastic marriages, 223–4; suppression of liberalism, 224; break up of the Empire, 225, 228; and the *Ausgleich*, 236; residual power, 242
Hamburg, 108
Hanover, 107, 118
Hardenberg, Karl August, Fürst von, 106 and n.

Hasties, William, and Russian planning, 187 n.
Hayes, and transfer of competition to states, 33
Haynau, General, reputation for brutality, 230 and n.; in England, 230 n.
Henry VII, 8 n., 18 n. 2
Henry VIII, 12 n., 18
Hertz, Cornelius, and Panama Canal, 97 n.
Herzen, Alexander, on the modern state, 261
Hesse-Nassen, 118
Hitler, Adolf, parody of civilized society, 8, 79; fellow-countryman of Freud, 13; *Mein Kampf*, 241 n. 1
Hobbes, Thomas, his uncivilized society, 1; on postures of war, 45; *Leviathan*, 45
Hobson, J. A., economic theories, 39 and n. 2
Hohenzollerns, 107; and Spanish crown, 85, 119-20; territorial ambitions, 222
Hohenzollern-Sigmaringen, Prince, 85
Holstein, its status, 52, 116, 117, 147; and German Confederation, 145
Holy Roman Empire, Dante and, 47; Voltaire on, 105; abolition by Napoleon, 107, 224; Charles V and, 220; reduction to titular sovereignty, 222
Hong Kong, 36
Housman, A. E., his 'mercenary army', 37
Hubbe-Scheiden, *Deutsche Kolonien*, 39
Hundred Years War, 22 n.
Hungary, 221; rebellion of 1849, 203, 230; cattle plague, 225; Kossuth and, 225-6; and Croatia, 228; discontent under Francis Joseph, 233, 234; and the *Ausgleich*, 235 and n. 4, 236; Magyar domination, 237, 245; distribution of nationalities, 244; position of Jews, 245 and n.
Hus, John, 221 and n., 222

Imperialism, projection of economic nationalism into untouched areas, 34, 40-1; use of term, 34, 35; present-day tendency to denigrate, 36, 39; decline after S. African War, 37; economic advantages, 40; contributory cause of two great wars, 41
Independent Labour Party, 285 n. 1
Independent Socialist Party, 128
India, protection of rulers against exploitation, 31 n. 2; extension of British authority into 'power vacuum', self-government, 38 n. 2; English and French expansion, 50; control of overland routes, 190
Individual, the, freedom of choice in high civilizations, 4, 6; misuse of power, 9; adjustment to civilized life, 12; lack of participation in modern state, 12; increasing isolation, 41
Industrial Revolution, 2, 4, 15, 73-4
Industrialization, 12, 27, 33, 163
Industry, in France, 64 and n., 73-4, 100, 103; German advances, 126; in Italy, 162, 163; Russian backwardness and later advance, 185, 211, 215
International organizations, 53; and freedom from fear and jealousy, 46; and overriding authority, 47; Postal Union, 46 and n. 1
Intervention, corollary to idea of balance of power, 47, 50, 53; used to exterminate lesser states, 50, 54; used against liberal reforms, 54; British resistance to absolutism, 54
Ireland, hostility to British rule, 38 n. 1
Isabella, Queen, 85
Ismail Pasha, 131
Italian Government, Napoleon III and, 160; corrupt practices, 164-5; particularist difficulties, 165; southern protection in return for votes, 165; papal refusal of Law of Guarantees, 166; effect of Catholic laity abstention, 168; and change to nation-state, 170-1; handicaps in its foreign policy, 171, 172; neutrality agreement with France, 175 and n.; Racconigi treaty with Russia, 176 and n.; and approach of First World War, 178

Italians, 149; middle classes, 150, 151-2; influence of Napoleonic conquests, 150-1; in Russia with him, 151 n.; desire for constitutional reform, 151; and national unity, 154, 165, 166; illiteracy, 162, 164, 166; absentee landlords, 162; low standard of living, 162-3; money sent home by emigrants, 166; north/south comparison, 166; division between revolutionaries, 168, 169; European denigration, 171 and n.; desire for grandeur, 171-2; emigration to France and U.S., 171-2; and Adowa defeat, 174 and n., 177; contribution to cult of violence, 177; percentage of Austro/Hungarian population, 238; and Futurism, 267-8

Italy, vii, 61; earlier 'waste lands', 5 n.; linguistic boundaries, 17, 148; collapse of revolutionary movement, 26, 153-4; and political unity, 26, 149, 150, 151-2, 154; tariff impositions, 32; nationalist cause, 81, 154, 155, 177; and Napoleon III, 81-2, 154, 156; effect of French revolutions, 108, 150; formation of a nation-state, 148-9, 170-1, 220; natural boundaries, 148; strength of city life, 149; Austrian predominance, 151-2, 154, 229; north/south disagreements, 152, 165; union under house of Savoy, 155, 160, 161; choice of a capital, 160; ancient glory, 161; centre of universal Church, 161; natural resources, 161-2; malarial regions, 161; poor communications, 162; brigandage, 162 and n. 2; corrupt political life, 164-5, 165-6; centralization (Piedmontization), 165; general strike, 169; underlying tradition of violence, 170; efforts to achieve grandeur, 171; colonial expansion, 171-2, 173-4; claims to *terra irredenta*, 172, 176, 177; membership of Triple Alliance, 172-3, 175; relations with Germany, 173, 176; tariff war with France, 173, 175; renewed outbreak of megalomania (*sacro egoisme*), 177; and Tripoli, 177-8; violation of treaties, 178 n.; and First World War, 178, 179; suppression of liberalism, 224; anti-Austrian outbreaks, 225

Izvolsky, meeting with Aehrenthal, 141, 251; and Balkans, 250

Jacobins, 25, 50, 61, 107; and external aggression, 54
Japan, British alliance, 130, 133, 208; victory over Russia, 136, 140; and Russian encroachment in China, 208-9, 263
Jaurès, Jean, and social reform, 99, 101 n., 264; assassination, 101 n.; and use of violence, 102
Jellacic, Count Josip, Ban of Croatia, 228
Jesuits, 94, 97; in China, 182 n.; and Counter-Reformation, 222
Jevons, W. S., 270
Jews, in France, 96; financial disrepute, 96-7, 97 n., 241; in Austria-Hungary, 241, 245 and n.; expulsion from Spain, 247 n.
Joan of Arc, 22 n., 44
John III Sobieski, 222
Joseph II, emperor, 43, 222-3

Kamchatka, 180
Karageorgevich dynasty, 209-10
Keble, John, sermon on 'National Apostasy', 271 and n.; and religious indifference, 271 and n.
Kiaochow, German occupation, 208
Kidd, Benjamin, *Social Evolution*, 269 n. 2
Kiel, mutiny of German navy, 138
Kingsley, Charles, *Two Years Ago*, 3, 276 n. 1
Kipling, Rudyard, literary exponent of imperialism, 36-7; and *Pax Britannica* in India, 37; truthful portrayal of British soldier, 37
Kitchener, Lord, victory at Omdurman, 174; and trench warfare, 266 n. 3
Kokovtsev, and Rasputin, 215
Königgrätz, battle of, 83, 118
Korea, Russian interests, 207, 208, 209

Kossuth, Louis, and Hungary, 225–6, 230; escapes to Turkey, 230; denounces *Ausgleich*, 235 n. 3; biog., 225 n.

Ladin, 238 and n. 2
Lamennais, F. R. de, and Church of France, 271–2; view of society, 272
Lansdowne, Lord, 139
Latin, 10; ceases to be international language, 23; use on China–Russian boundary posts, 182 n. 2
Latin American Republics, economic measures, 33–4
Laviegerie, Cardinal, 94 and n.
League of Nations, 20, 256; foreshadowed in Concert of Europe, 53
League of Three Emperors, Bismarck and, 247
Lena goldfields, political strike, 215
Lenin (Vladimir Ilyich Ulianov), biog., 197 n. 2; influence of Hobson, 39; joins Marxist revolutionaries, 197; his own plan, 198, 199, 219 (*What is to be done?*); in exile, 210; and Mensheviks, 216; on Trotsky, 216; arrival in St Petersburg, 218; assessment, 219
Leningrad, 183
Leo XIII, Pope, election, 94; and French Church, 94; proposes Church/Republic *rapprochement*, 94–5; and kingdom of Italy, 166–7; encyclical *Rerum Novarum*, 167 and n.
Leonardo da Vinci, and misuse of inventions, 12
Leopold II (Grand Duke of Tuscany), emperor, 223
Leroy-Beaulieu, P. P., *De la colonisation chez les peuples modernes*, 39 n. 1
Levantines, loans to potentates, 31 n. 2
Liaotung peninsular, 207, 208, 209
Liberalism, long and changing history, 24; attainable demands, 25; a defence against anarchy, 25; attacked from left and right, 25–6; short-lived triumph (1848), 26, 113; subsequent political reaction, 27; papal opposition, 27, 153, 154, 156;

Austrian, 224, 239–42; German 109, 111, 113, 118–19; Italian, 155
Liberals, on the side of property, 25–6; inability to defeat vested interests, 26
Libya, 178
Lisbon, 14
List, Friedrich, *Das Nazionale System der Politischen Ökonomie*, 32 and n. 2
Lithuania, 104, 201
Lloyd George, David, Earl Lloyd-George, and Agadir, 134
Lombardy, Austrian domination, 26, 81, 149, 151, 153, 224; and expulsion, 82, 155, 158, 232; invasion by Charles Albert, 153, 225, 226
London, compared with Paris, 62, 66–7
Louis XIV, 'L'Etat c'est moi', 19 and n. 1; and balance of power, 48
Louis XVI, 67, 68
Louis XVIII, 71; character and reign, 67–8
Louis Napoleon; *see* Napoleon III
Louis-Philippe, Duke of Orleans, 77; character and reign, 69–70, 73; abdication, 69, 75, 109; period of intellectual freedom, 71–2; supporters of his grandson, 78 and n. 2
Lucca, 149
Lueger, Dr Karl, and Vienna, 240–1
Lutherans, territorial establishment, 48
Luxembourg, 44; neutralization, 84

MacDonald, Ramsay, 265
Macedonia, 206, 247
Machiavelli, Niccolò, theme of 'power', 18, 19
Magenta, battle of, 157 and n. 2
Magyars, 84, 112, 203; their Golden Bull, 221; Turkish menace, 221; and other minorities, 227, 245–6; and Austrian domination, 230; and the *Ausgleich*, 235 and n. 2, 246; domintion of Hungary, 237, 245; percentage of population, 244; and the Jews, 245, 246
Maistre, Joseph, comte de, neo-Catholic, anti-revolutionary, 68; (*Considerations sur la Revolution française*)

Malthus, Thomas, biog., 270 n; view of the future (*Essay on Population*), 270
Manchester School, 25, 35 n.
Manchuria, 207, 208, 209
Manufacturing industry, development after 1850, 29; accompanying finance, 30–1; unfitness of French workers, 74; in German Confederation, 108
Manzoni, Alessandro, *I Promessi Sposi*, 149
Maria Theresa, empress, germanization, 222–3
Martin, John, *Satan in Hell*, 30 n.
Martin, Richard, and protection of animals, 259 and n.
Marx, Karl, 8; assumption of automatic progress, 9; and overthrow of capitalism, 9; and Communist Manifesto, 26 n.; and Commune insurrection, 90 n.; opposed to Bakunin, 197 n. 1; *Address to the Commune*, 90 n.; *Das Kapital*, 90 n.
Marxists, view of history, 10; and the social revolution, 198; prognosis on war, 263; Morris and, 273; Austrian, 240; Italian, 168; Russian, 197
Masaryk, Jan, 44
Masonic Assembly of the Grand Orient, and belief in God, 95
Maximilian, archduke of Austria, emperor of Mexico, 82–3
Mazzini, Giuseppe, 153; beliefs, 19, 20, 25; idealized European community, 27, 152; birth in Genoa, 44; and Italian patriotism, 152; republican revolution, 154, 158; death in exile, 155; *Giovane Italia*, 152
Mechanics' Institutes, 30
Mehemet Ali, Pasha of Egypt, 204
Menelik, emperor of Abyssinia, 173, 174 and n.
Mensdorff-Pouilly, Count, 234
Mensheviks, dispute with Bolsheviks, 199, 216; Lenin and, 216
Metternich, Prince, 51, 55; and constitutional reforms, 25, 109, 224; and Communist Manifesto, 26; on Napoleon, 223; resignation, 226, 227; biog., 223 n.
Metz, key fortress, 63, 87; surrender, 88, 89; railway station, 114 n.
Mexico, Napoleon III and, 82–3
Michaelangelo, Sistine chapel, 6
Middle Ages, Christian belief in temporal society, 2; exercise of power, 6; a feudal miscellany of kingdoms, etc., 18, 43; boundary demarcations, 19 and n. 2, 43 n. 1; unity of Christendom, 22; group life, 22; total wars, 22 and n.
Middle East, 138, 139, 184, 209
Milan, tobacco-boycott revolution, 153 and n. 2; socialist paper (*Avanti*), 169, 170; general strike, 169; anti-Italian riots, 225, 226
Mill, John Stuart, 269–70; and order of progress, 11, 258; and colonial self-government, 38 n. 2
Milton, John, the sin of Lucifer (*Paradise Lost*), 6; and contemporary clergyman (*Lycidas*), 273
Minorca, 42
Modena, 82, 158, 224
Mohacs, battle of, 221
Moltke, Helmuth, count von, 118 n., 143; campaigns, 118, 120, 234
Moltke, Helmuth, nephew of above, and Schlieffen plan, 143
Mommsen, Theodor, 243
Mongol invasions, 202
Mongolia, 209
Montenegro, 294, 253; and Scutari, 253 n. 2
Moravia, 238, 243
Morocco, French predominance, 131 and n. 132, 175; German intervention, 132, 133–4, 176, 253; rebel pretender, 133–4; Franco-German agreement (1911), 177
Morris, William, and contemporary living, 273–4; *The Dream of John Ball*, 274 n. 1; *News from Nowhere*, 274
Moscow, 180, 185; Patriarchate, 181; 1905 riots, 212; industrial concentration, 215

Moslems, repulsed by Charles Martel, 21–2; Russian absorption of Asian khanates, 183; rebellion in Herze-Govina, 249
Münster, 48 n. 2
Murat, Joachim, and Two Sicilies, 82 and n. 2
Mussolini, Benito, 79, 102, 268; and use of violence, 170
Mutiny Act, and standing army, 48–9

Naples, 14, 108, 220; return of the Bourbons, 26, 149 n. 1, 151, 152; union with Sicily, 149 n. 1; and a new constitution, 153 and n. 1; rebellion against Francis I, 158, 225; Garibaldi and, 159–60; and unification, 160
Napoleon I, 60 n., 82 n. 2; and map of Europe, 44, 50; military dictatorship, 61, 259; self-interpretation, 80; Concordat with papacy, 92–3; and German sovereigns, 106; influence on Italy, 150–1; marriage to Marie Louise, 224
Napoleon III, 61; supplants Second Republic, 26, 77–8, 109, 154; anti-parliamentary rule, 27, 62, 78, 79; supports Cobden Treaty, 31, 32; imperialism, 35, 78, 79; proposes an International Council, 55; and Slesvig-Holstein, 55, 83, 146–7; planning of Paris, 66; fall of, 69; and social questions, 73; ambition to impersonate Napoleon I, 77, 80–1; popular image, 77; royalist and Church support, 78; 1870 plebiscite, 80; career, 80–1; 'doctrine of nationality', 81; relations with Italy and Austria, 81–2, 82 n. 2, 84–5, 94, 154, 156–7; and Bismarck, 83–4, 119–20; and Spanish crown, 86–7, 120; tricked by Cavour, 156, 157–8; choice of an Italian capital, 160; and Franco–Prussian War, 187
Nation-states, necessary attributes, 17–18, 220; historical application, 18; continuing popularity, 20; an advance on medieval entities, 22–3; and maintenance of peace, 23, 45–6; and political uniformity, 24; impact of French Revolution, 24; pursue individual power politics, 27–8, 32–3; and non-metropolitan areas, 40–1; disputes leading to two Great Wars, 41; consolidation of independent sovereignties, 44; and element of aggression 45; emergence of Great Powers, 47; are they now an anacronism?, 257; influence of technical advance, 261

National Guard, 70, 74, 89; defeat of *fédérés*, 90–1
National Liberal Party, 119
National Sovereignties, expression of European civilization, vii; failure to avoid war, viii; boundary demarcation, 17, 19 n. 2, 43 n. 1; formation, 18, 19, 24; and maintenance of peace, 19–20, 45–6, 261–2; aspirants to independence, 20, 23; extinctions due to French wars, 50; and balance of power concept, 52
National Workshops, 227; insurrection following closure, 66, 76 and n.; co-operative organization, 76
Nationalism, nationalist movements, nineteenth century origin, 18 n. 1; first phase in Europe, 24; adaptation of economics, 28; element of fear after 1815, 41; development from group loyalty and patriotism, 41–2; emergence from revolutionary changes of sovereignty, 43–4; border-country origin of leaders, 44; defensive assertion of separateness, 44, 45; cultivation of the vernacular, 44; a cause of European decline, 257
Naval control, Anglo/French rivalry, 7; British supremacy, 34; and the slave trade, 34; effect of Franco/Russian alliance, 130; Anglo/German competition, 135–8; Austrian/Italian competition, 177
Near East, 57, 138, 209
Netherlands, Dutch, 42, 84; Habsburgs and, 220, 223; Estates of Flanders rebellion, 223; stable society, 262
New Zealand, British annexation, 35–6

New Statesman, 265 n. 1, 267–8, 268 n. 1
Newman, Cardinal John, and liberalism (*Apologia*), 24; in Naples, 153 n. 1
Newton, Isaac, view of the universe, 49
Nice, 61, 148, 159
Nicholas I, tsar of Russia, arch-enemy of liberalism, 109, 188, 189, 230; and imperial chancery, 187; and Crimean War, 189, 190; and Poland, 200; and Ukrainian nationalism, 202; assists Austria, 203, 230; and Turkey, 203–4
Nicholas II, tsar of Russia, 133; palace at Tsarkoe Selo, 195; and political changes, 195, 210, 213–14, 215; and 1905 revolution, 211–12; and the Duma, 212, 213–4, 243 n. 2; and Rasputin, 216; deaf to revolutionary warnings, 216; abdication in First World War, 217
Niebuhr, Barthold Georg, 106 and n.
Nietzsche, Friedrich Wilhelm, 'living dangerously', 10
Nikon, Patriarch, reforms, 181
Nobles' Land Bank (Russian), 215
North Africa, earlier 'waste lands', 5 n.; Christian/Moslem hostility, 22; French opportunities, 63, 172
North America, Anglo/French disputes, 7, 50; French colonialism, 63 and n.; Italian emigration, 171; Russian forts and traders, 180
North German Confederation, 83, 84; Bismarck and, 117, 118, 235; constitution, 118–19, 120; new *Zollverein*, 118

Odessa, 183; *Potemkin* mutiny, 213
Ollivier, Émile, and Ems telegram, 87
Osnabrück, 48 n. 2
Otto the Great, and Austria, 220
Ottoman Empire, 22, 49, 189; moribund state, 209; boundary with Habsburg dominions, 222; overthrow, 249; surviving sultans, 262
Owen, Robert, and 'socialism', 70 and n. 1; and child labour, 259–60
Oxford Movement, 24, 271 and n.

Palestine, dispute over Holy Places, 189
Palmerston, Henry Temple, Viscount, 35; and Slesvig-Holstein, 55 and n. 2, 146; and Haynau, 230 n.; and Kossuth, 230 n.
Pan-Germanism, 36, 239–40
Pan-Slavism, 36, 202–3
Panama Company, failure, 96–7; Jewish employees, 97 n.
Papacy, the, 48, 93; universal recognition, 22, 150; regains temporal power, 26, 94; and a federated Italy, 81–2, 150, 153, 158; and Italian liberal demands, 153–6 *passim*; and Church control of education, 155; encyclical opposing progress, 156; and annexation to Piedmont, 158; and Rome as the capital, 160; and separation of Church and State, 160; declaration of infallibility, 161; dislike of kingdom of Italy, 166–7; and Law of Guarantees, 166; and social questions, 167; and Italian franchise, 167–8
Papal states, 81, 149, 158; extent, 149–50; misgovernment, 151
Paris, centre of civilized Europe, 60; compared with London, 62, 66–7; hub of French Revolution, 66; immense political predominance, 66, 78, 91; factors reducing mob mobility, 66; defeat of Commune, 66, 90–1; republican declaration, 70; and German peace terms (1871), 89; effect of 1871 civil war, 91; one-day protest strike, 102–3
Parliament Act 1911, 134 n.
Parma, 82, 158, 170, 224
Partito Operaio Italiano, 168
Paul I, tsar, and serfdom, 186
Peasantry, source of conscript recruits, 27–8, 66, 171, 264; Austrian, 223; and abolition of *robot*, 225, 227; Francis Joseph and, 232; French, 64–5, 65 n.; and land ownership, 65–6; physical unfitness, 74; German, 106; Italian, 150, 162, 171; Polish, and 1830 revolution, 200; resistance to russification, 201; Russian, 180–1, 181 n.; characteris-

Peasantry, *cont.*
tics, 184, 185; and 'Time of Troubles', 186 n.; indebtedness to landowners, 186; compared with serfs, 186; and abolition of serfdom, 191; belief in communal land ownership (*mir*), 191–2, 196–7; and Emancipation, 192–3; undermining of their communities, 193; kulaks or *mir*- eaters, 193; increased numbers, 193, 215; and *Zemstvos*, 194; and revolutionary movements, 196–7, 198, 215; Stolypin's improvements, 214; increasing poverty, 215; seize the land after revolution, 218

Peel, Sir Robert, penal reforms, 259
Pellico, Silvio, *Le mie Prigione*, 152
Persia, Russian high-handedness, 141 n. 2, 190, 210, 251 n.
Persian Gulf, 138, 139
Peschiera, 228
Peter the Great, 180; westernization, 181–2; and Russian Church, 181; 'Table of Ranks', 185; poll tax, 186
Peter I, king of Serbia, 250
Philippines, U.S. annexation, 37
Piedmont, 26, 81, 151, 228; annexations by plebiscite, 82; and unification, 152, 154–6, 158–9, 165, 166; constitution, 153–4; anti-clericalism, 154 n., 155; Church control, 155; Austrian ultimatum, 157–8; confiscation of Church property, 166
Pisa, 149
Pitt, William, and a 'balance of power' treaty, 52, 55, 57
Pius II, Pope, 22
Pius IX, Pope, opposed to liberalism, 153, 154, 155, 156; leaves Rome, 154, 158; rejects Cavour's proposals, 160; and kingdom of Italy, 166–7; belief in his anti-Austrianism, 225
Pius X, Pope, 98–9; fear of revolutionaries, 167–8
Plehve, Minister of Interior, assassination, 211
Poland, 52, 111; partitioning of, 42, 43, 50 and n., 183–4, 222; unsuccessful rebellion, 119, 184 n., 200; repression and russification, 184 n., 201; revolution (1830), 184 n., 189, 199, 200; Catholic Church, 199, 201; and Prussian domination, 200; land settlement, 200–1
Poles, the, and independence, 199–200; and land reform, 200; and Western intervention, 200; Ukrainian hostility, 202; and Pan-Slavism, 203; % of Austro/Hungarian population, 237; 'submerged' nationality, 238
Polignac, Prince de, 93
Polybius, and 'balance of power', 46, 50
Port Arthur, 207, 208, 209, 211
Portugal, 42
Posen, 104, 184 n.
Potemkin mutiny, 213
Power, organized state/barbarian comparison, 6; misuse of, 6; noble side as instrument of right, 6; becomes an end in itself, 9; implied in 'sovereignty', 18, 19; compulsory surrender by European princes, 18–19; economic return, 28; attribute of great nations, 171
Prague, 225; Austrian bombardment, 111, 112; suppression of revolt, 227–8; Czech University, 239; Congress of Nationalities (1905), 235
Progress, implies possibility of regress, vii, 8, 257; modern belief in, 2; disconnected from material invention, 2–3; applied to quality of life, 6–7; relationship to geographical and other facts, 7; has the concept a lasting value?, 9 ff.; implies increasing danger, 10; unequal pace of advance, 10–11; allegedly based on exploitation, 11; technological/socio-political comparison, 11–12, 258; analysis of regress, 13
Protection, 32–3, 35 and n.
Protestants, Reformation, 8; and Treaty of Westphalia, 48 and n. 2; defeat in Bohemia, 222
Proudhon, Pierre Joseph, 197 n.; attack on property, 72 (*Qu'est-ce que la propriété?*)

Prussia, 25, 106; withdrawal of political concessions, 26; becomes a Great Power, 49, 52; autocratic 'intervention', 54; annexes Slesvig/Holstein, 55, 116–17; military predominance, 56, 113–14; and war with France, 85–7; and Spanish crown, 86; army predominance, 113, 115, 116; leading figures in revival, 106 and n.; and 1848 liberal revolutions, 109–10, 112; franchise reforms, 112–13; anacronistic ideals, 114–15; and leadership of Germany, 115 ff.; and war with Austria, 118, 122, 157–8, 234; domination of Reichstag, 120, 121; merges with Germany, 226; a police state, 237; *see also* Bismarck

Radetzky, field-marshal Count Josef, 228 n.; retires to Quadrilateral, 226 and n.; Italian victories, 228, 230; and Hungary, 228
Railways, influence on education, 3; advantages to all classes, 28; underestimation of usage, 28–9; European development, 29, 74; German concessions in Asia Minor, 127, 138; Baghdad project, 138–9, 210; Russian ambitions, 140, 210–11; Italian backwardness, 162; Djbouti to Addis Ababa, 174; Trans-Siberian, 193, 207; Chinese Eastern, 207; South Manchurian, 208, 209; Austro/Russian rivalries, 250
Rasputin, Grigori Yefimovick, 215–16
Red Sea coast, Italian, settlements, 172, 173
Reeve, Henry, and old balance of power concept, 56–7
Reinach, Jacques de, and Panama Canal, 97 n.
Religious orders, exclusion from French schools, 94; Republican attack, 96, 97–8
Renan, Ernest, study of American democracy (*Souvenirs d'enfance et de jeunesse*), 274–5
Revolutionaries, 8; freemasonry and, 95; Italian division, 168, 169; motivation in economic improvement, 170; use of terrorism, 195; changes in intellectual fashions, 195–6; development of intelligentsia, 196; Populist movement, 196 and n. 2, 197; optimism concerning technology, 268–9; and change by violence, 269
Russian, development underground, 194–5, 215; left-wing industry-based, 197; rise of Lenin, 197–9; origins of in *zemstvos* (1905), 211–12; total hostility to regime, 216; need for European support, 216–17; events of 1917, 217–18; and military defeat of Russia, 263–4
Revolutionary syndicalism, 102 n.; spread in Italy, 169–70; doctrine of general strike, 169, 170; split with socialists, 170; revival, 170
Rhineland, 50, 84
Rhodes, Cecil, 36
Roman Empire, 20; short-lived *pax romana*, 20–1; political collapse, 21; an 'overriding authority', 46–7
Rome, 82, 160; Italian seizure, 83, 161; presence of French troops, 158, 160–1; fear of demonstrations, 158 n.; Garibaldi and, 159, 161
Roosevelt, President Theodore, 209
Rothschild family, and French finance, 96
Roumania, 206 and n. 1, 245, 247
Roumanians, 221, 244; aristocracy, 246
Rousseau, Jean-Jacques, 5, 27
Royal Colonial Institute, 39
Royalists, French, 78 and n. 2, 91 and n., 92, 94–5
Rumelia, 247
Ruskin, John, 3, 72
Russell, Lord John, and Balance of Power questions, 52, 55
Russia, vii; social revolution, 8; retention of princely power, 19; political restraints, 25; tariff restraints, 32–3; territorial threats to Britain, 36; relations with Germany, 40, 133; autocratic 'intervention', 54; alliance with France, 57–8, 123, 124;

Russia, *cont.*
  nineteenth century pogroms, 96; and Poland, 119; Balkan rivalry with Austria, 122, 203, 248, 252; and Black Sea, 123, 140 and n. 3., 204, 251; inroads into China, 130, 208, 209; driven into Anglo-French arms, 138–40; relations with Turkey, 139, 203–4; and Austria-Hungary, 140, 203; and Sarajevo assassination, 143; supports Menelek, 173, 174 n.; relations with Italy, 176 and n.; late entry into Europe, 180; early history, 180; three great rivers, 183; port facilities, 183, 207; three main regions, 184; route to the Pacific, 207; politico/economic recovery, 210, 215; drift towards anarchy, 217; and Far East, 248–9

Russian Empire, 180, 182; Westernization, 181–2; peasant loyalty, 181 n.; physical features, 182, 184; Pacific coast claims, 182 n. 3; population distribution, 184–5; industrial backwardness, 185; social class structure, 185–6; character of bureaucrats, 186, 261; administrative uniformity, 187 and n. 1, 201; secret police, 187 and n. 2, 237; Decembrist conspiracy, 188–9, 189 n., 196; 1905 revolution, 193, 199, 211–12; a police state, 194–5, 212, 237; gulf between tsar and subjects, 195; capitalist bourgeoisie, 198; economic advances, 210; collapse of autocracy, 217–19; defection of the army, 217–18

Russian Government, and Orthodox Church, 181; remoteness from peasantry, 186–8; centralization, 187; and abolition of serfdom, 192 and n.; and communal system, 193; and *zemstovs*, 194, 211; and revolutionary movements, 197; and non-Russian nationals, 199–203; formatipn of the *Duma*, 212–13, 218; alleged use of *agents provocateurs*, 212–13

Russian Social Democratic Workman's Party, split in, 199

Russians, character and history, 180; concept of Christianity, 180; in Siberia, 182; and colonization, 182 n. 3; middle and merchant classes, 185; ennoblement by service, 185 and n. 2, 186; illiteracy, 187: use of violence, 194; alienation of educated classes from bureaucrats, 210; *see also* Peasantry

Russo-Japanese War, 132; Russian defeat, 136, 140, 184, 209, 249; U.S. mediation, 209; effect on Russia, 210; an impetus to revolution, 211, 217; indirect political results, 263

Russo-Turkish War, 123, 203, 205
Ruthenians, 237 and n., 244

St Cuthbert, 21 n.
St Petersburg, 180, 183, 185; Decembrist conspiracy, 188–9, 189 n.; communal land owners, 192; first Soviet, 212; industrial concentration, 215; riots of 1917, 217–18; arrival of Lenin and Trotsky, 218
Saint-Simon, Claude Henri, comte de, and French socialism, 70 and n., 71; his followers, 71–2
Salisbury, Lord Robert Cecil, earl of, 117, 122, 130
Salonika, 17, 140; approach corridor, 205; Greek population, 247; Spanish Jews, 247 n.; projected railways, 250
Salzkammergut, 238
San Marino republic, 42, 149
Sanjak of Novi Bazar, 140, 204–5; railway project, 250
Sarajevo assassination, 58, 142–3
Sardinia, 68 n., 148, 220
Savoy, 61, 81, 172
Savoy-Piedmont (Sardinia), 44, 68, 148
Saxony, 52
Sazonov, succeeds Izvolsky, 252
Scandinavia, 40, 262 n. 1
Scharnhorst, Gerard von, 106 and n.
Schlieffen, Alfred count von, invasion plan, 125–6, 126 n., 143, 144
Schwarzenburg, Prince, 112, 113, 229 and n. 2; and Hungary, 229; death, 232

306 Europe 1815–1914

Scotland, 18 n. 1, 42–3
Scutari, 253 n. 2
Sebastopol, 190, 204
Sedan, French surrender, 87 and n. 2
Seeley, Sir John Robert, *The Expansion of England*, 39
Serbia, and annexation of Herze-Govina, 141–2, 204, 206, 251; relations with Austria, 142, 206, 210, 248, 249–50; Sarajevo assassination, 142–3, 254 and n.; and the Balkans, 246, 248, 249, 250; indigenous dynasties, 247; murder of king and queen (1903), 250; and Bulgaria, 250; and Balkan wars, 253
Serbs, % of Austro/Hungarian population, 238, 244; relationship with Croats, 238 n. 1; nationalist demands, 238, 245; Orthodox Church in Bosnia, 239 n. 2, 250
Serfdom, 5, 21, 106; formalization in Russia, 184, 186; 'private' and 'state' serfs, 186, 188, 191, 193; efforts to abolish, 188, 191; compensation of landlords, 191, 192 and n., 193; outbreaks of violence, 191; Emancipation Edict (1861), 192–3; abolition in Poland, 200, in Austria, 223
Seton-Watson, C., and Italian politics, 165 and n.
Shakespeare, William, words conveying loyalty, 41, 42
Shipbuilding, German advances, 126; British programme, 1894, 130 and n.; Anglo/German naval competition, 135–8; introduction of *Dreadnought* class, 137 and n., 177; outclassed by super-*Dreadnoughts*, 138
Siberia, Russian occupation, 182, 183, 193; economic development, 297; Lena goldfields strike, 215
Sicily, 220, 225; Garibaldi and, 82, 158, 159; union with Naples, 149 n. 1; and independence, 152; presence of the Mafia, 162 and n. 2; underprivileged position, 166, 168–9
Siena, 149
Silesia, 222, 225, 238
Singer, C. *et alia*, *History of Technology*, 28 n. 1

Sino-Japanese War, 207
Slavery, abolition, 35
Slavophil movement, 202–3
Slavs, 112, 177, 221; and Habsburg empire, 142, 234, 246; in the Ukraine, 202; revolution in Bosnia-Herzegovina, 204; neglected by Kossuth, 225 n.; position in Austria, 235, 238
Slesvig, duchy of, 52, 104, 111, 147
Slesvig-Holstein, 55 n. 1; Danish rights, 55, 83, 145–6; area of political dispute, 116–18, 145–7; population, 145; prussianization, 146–7
Slovakia, 44
Slovaks, 221, 237, 244
Slovenes, 237, 238
Smith, Adam, *Wealth of Nations*, 32 and n. 1
Smolensk, 180
Social Democrats, Austrian, 240, 244; German, 121, 124, 128, and n. 2
Social reform, 73, 99; weapon against socialism, 129; dependent on ordered advance, 258; nineteenth century achievements, 259; inconsistencies of reformers, 259; necessary legislation, 261
Socialism, distrust of liberalism, 25; characteristics in France, 70–2, 99; little threat from intellectuals, 72–3; gulf between leaders and politicians, 100–1; middle class origins, 101; and a war with Germany, 101–2; doctrinal quarrels, 240; and avoidance of war, 264; identification of war and capitalism, 264; domestic preoccupations, 264–5; Austrian, 241; German, 121, 128, 129; Italian, 168, 169, 170
Sociology, a new science, 269 and n. 1
Solferino, battle of, 157; and formation of Red Cross, 157 n. 2
Sophocles, on the terrible nature of man, 10 n., 13
Sorel, Georges, biog., 102 n. 1; approval of Mussolini, 102; *Reflexions sur la violence*, 102 and n., 267
South Africa, 'mining millionaires', 37 and n. 2

South African War, 37, 130, 175
South America, Italian emigration, 171-2
Soviet, creation in St Petersburg, 212; arrest of leaders, 121; use of political strikes, 212-13; re-established in 1917, 218
Spain, 24, 220; tariff impositions, 32; and European community, 49; American possessions, 50; search for a monarch, 85-7; expulsion of Jews, 247 n.; separation from Portugal, 262
Spencer, Herbert, biog., 269 n. 2; assumption of 'automatic' progress, 9; immense influence, 269 and n. 3
Stael, Mme de, biog., 60 n.; *De l'Allemagne*, 60 and n.
Stalin, Josef, 8, 44, 79
Stein, Heinrich Baron von, 106 and n., 107
Stockholm, 14
Stolypin, Piotr Arkadevich, 193 and n.; and the *Duma*, 214; assassination, 215
Straits, the, Russian aims, 123, 140 n. 3, 141 and n. 2, 204, 251 and n.
Straits of Shimonoseki, Japanese control, 208
Strasbourg, 43
Styria, 238
Suez Canal, 29 n. 1, 71, 131 n.
Sweden, 18 n. 1, 48, 49; and Russia, 183, 201
Switzerland, Confederation, 17; and Romansch language, 44; French-speaking peoples, 61; Ladin language, 238 n. 2; stable society, 262
Sybel, Heinrich von, 117

Tartiglia, and misuse of gunfire, 12 n.
Technological skills and inventions, mark of high civilizations, 3, 6; need greater rationalization of life, 4; demand elaborate training of the few, 4; employment for destruction, 8, 11; rate of progress compared with socio/political skills, 11; lack of secrecy, 12; inherent dangers, 12; East/West comparison, 21 n.; cause interconnected changes, 28 and n. 2; good and evil results, 30 and n.; order of progress, 258 and n.; evidenced in Great Exhibition, 268
Tel-el-Kebir, battle of, 131 n.
Tennyson, Alfred, Lord, bellicose sentiments (*Maud*), 267 and n. 1
Theirs, Adolphe, 87; and Third Republic, 69, 88; on Louis Napoleon, 77
Third International, expulsion of Bakunin, 197 n. 1
Thirty Years War, 48, 222
Thorn, 184 n.
Thrace, 206, 247
Times, The, 266 n. 3; reports Crimean War, 190 n. 2
Tirpitz, Grand-Admiral A. von, 135 and n. 2, 138; his 'risk theory', 136
Tocqueville, Charles Alexis de, *Democracy in America*, 275-6
Tours, 88
Transylvania, 296, 221, 244, 245
Treaty of Augsburg, 48
Treaty of Berlin, 251
Treaty of London, 179
Treaty of San Stefano, 123
Treaty of Unkiar Skelessi, 203-4
Treaty of Utrecht, 42, 48, 49
Treaty of Versailles, 42
Treaty of Vienna, 42, 203, 223; aims, 52, 53; signatories, 53; deficiencies in execution, 53-4; loses its validity, 54; and nationalist hopes, 80
Trieste, 162, 238
Triple Alliance, 58, 172-3; Bismarck and, 172-3; Italy and, 173, 175, 176; renewals, 173
Tripoli, 172, 175; Italian acquisition, 177-8
Trotsky, Leon, dispute with Lenin, 216; arrival in St Petersburg, 218
Tunis, 172
Turgot, Anne Robert, on colonies, 35
Turkey, financial defaults, 31 n. 2; and Crimean War, 54; German railway concessions, 127, 138-9; Russian

Turkey, *cont.*
designs, 140, 203, 252; Young Turks, 140, 177, 249 and n. 1, 253 n. 3; European intervention, 189-90, 204-5, 252-3; Bashi-Bazouk irregulars, 204; German domination, 221-2; and Bosnia/Herzegovina, 246; conflicting Greek/Bulgarian claims, 247; denounces armistice, 253 and n. 3
Turin, 160
Tuscany, 82; Grand Duchy, 149, 151, 158; Habsburg possession, 149 n. 2, 224
Two Sicilies, 48-9; union of Naples and Sicily, 149 n. 1; misgovernment, 151; Piedmont acquisition, 155; Austrian predominance, 224
Tyrol, North, 238

Ukraine, 202
Umbria, 159
Union Générale bank, collapse in 1882, 96
Union organization, Austrian, 240; French, 65; compared with English, 99-100; slow growth, 100-1; formation of C.G.T., 101; and a general strike, 101 and n., 102-3; and use of violence, 102; German, and growth of socialism, 128; Italian, 168; strikes, etc., 169-70; Russian, 'police socialism', 211, 215
United Empire Loyalists, 35
United Nations, 20, 53, 256
United Netherlands, 49
United States, 15; increase in political barriers, 33-4; reaction against annexation of Philippines, 37; British investment, 40; lack of 'French' vote, 63 and n.; and Napoleon III, 82-3
United Workers' Party (Italian), 168
University of France, 93
Uppsala, 14
Ural Mountains, 13-14
U.S.S.R., 5, 20; extent, 180

Vattel, Emmerich de, and balance of power, 47, 49, 57
Venetian republic, Austrian domination, 26, 81, 82, 116, 149, 151, 224; secession, 161, 226
Venice, 42, 48, 153
Vergennes, Charles Gravier, 50
Vergil, on Rome, 6
Verona, 228
Versailles, 89 and n., 120 and n.
Vicenza, 228
Victoria, Queen, 154 n., 230 n.
Victor Emmanuel I, king of Sardinia, *ancien régime*, 151
Victor Emmanuel II, king of Sardinia, 82, 153-5; visits Windsor, 154 n.
Vienna, 14, 225; and 1848 revolution, 26, 109, 112, 225-7, 228-9; population, 108; Turkish siege, 222; Committee of Security, 227; student riots, 228; treatment of rebels, 229 and n.; three nobilities, 232; Municipal Council, 240; Jewish problems, 241 and n. 2
Virchow, Rudolf, 117
Viviani, René, 99 n.
Vladivostok, 180, 183, 207, 208
Vogelsang, Freiherr von, 240
Voltaire, on Germans, 60 n.; on Holy Roman Empire, 105
Vorarlberg, 238

Wagram, battle of, 223
Wallachia, Hospodars, 51
Warsaw, Grand Duchy, 184 n., 199, 200
Watt, James, 29
White Mountain, battle of, 222
Wilberforce, William, inconsistency in reform, 259
William I, king of Prussia, and Spanish crown, 86-7; proclaimed emperor of Germany, 89 n., 120 and n.; Regent, 115 n.; and army reform, 115-16; belief in divine right, 120; death, 124
William II, emperor of Germany, belief in Britain's war intentions, 58 n., 139-40, 140 n. 1; and Bismarck, 124-5; and social reform, 124; character, 125; and fall of

William II, *cont.*
Second Reich, 129; and foreign affairs, 132, 133, 142, 143, 208 n., 253 n. 1; and a large battle fleet, 135 and n. 2, 138

Wilson, President, belief in 'self-determination', 19–20, 81

Windisch-Graetz, field-marshal Prince, 227 and n., 228–9 and n. 1

Witte, count Sergius, economic policy, 207 and n., 210–11; and French loan, 213; President of *Duma* Council, 213; *Memoirs*, 213

Wordsworth, William, 273

Working classes, 3; Austrian, lack of social legislation, 240; French, armed insurrection, 76–7; disenfranchisement, 78, 79; under Napoleon III, 80; and the Commune, 90; and social reform, 99; and union organization, 100–1; Italian, traditional loyalty to the Church, 166, 167; lack of opposition party, 168; German, 110; and use of violence in revolution, 128–9: Russian, 185; habit of communal action, 192 (*artels*), 192, 197; increasing poverty, 193–4; subject to revolutionary propaganda, 211, 215; set up a Soviet (Committee) of representatives, 212, 218; and improved economy, 215

For Product Safety Concerns and Information please contact our EU representative GPSR@taylorandfrancis.com
Taylor & Francis Verlag GmbH, Kaufingerstraße 24, 80331 München, Germany